CHANGING DYNAMICS OF INDIA-JAPAN RELATIONS

Buddhism to Special Strategic Partnership

CHANGING DYNAMICS OF INDIA-JAPAN RELATIONS

Buddhism to Special Strategic Partnership

Shamshad Ahmad Khan

Foreword by

Professor Yasushi Watanabe, Ph.D.
Professor, Graduate School of Media and Governance
Keio University, Japan

PENTAGON PRESS

Changing Dynamics of India-Japan Relations: Buddhism to Special Strategic Partnership

By Shamshad Ahmad Khan

ISBN 978-81-8274-936-8

First Published in 2017

Published by
PENTAGON PRESS
206, Peacock Lane, Shahpur Jat
New Delhi-110049
Phones: 011-64706243, 26491568
Telefax: 011-26490600
email: rajan@pentagonpress.in
website: www.pentagonpress.in

Printed at Avantika Printers Private Limited.

Dedicated to

My daughter Taiyaba Fatima and My wife Nelofer

CONTENTS

FOREWORD

In his book, Towards a Beautiful Country, Shinzo Abe, the then Chief Cabinet Secretary of Japan who later became prime minister, had identified India as a pivotal partner and described how Japan could advance its "national interests" by strengthening "ties with India." Abe also speculated that "it will not be a surprise if in another decade Japan-India relations overtake Japan-US and Japan-China ties." Given the layers of relations between the US and Japan, it is difficult to envisage that India-Japan relation will overtake the US-Japan relations in the near future. But it cannot be denied that the bilateral relationship between Japan and India has deepened faster than expected. It is one of the most talked about and discussed bilateral relationship in the strategic and academic circles of India, Japan, China and the US. As the bilateral relationship is evolving, examining the past and present aspects of Japan-India relations was needed. I am happy that Dr. Shamshad A.Khan took the effort to assess and analyse the changing nature of bilateral relationship during his affiliation at Keio University on a prestigious Japan Foundation's post-doctoral fellowship. He has brilliantly analysed not only contemporary aspects of deepening Japan-India relations in the fields of maritime security, trade and economics, energy security and infrastructure development but also the history of Japan-India relations starting from interactions among Buddhist monks with the Japanese society.

It is interesting to note that the author points that the present ties between Japan and India is based on strong pedestal of cultural and religious linkages that started between the two Asian civilizations following the introduction of Buddhism in Japan. Whenever, Japan-India bilateral relations drifted from its course due to various domestic and external factors, cultural and religious ties played a pivotal role in binding them together, the author rightly argues. Followed by Buddhism, a dialogue between Indian and Japanese intellectuals started and scholars such as Swami Vivekananda, Rabindranath Tagore and Okakura Tenshin and his disciples visited each other's country, exchanged views and envisioned a partnership between Japan and India based on common spiritual linkages. Though they could not succeed in achieving their envisioned ideals, the dialogue between them which has been given adequate coverage in this book, will fascinate the readers and will help them understand evolving nature of the bilateral relationship. It is a must-read book for anyone seriously interested in this unique relationship whether inside or outside of academia.

Japan became a source of inspiration for many young Indian who wanted to liberate India from British rule. Since it was the first Asian nation to defeat a European power, many started visiting Japan, established their base in Japan and launched their campaign to achieve India's liberation. Their interaction with Japanese officials later led to creation of Indian Independence League and its military wing Indian National Army. This aspect is well recorded in the books of history but the author has tried to examine the same from the prism of India-Japan relationship bringing some new fact to the fore.

Since the Japanese and Indian society has deepened their interactions, it was expected that following emergence of India as an independent state, the relationship between India and Japan would transform into a stronger partnership. But after an initial bonhomie at the level of political leadership, the relationship drifted away from its course. The author has elegantly analysed the various internal and external factors to assess why it strayed from its path?

The relationship between the two countries started strengthening after the end of Cold War period which coincided with India's economic liberalization. In this period cooperation between India and Japan strengthened in the fields of security, economic partnership and creating a regional order based on rule of law. The author has devoted one chapter each to understand the aims and objectives of the partnership in these two countries. Singing a civil nuclear cooperation is one of the most debated issues between the two countries. The author has devoted one chapter to understand various factors that delayed the conclusion of a deal between the two countries. The final chapter summarizes that debate and offers few recommendations for both the governments on how to deepen the relationship further.

I am hopeful that this book will be one of the important sources for those who want to understand evolution of Japan-India relationship and areas of their cooperation. I congratulate Dr. Khan for writing this book during his association with Keio University. We at Keio are all proud and appreciative of having had a chance to work with him. I also hope that he will continue to study and write on various aspects of Japan. Those in policy and intellectual circles will be keen to know what he has to say about Japan and the bilateral relationship, as he is already widely recognized as a rising star in this field. I wholeheartedly wish him good luck for his future endeavors in academics.

Professor Yasushi Watanabe, Ph.D.
Professor, Graduate School of Media and Governance
Keio University, Japan

Preface

After witnessing various phases of "estrangements" and "engagements," India-Japan relation has transformed into a "special strategic and global partnership." Many contemporary scholars have viewed the ongoing bonhomie between the two nations as driven by the US factor and propelled by the "Rise of China." No doubt, the external factors have played an important role in pushing the two Asian countries closer. But there are various factors such as old historical and civilisational ties between the two countries built around the dialogues among the intellectuals of the two Asian nations that bound them together even when there were minimal political interactions between the two. Then there were interesting dialogues between the personalities and thinkers of India and Japan including between Rabindranath Tagore and Okakura Tenshin who argued to create an Asian identity based on common civilisation and culture.

It may be noted that when the two countries were trying to give new shape to their relationships, Japanese Prime Minister Shinzo Abe in his address to Indian Parliament (in 2007), talked about "confluences of two Seas" to revive old ties. Therefore, it can be said that present day India-Japan relation is not a fresh beginning as it is widely believed; rather it is re-integration of ties between the two civilisations that got disrupted because of various domestic and external factors. Then there are economic factors that are compelling the two Asian nations to revitalize their relationship. Japan is looking India as one of the favourites investment destination and India looks at Japan for cutting edge technology. All these factors can be counted among the catalysts that bring and bind the two Asian nations together.

In this book, an attempt has been made to study how the relationship between the two Asian civilisations has evolved over the centuries, putting the three aspects viz. political, economic and cultural/religious together. It is important to establish the fact that what are the factors that drive India-Japan relations? Is it the "Rise of China" which has compelled the two Asian nations to seek a closer partnership or it is the continuation of the old civilisational ties between the two which was disrupted due to circumstances such as the two World Wars and the Cold War period that followed the World War II?

Since the two countries have signed a special strategic partnership and have pledged to work closely on various international and multilateral fora, the study looks into various areas where their perceptions converge and diverge. Particularly, on the nuclear issue, their perceptions diverge. Although India and Japan are in favour of elimination of nuclear weapons, their approaches are different. India considers Nuclear Proliferation Treaty discriminatory as it accepts nuclear power status of P-5 countries, while Japan has accepted NPT in present form. Although it is generally perceived that the approach of the two governments are identical to set global norms and agenda, an analysis of Indian intelligentsia and their writing suggest (analysed in one of the chapters of this book) that there are various opinions when it comes to the issue of aligning with Japan on certain international issues including securing the global commons or taking joint efforts to secure seat in the expanded UN Security Council. The researcher has tried to bring these issues into a comprehensive study on India-Japan relations to give a clear understanding to the policy planners.

Over the last few years, the researcher has spent time at Slavic Research Centre in Hokkaido University, Institute of Developing Economies in Chiba, Japan Institute of International Affairs in Tokyo and most recently at the Keio Research Institute, Keio University and has collected study materials related to the different aspects of India-Japan relations. These research materials have been thoroughly analysed and researched during author's affiliation at the Keio University on a Japan Foundation supported fellowship. These materials have helped a lot in shaping the arguments on India-Japan relations. It is hoped that finding and conclusion of this study will be of some use for those who keenly follow different aspects of India-Japan relations. I also hope that the study would inspire other researchers to undertake further research on this issue in an effort to deepen understanding on the entire gamut of India and Japan relations.

Shamshad Ahmad Khan

Acknowledgment

This book is a result of my consistent efforts to understand Japan and India-Japan relations. I started taking interest in India-Japan relations in 2007 when I joined Waseda University's Department of Political Science as a Special Research Student on Mombukagakusho Fellowship. During the fellowship, my main task was to research on Japan's Constitutional revision debate. But the people in Japanese academia were asking lots of questions about the ongoing summit level interactions between the prime ministers of the two countries and the areas of their bilateral cooperation. To respond to their queries, I started following the developments in India-Japan relations while the core of my interest still remained in the Japanese security policy and later when I joined Institute of Defense Studies and Analyses in New Delhi I started writing small articles and opinion pieces on contemporary India-Japan Relations.

The suggestion to write a book on India-Japan relations was given to me by Professor Srinath Raghavan when I visited him for an interview at his office in the Centre for Policy Research, New Delhi. It was November 2010 and I was preparing to undertake a Visiting Research Fellowship at the Slavic Research Centre (SRC) at the Hokkaido University. I undertook a research project on India-Japan strategic cooperation under the guidance of Professor Akihiro Iwashita. He was very impressed with the draft of my research project and asked me to present the findings before the Japanese Indologists in Tokyo. I must sincerely thank Professor Raghavan and Professor Iwashita for inspiring me to develop interest in India-Japan relations. During my presentation in Tokyo in February 2011, I found renowned Indologists in attendance including Professor Takenori Horimoto, Professor Makoto Kojima, Dr. Marie Izuyama and Dr. Toru

Ito and many other young Japanese scholars. To my surprise, they liked my research and suggested me to continue pursuing this subject. I later developed a good academic network with the persons mentioned above and they had been very helpful in sharing their research, writing recommendations and introducing new people in the Japanese academia. I owe a lot to Professor Takenori Horimoto, Professor Makoto Kojima, Dr. Marie Izuyama and Dr. Toru Ito for helping me understand new and emerging aspect of India-Japan relations.

I am also indebted to Dr. Rajaram Panda, presently India Chair and Visiting Professor at Reitaku University, Japan who had been my senior colleague at the IDSA and has never hesitated to write recommendation letters for me and have read almost all my writings and offered sincere advice to improve them further. I am indebted to various people including Dr. Alexander Bukh, Associate Professor at Victoria University, Willington, Dr. Norio Kondo, Director Asian Studies Division at the Institute of Developing Economies, Chiba and Professor Yasushi Funabashi, Keio University. Despite their busy schedule they have never hesitated to write recommendation letters to me.

I am also thankful to Dr. Pankaj Jha, who read the previous version of this book draft, which mostly focused contemporary aspects of India-Japan relations and suggested me to add few chapters on the history of the two Asian nation's bilateral relations. This suggestion though delayed the process of book publication; I learnt a lot by reading the historical relations of India-Japan and the context of their interactions. I am also thankful to Japan Foundation for offering me a fellowship during which I studied historical and cultural aspects of India-Japan relations and gave final shape to this book.

I am also thankful to various institutions and colleagues both in India and Japan where I have worked and have been associated with in different capacities including Institute of Defense Studies and Analyses and Indian Council of World Affairs, New Delhi, Slavic Research Centre, Hokkaido University, Institute of Developing Economies, Japan Institute of International Affairs and Keio Research Institute, Keio University. While working in each of these institutes, I have enriched my understanding on various aspects of Japan and India-Japan relations which helped me give shape to my thoughts resulting into publication of this book.

My special thanks go to various persons who gave their time to share views on India-Japan relations. Many of them have witnessed the evolution of India-Japan relations and have directly or indirectly been part of the process of transformation of the bilateral relations. I would start with Hiroshi Hirabayashi and Yasukuni Enoki, the two former Japanese ambassadors who were posted in New Delhi during crucial periods of India-Japan relations. I am also thankful to Professor Tomohiko Taniguchi, special advisor to Prime Minister Abe and his cabinet. I had interviewed him twice on various aspects of India-Japan relations. I am also thankful to Mrs. Yoshiko Sakurai of Japan Institute of National Fundamentals, considered closer to Prime Minister Abe and have played an influential role in shaping India-Japan relations. Special thanks to Takeshi Shiraishi, President of Institute of Developing Economies as well as GRIPS, whom I interviewed thrice from 2012 to 2015. In almost all these interviews, Y. Ishida, my Japanese friend from JNU days, accompanied me. Special thanks to Ishida for giving his time and company to me. I am also thankful to my Japanese language teachers Etsuko Hagiwara, Tomoko Tsuro, Takeda Mayu, Shima sensei and others. Among the academicians following India-Japan relations, I must thank Professor Hiroshi Sato, Professor Takenori Horimoto and Dr. Marie Izuyama for providing reading materials on different aspects of India-Japan relations which were very helpful in building arguments.

I am also thankful to Professor Umemori Naoyuki and Professor Tsuboi whom I met in 2006 while they were visiting different institutions in Delhi as part of their academic engagements. I was thinking to pursue journalism after completing my Master of Philosophy course. But my interactions with them dramatically changed my career path. They suggested me to come to Waseda and gave recommendations for Mumbukagakusho fellowship to study at the prestigious university. I studied at the department of political science as special research student under Professor Umemori. Thereafter, Professor Umemori has always been encouraging me to visit Japan and attend his seminars at Waseda University. I am also thankful to professors at the Centre of East Asian Studies, Jawaharlal Nehru University including Professor H.S. Prabhakar and Professor Srabony Roychaudhury who taught me various aspects of Japan. I am also indebted to Professor Sreemati Chakravarty and Professor Anita Sharma of Department of East Asian Studies, Delhi University for offering me to teach courses at the Department as a guest faculty including a course on India-Japan relations. This helped me broaden my reading on different aspects of bilateral relationship and thus also helped me formulating ideas for this book. I am also thankful to my students at the Department who asked thought provoking questions. I still remember questions posed by Parul, Kiso, Ashwarya, Remya, Bikramjit, Nidhi, Amlan, Elsa, Shruti, Surbhi, Balram, Lakhanbir and others.

I also thank Mr Rajan Arya for liking the contents of the book and considering it to publish at Pentagon Press. Special thanks to the library staffs of the Japan Foundation Library and Hiyoshi Campus Library of the Keio University, where I used library facilities to complete the first draft of the book. Thanks to my wife Nelofer and my daughter Taiyyaba Fatima for accompanying me to Japan and encouraging me to complete this book.

Shamshad Ahmad Khan

INTRODUCTION

INDIA-JAPAN RELATIONS: REINTERPRETING THE TIES

Introduction

Various scholars studying India-Japan relations have pointed that the Japanese society has held a strong affinity with the Indian subcontinent as the cradle of Buddhism, which arrived in Japan during the sixth century. Indian subcontinent, referred to as *Tenjiku* in Japan during that time, became an integral part of Japanese people's global image. They held *Tenjiku,* from where Budhism originated and spread to different parts of the world, in high esteem. This link got stronger when Indian monk Bodhisena visited Todaiji temple in Nara during the 8th century.

Studies suggest that a number of Japanese visited India to understand the Buddhist philosophy, but this early religious/cultural linkage could not transform into a stronger relationship between the two countries. Interactions between India and Japan witnessed two major intermittent phases thereafter—Japan's self imposed isolation from the world (1633 to 1868), and the Cold War period (late 1950s to 1990s). Prime Minister Jawaharlal Nehru's decision to waive off war reparation on Japan, generated goodwill towards India among Japanese people and Japanese Prime Minister Kishi Nobusuke's visit to New Delhi generated a hope that both the Asian democracies will forge strong bilateral ties. However, Japan's decision to join the US led bipolar world and India's decision to spearhead a Non-Aligned Movement created a political barrier between the two countries. The psychological fencing between the two countries started weakening after the Cold War period—which coincided with India's economic liberlaisation—got over. Japan and especially its investors saw opportunities in newly liberalised Indian market. But the relationship again touched the lowest ebb following 1998 Pokhran nuclear test as Japan imposed economic sanctions on India. India made consistent efforts to put the relations back on the track politically and economically by engaging Japan. This resulted in softening of Japan's attitude and as a result the two countries signed various agreements to take the relationship to a new height during Japanese Prime Minister Yoshiro Mori's visit to India in 2000 and later during Prime Minister Koizimi Junichiro's visit to India, the relationship was transformed into a strategic partnership in 2006.

Japanese cabinet's decision to send Japanese Emperor Akihito on an official visit to India in December 2013 was indicative of the fact that Tokyo attaches great importance to its ties with New Delhi. The Emperor's visit was followed by Japanese Prime Minister Shinzo Abe's visit to New Delhi as the chief guest of India's Republic Day ceremony on January 26, 2014. These two high-level visits from Japanese side are indicative of the fact that India and Japan have cemented their ties for a stable and peaceful Asia.

An analysis of India-Japan relationship from the Indian perspective makes it evident that New Delhi too attaches an equal importance to its ties with Tokyo. Indian has signed strategic partnership with 29 countries including Japan, but Japan is among the few countries with which it has institutionalised Prime Minister level talks, which means the change of government and leadership in both the countries will not derail the partnership. Both the countries have established a 2 plus 2 dialogue, in which an annual interaction takes place at the levels of India's Foreign Secretary and its Japanese counterpart and India's Defense Secretary and its Japanese counterpart. Although Japan has established two plus two mechanism with a number of countries, India, as of now, has this arrangement only with Japan. Moreover, the then Indian Prime Minister Manmohan Singh appointed a special envoy on Japan with a Cabinet Minister rank in his cabinet to expedite the process of implementing the agenda identified in the strategic partnership.

Prime Minister Modi continued the momentum in the bilateral relationship and gave special priority to Japan in India's Foreign policy by upgrading the existing partnership between India and Japan to a "special and strategic partnership." A special "Japan Cell" has been established in Prime Minister's Office after his first visit to Japan in September 2014. These developments suggest that India no more sees Japan as a 'camp follower' of the US as was seen during the Cold War period. Similarly, Japan also does not dismiss India as a 'poor and dysfunctional country' not suitable for a partnership. In this context, the inevitable question that arises is: what are the factors that are driving this unexpected turn in the relationship and what does it portend for the future of India-Japan bilateral relationship?

This research project, located within the discipline of International Relations (IR) and history aims at deepening academic understanding of India's interactions with Japan. India-Japan relations, over the centuries, have been driven by religious/cultural factors ever since Buddhism was introduced in Japan. The other two prominent factors—politics and economics, which drive the bilateral relations today, come much later. However, the literature on India-Japan relations from Indian scholars in recent times has laid more emphasis on political and economic aspects of the relationship. They have either given less importance to cultural/religious factor or have totally missed this factor in their discourse. The fact cannot be ignored that when India and Japan had least or almost no interactions during Japan's almost two hundred years (1633 to 1868) of self-imposed isolation, it was cultural/religious aspects that kept Japanese imagination towards India alive. Therefore, when Japan transformed itself from a closed country to an open country, India was no stranger to the Japanese people. It was because of this existing bonhomie between the two civilisations, a number of Buddhist scholars traveled to India after re-opening of Japan to search for true teachings of the Buddha. It was followed by dialogues between the two great thinkers—Rabindranath Tagore of India and Japanese thinker Okakura Tenshin—who forged a personal bond and held discourse on a new Asian identity.

A literature survey on India-Japan relations reveals that research on this subject remains very fragmented. Maybe because India-Japan relations were not as strong in the past as they are today; and thus it remained off the academic discourse. Indian Japanologist P A Narsimha Murthy (1986) had attempted to comprehensively cover various aspects of the India-Japan relations in his book *India and Japan relations: Dimension of their relationship.* The book explores various facets of India-Japan relations such as economic engagement and cultural exchanges. However, the book deals with developments in the bilateral relationship only till late 1980s. Evidently, till late 1980s, India-Japan relations were driven by Japan's entrepreneurial interests, and there were less political interactions between the two countries during the Cold War period. Therefore, Murthy did not focus on these aspects.

Similarly, Toshio Yamanouchi (1990), in his book *India through Japanese eyes,* highlights various phases of Indo-Japan relations. He divides India-Japan relations into "bright and dark" periods. He describes, "end of Nehru era" heralded into a dark period of Indo-Japan relations as the Japanese who were mainly interested in business and investment in India felt uncomfortable with Indira Gandhi's nationalisation drive and license raj. However, Yamonouchi's study does not touch liberalisation of India and the end of Cold War period; the changes that generated Japan's interest back towards India mainly because the study was completed much before the signs of liberalisation had emerged.

Takenori Horimoto and Lalima Varma (2013) in their co-edited book; *India-Japan Relations in Emerging Asia*, partially fill the gap in the existing literature on India-Japan relations. They argue that a major breakthrough in relations between India and Japan was witnessed after 1991. India initiated the process of liberalizing its economic policy which attracted the Japanese businessmen. They argue that following India's liberalisation, economic ties between the two countries have improved greatly. Moreover, they opine that "strategic aspect of the relation in particular has gradually assumed great relevance." They are of the view that "developments such as the rise of China" has necessitated strategic relations between the two countries and it "expanded and consolidated further." They firmly believe that the expanding relations between India and Japan have to be viewed against this background.

An attempt to fill the void in existing literature has also been made by Rohan Mukherjee and Anthony Yazaki in the recently published book (*Poised for Partnership: Deepening India–Japan Relations in the Asian Century*). This edited book, published in 2016, consists of various chapters contributed by scholars who follow Japan from an IR perspective. Also it follows the developments in bilateral relations from the 1990s onwards and does not touch on the relationship between the two countries that existed before the 1990s. This book came on the shelf of the libraries in late 2016 and by the time this researcher had already given final shape to this project. Therefore, the arguments made in the book by Rohan Mukherjee and Anthony Yazaki could not be utilised fully.

A number of scholars have made their individual efforts and tried to understand the burgeoning relationship between India and Japan by contributing chapters in edited books and contemporary journals. K.D. Kapoor (2007) for example in his article on *India-Japan: Strategic Partnership in the Emerging Global Scenario* examines the strategic partnership between India and Japan. He opines that Japanese Prime Minister Yoshiro Mori's India visit in 2000 proved to be a catalyst in opening a new chapter in India-Japan relations. He also examines the upswing in the diplomatic relations between the two countries by analysing bilateral visits and highlights the importance of continuing dialogues in the contemporary world situation. Purunendra C. Jain (1997), analysing Japan's overall relations with India and South Asia (*Japan's Relations with South Asia*: The Asian Survey) argues that following the end of the Cold War period, there has been renewed interest on both sides. Strengthening politico-diplomatic relations will serve as 'icing on the cake' for Japanese business interests in the region. Improvement in domestic economic, social, and political conditions in South Asian countries will be more appealing to Japan than any strategies.

A close look on survey of literature on India-Japan relations suggest that study on recent phase of India-Japan relations remains scattered in book chapters and articles. In this book, an attempt has been made to analyse the existing literatures for this study. Secondly, the last comprehensive study on India-Japan relations was published by P.A. Narsimha Murthy in 1986. Many more developments have taken place thereafter. Many scholars believe that in the 1990s, India's economic reform is the "take off" period of India-Japan relations. In fact political, cultural and economic interactions have increased manifold between the two Asian countries since 1990s. Thus, an effort has been made to bridge the gap that exists in the available literature on Japan-India relations by anaylysing the new developments in the bilateral relationship.

Apart from the existing literature on India-Japan relations the book analyses bilateral treaties and cooperation agreements in economic, political and security fields the two countries have signed. An effort has been made to examine, policy statements by Japanese Prime Ministers, Foreign Ministers and other key leaders as well as important policy papers/ documents to assess what are the divergence and convergence in their ideas and formulations. Selected writings of key Indian and Japanese policy makers and diplomats have been analysed in the study, and to ascertain the policy priorities of both India and Japan towards each other, various interviews with the Japanese ambassadors and key figures in Japanese academia have been conducted and used in this book.

Analysis of the existing literature on India-Japan relations, suggest that researchers in their studies have analysed bilateral relations based on events such as Japanese Prime Ministers' visits to India, signing of key agreements etc. What has been policy thinking in the official documents and how India has figured in Japan's strategic thinking have not been analysed adequately in the previous studies. This book tries to fill the existing gaps by bringing these aspects into India-Japan relations.

An attempt has also been made to analyse the contents of the treaties and agreements to deduce the importance Japanese foreign policy makers have given to India and vice a versa. Hopefully, the study would be helpful to different government departments, decision makers and general public of both the countries, and would prove an important guide to know about the two countries' evolution of relations and the future direction of the relationship.

Finally, here is a cursory look at the contents of the book. Following this introductory chapter which sums up the reasons behind choosing India-Japan relationship as subject of this study, the first Chapter examines evolution of civilisational ties by looking into spread of Buddhism in Japan and how it helped strengthen a kind of spiritual bonding between the two countries. It also delves into introduction of Buddhism in Japan and visits by Indian monks as well as visits undertaken by Japanese Buddhist scholars two centuries later. Chapter 2 looks at India-Japan relations starting from Meiji Restoration of 1868 up to World War II during which personal bonding between Okakura Tenshin of Japan and Rabindranath Tagore of India was established and that resulted into mooting of a proposal of a "Pan Asian" identity. A section of Chapter 2 has analysed Japan's motives and objectives in supporting India's liberation movement by forming the Indian Independence League and its military wing, the Indian National Army. It also looks at the factors that bound Japan and Indian revolutionaries together up to the end of World War II.

Chapter 3 of the book analyses India-Japan relations during the Cold War period, wherein the political relationship between the two countries witnessed various ups and downs owing to the external factors. Chapter 4, evaluates the strategic partnership between the two countries that they signed in 2006 and how it has evolved over the years. It maps the strategic priorities of the two countries, cooperation in security fields as well as how this partnership has been viewed in China and in other countries in the region. Chapter 5, analyses India-Japan Comprehensive Economic Partnership forged in 2011 and how it has changed the ODA driven economic relations between the two countries. An effort has been made to analyse flow of trade and investment from Japan and vice a versa. One of the priorities of India and Japan is to create a new security order in the Asia-Pacific Region. Chapter 6 of this book analyses the factors which compelled them to think for a rule based architecture in this region. How they approach it and how different constituencies within Indian and Japan view this emerging architecture, and whether can it be achieved? Signing of a civil nuclear cooperation between India and Japan has been one of the most debated issues. There are diverging perceptions in Japan over the nuclear cooperation that has been signed in November 2016. Chapter 7 tries to analyse the perceptions of the pro and anti-nuclear lobbies to assess why the two countries took almost a decade to sign the nuclear cooperation agreement. It also analyses the texts of the Civil Nuclear Cooperation agreement signed between the two countries in 2016. The final chapter of this book summarises the key finding of the research, and offers some policy recommendations to both the government on how to deepen the relationship further.

1

INDIA-JAPAN RELATIONS: TRACING THE CULTURAL AND RELIGIOUS ROOTS

Introduction

India-Japan relations of present time is based on the strong pedestal of centuries old historical, cultural, religious and civilisational ties between the two countries. Various historical accounts suggest that the Japanese society has held a strong affinity with the Indian subcontinent, referred to as *Tenjiku (India)*. In their imagination, the world was divided into three parts or *Sangoku,* meaning three states. The three states were: Yamato (Japan), Kara (modern China and Korean peninsula) and Tenjiku (India). The Japanese had direct links with Kara but with *Tenjiku*, they had no direct contacts till an Indian monk visited Japan in 7th century. This chapter tries to knit the information together to assess how and when India's interactions with Japan started and evolved.

Arrival of Buddhism in Japan

It is said that during the period of Emperor Kotoku (645-654 AD), a seer called Hodo (Dharmamarga or Dharmapatha) came to Japan from Rajgraha of India;[1] his visit has not been verified by other sources though. But a number of sources vividly mention arrival of Buddhist monk Bodhisena in 730 AD in Nara via China. It may not be mistaken that the visiting Buddhist monk introduced the religion to Japan. A section of

Japanese society—mainly elites—were already practicing Buddhism much before the arrival of Bodhisena. Shun Saitoh writes that "Buddhism was first introduced by Korean immigrants. The King Parkchoi, of Korea, presented in the year 538 AD to the imperial court, a Buddhistic statue scripture."[2] With this scripture, King Parkchoi sent a message extolling merits of Buddhism which read as follows:

> The doctrines of this religion far surpass other doctrines. They bring unlimited and unfathomed blessing and happiness to believers, and teach the way to salvation. As the Chintamani jewel is sought by men, so the treasure of this teaching should be sought, as it will be freely bestowed upon those who seek for it. The holy religion came from India, very far away; and the peoples living in the countries between India and the Far East are all believers in it.[3]

The Buddhism, however, was not publicly recognized as a religion but some of the members of Japanese Imperial family, including Prince Shotoku Taishi devoted themselves to the Buddhist doctrine. With the ascendance of Shotoku as king in 593 AD, Buddhism was "nationalized" in Japan.[4] Shotoku also employed religion for political purposes. He promulgated an ordinance consisting of 17 articles. Various articles of the ordinance were influenced by the teachings of Buddhism and Confucianism.[5] The ordinance issued in 604 AD reads as follows:

1) Peace shall be respected above all things.
2) Respect shall be paid to the Buddhist priests.
3) The Imperial Decree shall be honoured.
4) Courtesy shall be the cardinal virtue among court retainers and officials.
5) Fasting shall be kept for the suppression of evil desires.
6) Evil shall be chastised and good encouraged.
7) Each man shall have his duty.
8) Courtiers and officials shall attend their offices early in the morning, and shall retire late.
9) Sincerity shall be considered foundation of righteousness.
10) Anger must be suppressed and malice cast out.
11) Merits and shortcomings must be considered.
12) Provincial lords and officials shall not overtax farmers.

13) All officials shall know their functions.
14) Courtier and officials shall not regard one another with jealousy.
15) The public must be served, even before self-interests.
16) The people's times shall be considered in demanding their service.
17) Decisions shall not be made single-handedly.[6]

Prince Shotoku took a "top down" approach to introduce ideals of Buddhism in Japan. Since the Japanese revere their emperors and considered them as the head of their family, they obeyed the commands of Shotoku as their filial duty. But practice of Buddhism remained limited to elite class of society.[7] The common people did not have time to do this. In Kamakura period (1185-1333), however, priests Honen and Shinran taught that having faith in Buddha is more important than making effort; and even common people could gain enlightenment if they just believed in his teachings.[8] But it cannot be negated that Shotoku played an important role in propagation and institutionalisation of Buddhism in Japan.

Buddhism and Direct Contacts with India

Shotoku encouraged the Japanese people to visit China and study Buddhism. It was these Japanese students who interacted with Bodhisena in China and asked him to come to Japan with them. Bodhisena, bracing the heavy storms reached Dazaifu in Kyushu, Japan, on May 18, 730 AD and then proceeded towards the province of Settsu (presently Osaka).[9] He participated in the inauguration ceremony of Todaiji temple in Nara. The then emperor gave him a residence in Daisan ji temple and provided him with whatever he wanted.[10]

Direct contact between India and Japan was established when Buddhist monk Bodhisena visited Todaiji temple in Nara and settled there for the remaining period of his life, and taught Buddhism to Japanese peoples. In the next few centuries, Buddhism flourished in different parts of Japan and various centers of Buddhism came to prominence in Japan, including in Kamakura, Kyoto and Nara. Buddhism not only introduced religious practices, but some of the Indian customs seeped into Japan with the introduction of the Indian religion too. These included the custom of cremation, ritual of ancestor worship and offering water, flowers, rice cakes and incense to the departed souls of their ancestors.[11]

However, this early religious linkage could not translate into a stronger relationship between the two countries. Japan's self-imposed seclusion policy also impeded the natural flow of people and interactions among the people of the two countries. It may be mentioned that Japan, in 1633 AD, adopted a policy of seclusion from the outside world apparently to maintain cultural purity; and the country neither allowed the Japanese to go outside, nor the foreigners to come inside Japan. It had opened only few of its ports through which the East Asian nation has been interacting commercially with the outside world. This policy ended in 1868 with Meiji Restoration, when Japan opened itself for foreign interactions and decided to re-engage with the world.

Reopening of Japan: Buddhist Scholars' Interactions with India

After the re-opening of the country, various Japanese monks and scholars visited India and South Asia to exchange views with their counterparts in the region. This included visits by Kitabatake Doryu, Shaku Kozen, and Shaku Soen.[12] Since Buddhism was introduced in Japan through Korea and China, there emerged various sects of Buddhism and the purpose of these travelers was to know true form and practices of Buddhism. Richard M. Jaffe notes that the visits "influenced the shifting Japanese understanding of their form of Buddhism and its relationship to the broader Asian tradition."[13] After their visits, they wrote their experiences in the form of travelogues and essays which helped increase awareness of other forms of Asian Buddhism and "marked the start of growing Buddhist cooperation within the region."[14] Kitabatake in his travelogue *Tenjiku Koroji Shoken* (Things Seen Enroute to India), published in 1886, claimed to have been the first Japanese to have traveled to Bodh Gaya and the tomb of Sakyamuni Buddha.[15]

Apart from interactions with Buddhist monks and scholars in India, Kitabatake, closely observed the Indian society and their economic condition. He viewed India's modern history as a "cautionary tale for the

Japanese—if they failed to compete with the west successfully, they would suffer a similar fate."[16] He also observed that "the brutal British colonial policy in India was hypocritical and shameful."[17] Apparently, Kitabatake was the first Japanese to inform the Japanese society about the sufferings of Indians at the hands of occupation authorities.

Kitabatake's main purpose, however, was to inquire about the location of Sakyamuni's (Gautam Buddha's) tomb. In 1883, Kitabatake, accompanied by his co-traveler Kurosaki reached Bodh Gaya. As per Kitabatake's account, Sakyamuni's tomb was discovered some ten years back, and was being excavated when the two Japanese reached there.[18] Richard M. Jaffe describes that Kitabatake Doryu, took the help of a stonemason to carve a stele (*Seikihi*) to commemorate his visit; it read:

> "Since the founding of Japan, I am the first to make a pilgrimage to the tomb of Sakyamuni. Doryu, December 4, Meiji 16 [1883]."[19]

Jaffe also points that the Japanese duo should have mentioned Bodh Gaya as a place where Sakyamuni got enlightenment not as Sakyamuni's tomb, as it stood at Kushinagara some hundred miles away, where he died. This was due to ignorance and little understanding about biography of Sakyamuni in Japan till mid-Meiji period.

Apart from penning his travelogue and describing his visit to India, Kitabatake delivered a series of lectures in Japan and narrated his observation about the state of Buddhism in India in general, and society in particular. This apparently, generated interest among the Japanese to visit Buddhist sites in India. In 1891, another Japanese traveller, Shaku Kozen visited Bodh Gaya and co-founded Mahabodhi Society with Dharmapala, a Sri Lankan Buddhist. Jaffe, quoting Jacob Kinnard, states that one of the objectives of the society was to "wrest control from the Hindus."[20] In fact, Kozen came to India with one of his associates Ato Yuji, who had collected funds in Japan to purchase Buddhist sites in India, but their plan failed.[21]

As has been mentioned in the previous paragraphs, Japanese severely lacked proper understanding of Buddhism and there emerged many variants of Buddhism in Japan. After the visits of the Japanese Buddhist scholars, they realized that in order to create a Buddhism that could flourish, it was necessary to establish Buddhism that was unified in belief, practice and purpose. They argued to return to the teachings of real Buddhism. Kozen argued:

> There is no true Buddhism that sets Sakyamuni's teaching aside. Therefore, in order to make clear the true teaching of a Buddhism that is really Buddhism, one must, at all costs, return to the living Buddhism of Sakyamuni.[22]

The Objectives of Buddhist Scholars visit to India

It can be said that as a result of series of visits made by the Japanese travellers to Buddhist sites in India and in the Indian subcontinent, the Japanese understood the true teachings of Buddhism and established a kind of Buddhism in which Sakyamuni's teaching was the core.

The visits were also aimed at achieving another objective; the creation of a coalition uniting all Asian Buddhists to repel colonialism and Christianity from Asia.[23] Kozen along with his disciple Nindo, was successful in organising a Buddhist congregation in 1940 to spread Buddhism in Japan. They performed this ceremony in the name of establishing Japanese-led order in Asia and Buddhism was one of the binding threads of all the Asian countries where Buddhism was practiced. Five years later, Nindo made another effort to call a *Vesak* (a gathering of Buddhists) and made the objective of Vesak explicit: "creating spiritual harmony with the people of Southern Asia is important foundation work for us, as we are aiming to construct the Greater East Asia Co-prosperity Sphere."[24] The announcement by the Japanese Buddhist that they want to create a Japanese led order in Asia was in line with the government of Japan which had adopted similar goals in the late 1930s, which has been discussed in the next chapter in details.

As has been analysed above, the visits of Japanese monks and scholars to India resulted in greater understanding of Indian society, and in carving the true biography of Buddha and his teachings. The Buddhists, in line with their government, tried to bring all Buddhists practicing countries into a Japanese-led order. However, this could not be achieved because of the defeat of Japan in the World War II.

Conclusion

When Japan lifted the policy of self imposed seclusion, a new interaction between the Japanese and Indian people began as they started engaging with each other but these engagements remained limited to religious scholars. Since Japanese government, post Meiji restoration wanted to emulate the European model of development, its thrust was to strengthen relationship with the West. On the contrary, people of the two countries looked each other with respect and established emotional connect among themselves. This emotional connect later became one of the binding factors between India and Japan whenever their relationship witnessed intermittent phases. After Meiji Restoration, India and Japan witnessed two intermittent phases; the Cold War period and period after India's 1998 Pokhran nuclear test, when the political relationship between the two countries remained below normal. However, the religious and cultural ties between the two countries continued to flourish.

When Japan decided to restore various interactions that were suspended between the two countries following India's Pokhran nuclear test, religious and cultural link was one of the factors that pushed Japan to re-think its decision. In Prime Minister Yoshiro Mori's word, "India is a Buddhist country and we have old civilisational ties, we could not ignore India for long and decided to normalize the relationship."[25] Therefore, role of Buddhism as a factor in India-Japan bilateral relations cannot be discounted. Apparently this is the reason that India and Japan are once again paying focus to strengthen the Buddhist link between the two states and the people.[26] With the government level backing, they have organized two Buddhist conclaves; one in Bodh Gaya in India in 2015 and another in Tokyo in 2016, to renew and reinvigorate their cultural and religious ties. Hopefully, these endeavours will help deepen the people-to-people contact and add fillip to their bilateral ties.

END NOTES

1. Hajime Nakamura, "Japan and Indian Asia: Their Cultural relations in the past and present," Firma K.L. Mukhopaddyay, Kolkata, 1961, p. 2.
2. Shun Saitoh, "Japan and India," The Japan, India and the Straits Trade Researchers' Association, 1912, Tokyo, p.74.

3. Shun Saitoh, 1912, p.74.
4. Shun Saitoh, 1912, p.75.
5. James M. Vardaman, "Japanese History in simple English," *The Japan Times Publication*, Tokyo, 2016, p.20.
6. Shun Saitoh, p.30.
7. The Confession of Lady Nijo, a famous novel based on autobiographical narratives of a 'wandering Buddhist nun' about her interactions with the peoples in the palace of emperor Go Fukakusa in 13th century Japan highlights various Buddhist practices during the birth ceremonies, prayers to get rid of ailments and customary eight lectures on *Lotus Sutra* which was an annual function, indicate that Buddhism indeed had been patronized by emperors and elites. For details see, "The Confession of Lady Nijo," translated by Karen Brazel, Stanford University Press, Stanford California, 1976.
8. James M. Vardaman, "Japanese History in simple English," p.54.
9. Hajime Nakamura, "Japan and Indian Asia; Their Cultural relations in the past and present," p. 45.
10. Ibid, p.46.
11. Hajime Nakamura, p.2.
12. The two Japanese monks Shaku Kozen and Shaku Soen, apparently chose their first name Shaku to show their affinity with Buddha who was also famous with the name of Shakyamuni.
13. Richard M. Jaffe, "Seeking Sakyamuni: Travel and the Reconstruction of Japanese Buddhism," *Journal of Japanese Studies*, Vol. 30, No. 1, 2004, p.67.
14. Ibid, p.68.
15. Ibid, p.73.
16. Ibid, p.74.
17. Ibid, p.74.
18. Ibid, p.75.
19. Ibid, p.76.
20. Ibid, p.86.
21. Ibid, p.86.
22. Ibid, p.91.
23. Ibid, p.93.
24. Ibid, p.96.
25. Yoshiro Mori's keynote address at the inauguration of 60th years of India-Japan relations, January 18, 2012, Embassy of India, Tokyo, authors personal note. The author participated as a panelist in a discussion on the occasion of inaugural ceremony celebrating 60th years of India-Japan relations.
26. Kanwal Sibbal, "How Modi Can usher Buddha era back to India," *The Daily O*, September 9, 2015 available online at http://www.dailyo.in/politics/global-hindu-buddhist-initiative-bodh-gaya-modi-shinzo-abe-dalai-lama-syria-isis-religious-intolerance/story/1/6144.html. (Accessed on October 2, 2016)

2

Prelude to a New Partnership: India-Japan Relations from Meiji Restoration to the End of World War II

Introduction

As has been discussed in the previous chapter, Japan started to re-engage with the world after 1868 Meiji Restoration. It was expected that Japan will engage officially with India, with which it had established strong religious and cultural bond. But since Japan, following its reopening, had adopted a policy to make the country military and economically strong with an objective to achieve parity with the West, Asia did not figure in its policy priorities. However, a number of Asian countries including India—especially Indian princely states—were inspired by Japan's spectacular achievements in the field of science, technology and education, and were keen to emulate examples set by Japan.[1]

Japan's victory over Russia during Russo-Japanese war (1904-05) was yet another phenomenon which drew Indian nationalists emotionally closer to Japan, and they started following it as a role model. At this juncture, a number of Indians visited Japan and a dialogue between the two civil societies began. The intellectual dialogue brought the two societies closer. Yet in Japanese policy priorities, India-which was administered by the UK—

did not figure prominently. Tokyo looked at India and its revolutionary leaders seriously only after it adopted a policy to break the "economic ring" surrounding Japan in late 1930s. With this strategy in mind, Japan started supporting India's freedom movement and helped establish Indian Independence League and its military wing—the Indian National Army. This chapter, against this context starts with the intellectual dialogue that began between the prominent personalities of the two countries and discusses their role in transforming India-Japan relations and captures the developments in their bilateral relationship post Meiji Restoration till the end of World War II.

The beginning of Intellectual Dialogues between India and Japan

It is interesting to note that during the Meiji Era (1868-1912) while the Japanese government adopted a realist foreign policy which aimed at joining the club of great powers, a section of people of civil society laid emphasis on creating Pan-Asian identity emphasizing on Japanese commonalities with Asia.[2] It also aimed at uniting Asian people from the encroachment of Western countries which posed a threat to erode the unique value based Asian Culture.

During this period, apparently impressed by the Pan-Asianism ideology, a number of Indian thinkers—including Swami Vivekananda and Rabindranath Tagore—held dialogues with their Japanese contemporaries. En route to his visit to Chicago, Swami Vivekananda made a stopover in Japan for three weeks. Moved by post Meiji restoration developments in Japan, he opined: "Japan is completely awakened to what modern age requires. The army is organized and the navy continues to be strengthened. The Japanese are working hard to produce all the essential goods domestically."[3] He was so much inspired by Japan that he wished that "every one of our young men could visit Japan once at least in his life time."[4]

Vivekananda encouraged Indian youth to visit Japan to learn from Japan's experience. At a time when the Indian youths had fascination to get degrees in England, he wanted to send "unmarried graduates" to gain "technical knowledge" from Japan and contribute back their experience and knowledge to Indian society. He urged Indian youths to prefer Japan over England. In his words, the Japanese "have taken everything from Europe, but they remain Japanese all the same, and have not turned European. While in our country terrible mania of becoming westernized has seized upon us like a plague."[5]

Back home, Vivekananda hosted Okakura Tenshin—the Japanese intellectual who was asked to visit India by the Japanese Imperial Art Commission to survey art and archeological remains. During his visit to India from November 1901 to October 1902, Okakura visited Bodh Gaya, Benares (Varanasi), Sarnath, Ajanta and Ellora.[6] Apart from visiting these places, he held a series of dialogues with Swami Vivekananda, Margret Noble (also known as Sister Nivedita) and Rabindranath Tagore. Prior to his India visit, Okakura has visited different parts of China to understand the uniqueness and similarities among the Asian nations. Based on his observations during his visit of India and China, Okakura talked of a "common Asia" having "shared aesthetic past anchored in Buddhism."[7]

In the opening chapter of his book titled *The Ideal of the East,* Okakura observed that "Asia is one." He wrote that the Himalaya only physically divides "two mighty civilizations" India and China "but not even the snowy barriers can interrupt for one moment the broad expanse of love for the ultimate and universal, which is the common through-inheritance of every Asiatic race..."[8]

Okakura, spent most of his time during his visit to India in Calcutta (Kolkata) and stayed in Tagore's house. Naturally, both Tagore and Okakura became good friends. Recalling his friendship with Okakura, Tagore wrote, "When I first met him, I neither knew Japan nor had I any experience of China. I came to know both these countries from the personal relationship with this great man whom I had the good fortune to meet and accept as one of my intimate friends."[9] Tagore's interaction with Okakura and dialogues about the Asian civilization, it seems, generated curiosity in him to know more about this part of the world. In a letter written to one of his acquaintances in Japan, Tagore wrote that he wants to know Japan "in the outward manifestation of its modern life and in the spirit of its traditional past." He expressed his wish to "follow the traces of ancient India" in Japan.[10]

Tagore's Visits to Japan

From 1916 to 1929, Tagore made five visits to Japan and during two of these visits; he stopped both, in Japan and China. Tagore's writing and speeches in Japan remains an important source to understand the post Meiji interactions between India and Japan. Since this aspect has not been adequately analysed from India-Japan bilateral relations perspective, this section of the chapter makes an attempt to bring this aspect to the fore to understand each others' perspective and expectations.

When Tagore established contacts with Okakura and a number of other Japanese intellectuals in Japan, he was not a renowned entity except among disciples of Okakura. But the Nobel Prize that was conferred on him made him famous not only in Japan but across Asia. He was awarded this coveted prize for his collection of poem titled *Gitanjali* (an offering of songs)—the first Asian to receive the Noble Prize for his literary work. It was followed by a knighthood conferred on him by the British monarch in 1915. Therefore, when Tagore arrived in Japan, he was an internationally—acclaimed person and was received by Prime Minister Okuma Shigenobu when he reached Tokyo.[11] During his visit to Japan, he met with a large number of people representing different fields of life. During his first interaction with the Japanese people in Kobe, he felt that there already existed feeling of "nearness" towards India among the people of Japan. He, thus, summarized his experience in his lecture; *The spirit of Japan:*

> And since then, I have had other opportunity of reaching the heart of the people; and I have come to the conclusion, that the welcome which flowed towards me...... was owing to the fact that Japan felt nearness of India to herself, and realized that her own heart has room to expand beyond her boundaries and the boundaries of the modern time.[12]

Additionally, during his visit to Japan, he wrote letters for his audience at home describing his experiences and what he saw there. These letters, written in Bengali, were collected and published later as Tagore's travelogue to Japan. The travelogue, *Japan Jatri* (A visit to Japan) introduced fascinating aspects of Japan to the Indian audience for the first time. In these letters, Tagore gave detailed accounts of traditional dress of Japanese men and women, Japanese short poetry; their way of cleanliness, the Haiku, the Japanese painting, and many more things. In one of the letters he wrote: "the first thing I learned was that I had to leave my shoes at the door of the house before entering. I was told that shoes are for the road, feet are for the house."[13]

Therefore, credits goes to Tagore for introducing fascinating aspects of Indian and Japanese culture and for bringing populace of India and Japan closer to each other. However, there were few aspects of Japan, which went beyond his imagined image of the East Asian country, which developed during his interaction with his friend Okakura Tenshin. In his travelogue, he notes that "when I see something that runs counter to their (Japanese) true spirit, I feel much pain. That Japan, having fought a naval war with China, should litter the countryside with memorials of its victory, is an evidence of barbarism. Japan ought to have known how ugly it is."[14]

When Tagore got the opportunity to speak before the Japanese audience, especially the intelligentsia, he gave his frank opinion about how he felt about Japan and what Japan should do. In one of his speeches at Keio University in Tokyo on July 12, 1916, he praised Japanese civilization terming it as a "civilization of human relationship."[15] But at the same time, Tagore reminded them that Japan's "national unity has not been evolved from the comradeship of arms for defensive and offensive purposes, but it is an extension of the family and the obligations of the heart in a wide field of space and time."[16] Tagore noted that the ideal of '*maitri*' [friendship] is at the bottom of Japanese culture; "*maitri*' with men and '*maitri*' with nature."[17] However, he was of the view that there are group of Japanese "who are not in sympathy with your [Japan's] national ideals; whose object is to gain, and not to grow. They are loud in their boast, that they have modernized Japan."[18]

He had been warning Japan not to recklessly, arm itself, but at the same time, he treaded cautiously so as not to offend his hosts. In the same speech, he observed:

> I do not for a moment suggest, that Japan should be unmindful of acquiring modern weapons of self-protection. But this should never

> be allowed to go beyond her instinct of self-preservation. She must know that the real power is not in the weapons themselves, but in the man who wields those weapons; and when he, in his eagerness for power, multiplies his weapons at the cost of his own soul, then it is he who is in even greater danger than his enemies.[19]

In the same breadth, Tagore suggested the Japanese to steadfastly adhere to the "moral law."[20] He said, "And Japan must have a firm faith in the moral law of existence to be able to assert to herself, that the Western nations are following that path of suicide, where they are smothering their humanity under the immense weight of organisations in order to keep themselves in power and hold others in subjection."[21] He observed that this was sheer imitation of the West and stated that "It is burdening her true nature and causing weakness, which will be felt more deeply as time goes on."[22]

During his visit to Japan, Tagore came to know that Japan was propagating patriotism in its schools. He noted with pain the kind of patriotism that was being instilled among students in its schools. He reminded his audience: "And nations, who sedulously cultivate moral blindness as the cult of patriotism, will end their existence in a sudden and violent death."[23] This observation made by Tagore proved prophetic as Japan's expansionist policies brought disaster for Japan and resulted in its defeat in World War II. While reminding that patriotism may lead to a "sudden and violent death" Tagore explained:

> Never think for a moment, that the hurts you inflict upon other races will not infect you, and the enmities you sow around your homes will be a wall of protection to you for all time to come. To imbue the minds of a whole people with an abnormal vanity of its own superiority, to teach it to take pride in its moral callousness and ill-begotten wealth, to perpetuate humiliation of defeated nations by exhibiting trophies won from war, and using these in schools in order to breed in children's minds contempt for others, is imitating the West where she has a festering sore, whose swelling is a swelling of disease eating into its vitality.[24]

Tagore was cautious not to hurt the sentiments of Japanese and qualified his sentences by adding that why the Japanese must heed to an outsider, a foreigner like him:

When Japan is in imminent peril of neglecting to realise where she is great, it is the duty of a foreigner like myself to remind her, that she has given rise to a civilisation which is perfect in its form, and has evolved a sense of sight which clearly sees truth in beauty and beauty in truth. She has achieved something, which is positive and complete.[25]

Tagore also added:

All these qualities are the outcome of a civilisation, whose foundation is in the spiritual ideals of life. Such a civilisation has the gift of immortality; for it does not offend against the laws of creation and is not assailed by all the forces of nature. I feel it is an impiety to be indifferent to its protection from the incursion of vulgarity of power.[26]

Tagore forewarned Japan not to enter into a power struggle and expansion as Europe has done:

[T]ere is always the natural temptation in us of wishing to pay back Europe in her own coin, and return contempt for contempt and evil for evil. But that again would be to imitate Europe in one of her worst features which comes out in her behaviour to people whom she describes as yellow or red, brown or black. And this is a point on which we in the East have to acknowledge our guilt and own that our sin has been as great, if not greater, when we insulted humanity by treating with utter disdain and cruelty men who belonged to a particular creed, colour or caste.[27]

In the next public address at Tokyo University, he yet again reiterated his views and asked Japan to "apply your Eastern mind, your spiritual strength, your love of spirituality, your recognition of social obligation, in order to cut a new path for this great unwieldy car of progress of discords as it runs."[28]

Tagore reminded his audience that there was an age:

When the whole of Western Asia, from Burma to Japan was united with India in the closest ties of friendship, the only natural tie which can exist between nations. There was a living communication of hearts, a nervous system evolved through which messages ran between us about the deepest needs of humanity. We did not stand in fear of each other, we had not to arm ourselves to keep each other in check, our relation was not that of self interest, of exploitation and spoliation of each

> others' pockets, ideas and ideals were exchanged, gifts of highest love were offered and taken, no difference of language and custom hindered us in approaching each other heart to heart; no pride of race or insolent consciousness of superiority, physical and mental marred our relations; our art and literatures put forth new leaves and flowers under the influence of this sunlight of united hearts; and races belonging to different hands and languages and histories acknowledged the highest unity of man and the deepest bond of love.[29]

It is interesting to note that while a section of Japanese, including Buddhist scholars, in line with the government policy, were trying to forge a new order in Asia led by Japan, Tagore suggested Japan to establish relationship based on ideals.

It may be noted here that the journey which Tagore started with much fascination to know Japan ended in despair. Commenting on Tagore's visit to Japan, PA Narsimha Murthy writes that "mystified by Okakura's single paragraph in *The Ideals of East*, Tagore set off to Japan and China in the hope of mobilizing support for the ideal of Asian spiritual unity only to find that the road to the ideal was long and full of obstacles."[30] To understand that why views and suggestions offered by Tagore did not elicit much support, one must not ignore the observations of Japanese Buddhists who visited India after the re-opening of Japan. One of the Japanese travelers and a Buddhist scholar, Kitabatake Doryu, after witnessing the poverty and the plight of Indians and their sufferings at the hands of their British rulers, looked India's case as a cautionary tale for the Japanese. "If they (the Japanese) failed to compete with the West successfully, they would suffer a similar fate,"[31] cautioned Kitabatake to his audience back home.

Tagore, however, must be commended to give frank advice to Japan; and by doing so he played the duty of a friend as only a friend gives an honest advice. Certainly, the dialogue did not elicit support from the Japanese intellectuals, and the Japanese audience responded by saying that Tagore has "cursed material civilisation of the West and had not offered a workable solution to it."[32] Murthy argues that "Asian unity and Asian civilization were to Tagore essentially a cultural concept whereas the people whom he addressed in Japan were inclined to give a political meaning to them."[33]

Tagore realized that his speeches had failed to produce response he expected, so he cut down his public engagements during the next few months he stayed in Japan. During the next few visits he made to Japan, he did not show similar enthusiasm to engage with the Japanese society; neither was he given the similar treatment in Japan as was given to him during his first arrival. However, during his last visit in March 1929, he delivered a lecture at a meeting organized by the Indo-Japanese Association. He confined himself to India-Japan relations and stated that Okakura had tried to establish a link between Japan and India through culture and understanding. If that friendly and peaceful contact was further expanded, then there will be developed some day "not only national cultures, national minds, but a continental mind of Asia, greatly needed and long waiting to be revealed."[34] Although Tagore's thoughts could not influence the Japanese people who were swayed by the then prevailed notion of patriotism and nationalism; but when his thought expressed through lectures proved true when Japan's expansions ended in defeat, he became a subject of study in Japan. In Japan, many scholars have emerged who studied Tagore, and thus, Tagore remains an important link in India-Japan relations.

The Indian Revolutionaries' Fascination towards Japan

Apart from the intellectuals, a number of revolutionaries were drawn towards Japan. In this section of the chapter, an attempt has been made to highlight of the individuals and their role in fostering ties that becomes a point of reference when India-Japan relations are described. As mentioned earlier, Japan's victory over Russia became a source of inspiration for the Indian youth who were active in India's struggle for independence. Following Japanese victory over Russia in 1905, Tokyo became a Mecca for revolutionaries[35] of all over Asia including Indians who visited Tokyo to seek support from Japanese Society to liberate their countries from British yoke. R.H. Caddock, the Home Member, Government of India was constrained to record subsequently that "the thing would have been much quieter in India during the last ten years (from 1935 to 1945) had Japan met defeat from Russia. It was Japan's victory that first started idea of Swaraj in India."[36]

By shifting their base to Tokyo and other parts of Japan, the Indian revolutionaries organized anti-British propaganda, highlighting the oppression faced by the Indian people at the hands of colonial power. Japan, by this time, had established a security alliance with Great Britain by signing a series of Anglo-Japanese treaties. Still, a number of Indians were successful to launch an anti-British campaign in Japan. It was mainly because many Japanese activists in Japan, motivated by Pan-Asianist ideology had established societies to support the revolutionaries who could oust the old regimes,[37] who they believed, were hand in glove with the western powers. The first known Indian revolutionaries who shifted his base to Tokyo for anti-British propaganda campaign was Maulvi Barkatullah. He took an assignment of teaching Urdu at School of Foreign Languages in Tokyo University in 1909.[38] He also used his time to unleash campaign against the British by publishing various articles aimed at informing the Japanese people about the treatment meted out by colonial rulers to his fellow Indians. Barkatullah had been associated with Indian revolutionaries abroad, and was well acquainted with political propaganda against the British rule. But his activities in Tokyo did not go unnoticed by the British government who treated Barkatullah as "sort of connecting link between three different movements, namely—the Pan-Islamic, Asia for Asiatics, and Indian militant nationalism."[39] The common aim of these movements in the view of British government was "the emancipation of Asia... from the European dominance."[40] The British government in India asked the Japanese government to deal with Barkatullah in a suitable manner.[41] Because of British government's pressure, Barkatullah's contract was not renewed on expiry of his tenure.[42]

Yet another Indian revolutionary who made his presence felt in Japan and campaigned for India's independence was Rash Behari Bose. Bose who was demanded by Britishers in number of anti-government cases, had escaped to Japan and landed in Kobe on June 5, 1915.[43] He established links with a number of Japanese journalists and told them stories of Indian people's sufferings under the British rule in India. These stories frequently appeared in the Japanese press, and thus, a number of people in Japan felt sympathetic about India and offered their moral and political support to the cause of India's struggle for Independence. While campaigning in Japan to gain support for India's independence among the civil society, Bose had been pursuing his goal of an armed rebellion in India by providing weapons to his Indian counterparts. He sent first consignment including some documents addressed to his comrades, to India using one of his associate Avani Nath Mukherjee, but these documents and consignments were confiscated by the British authorities in Singapore. The British discovered big secret; Rash Bihari Bose had escaped to Japan using a false name—P.N. Tagore.[44]

Notably, another revolutionary Heramba Lal Gupta (commonly known as H.L.Gupta), a member of Berlin Committee of the Indians in Germany, a renamed outfit of erstwhile Gadar Party[45] had also arrived in Japan. According to Takeshi Nakajima, Bhagwan Singh was the in charge of Gadar Party's activity in Japan, and was replaced by Gupta in Japan.[46] Both Bose and Gupta took their separate efforts to reach out to the Japanese press and political leadership, who could sympathize with Indian cause. In this process, Gupta met with Shumei Okawa, an Indologist, and befriended with him. He later introduced Bose to Okawa Shumei who later introduced these two Indians with a number of Japanese intellectuals—including Toyama Mitsuru, leader of the Black Dragon Society.[47] Toyama had links with members in the Japanese Diet. When deportation orders were served by the Japanese government to the two Indian revolutionaries in Japan, these linkages helped the Indian duo in evading the deportation.

Both Bose and Gupta took refuge in Nakamuraya, a famous bakery near Shinjuku.[48] It is believed that police knew whereabouts of the Indian duo but did not touch them because they were under Toyama's protection.[49] Japanese government withdrew deportation order in March 1916 when relationship between the United Kingdom and Japan strained. Bose lived freely in Japan thereafter till the end of his life.

Rash Behari Bose later married to a Japanese woman, and got Japanese citizenship and became an important link between Japan and revolutionaries of the Indian Independence League. His role and activities in this regard will be discussed later in this chapter.

India and the Economic Ring Surrounding Japan

Despite the individual support offered by a group of leaders, the Japanese government did not feel the need to give an official support to the cause of Indian freedom movement as it was bound by an alliance with UK. But after the lapse of the third Anglo-Japanese alliance in 1921,[50] the Japanese felt the need to utilize the Indian revolutionaries in their goal to drive the Western power out of the region. Around this time, a section of people in Japan, especially in the Japanese military were arguing to "break through the economic ring that surrounded Japan." In the 1930s it was proposed that "the ring formed by the Americans, the British, the Chinese and the Dutch had become so injurious to Japan that it should either break the ring or perish economically."[51] Japan adopted the former course with the event of a military rule in the country led by Tojo Hideki.

Moreover, Japan around this time was contemplating to create a "new order in East Asia" and unveiled a "greater East Asia Co-prosperity sphere" concept. The co-prosperity sphere remains one of the most contested and ambiguous concepts, and there are different accounts about how and when it started. Joyce C. Libra believes that the forerunners of the East Asia Co-prosperity Spheres and the New Order in Asia advanced during the Manchurian incident and the "concept was crystallized in the minds of various individuals, some civilians but mostly military, by late 1940s."[52]

Japanese Premier Tojo, in one of his speeches, explained that the aim of Japan was to end Anglo-American exploitation of South-East Asia, and to "help create a new order in which all peoples and all countries will be enabled to develop their distinctive character free from alien interferences and to attain security and prosperity through mutual aid and cooperation."[53] Japan's plan was to conquer British territories and put it under military administration and grant them independence as soon as local condition allowed. Though, India was not included in the official policy of "co-prosperity sphere" considering that administering India militarily because of its huge size would be difficult—the dominant view in Japan was that the presence of British Army in India would always be a threat to the stability of the region.[54]

Fujiwara Kikan and establishment of the Indian Independence League

Apparently, motivated by the aim of "breaking the economic ring" surrounding Japan, the Japanese military officials were given task to "consider future Indo-Japanese relations from the standpoint of establishing Greater East Asia Co-prosperity Sphere"[55] once an Anglo-Japanese war breaks out in the Malayan sector. This task was to be executed by Major Fujiwara Iwaichi, a middle ranking officer in the Japanese Imperial Army. Fujiwara assured his General that his team "will encourage Indian independence and Japanese-Indian cooperation beginning with operation in the Malay Sector.[56]

Japanese officers contacted various Indian organizations in Southeast Asian countries which were active in their efforts to bring an end to British rule in India. They were successful in contacting Independence League of India (also referred as Indian Independence League), consisting of Thailand-based Indians and of its prominent face-Pritam Singh. Apparently, after the rounds of talks between the active members of the League and Japanese officers, the League was revamped and a new agenda;-cooperation with Japan to liberate Asia was added among the goals of the league.

Pritam Singh, in one of his speeches, apparently overwhelmed by Japanese pledge to overthrow British rule in some of the South East Asian countries, stated that "Japan has taken pledge to stake her fate for the fulfillment of her incomprehensible spiritual aim of liberating the whole of Asia from the British yoke."[57] He was of the view that the "liberation of India would also emancipate the whole of Asia from British Imperialistic suppression."[58] On behalf of the newly revamped League, he appealed Indians to "refrain from helping the British War efforts and to stand up together to attain the glorious Indian freedom."[59] Later, a Memorandum of Understanding (MOU) between the Indian Independence League (IIL) headed by Pritam Singh and Col. Tamura was signed, and the IIL was given the task to weaken British Empire in Southeast Asia with the help of Indian nationalists based in the region. As per the MOU, the main objective of the cooperation between Japan and India would be to "establish India and Japan as an independent, sovereign and equal nation."[60] It was also agreed that once the Anglo-Japanese hostilities breaks out, "the IIL will proceed to South Thailand and Malaya along with the advancing Japanese forces and will enlarge its base in the area, rouse the Indian people and soldiers of the British Indian army in the area to join the anti-British independence movement, and propagate goodwill for the Japanese forces."[61]

Notably, it was also agreed that the Japanese authorities will "assist propaganda activities of the IIL by loaning the broadcasting facilities in Tokyo, Bangkok and other occupied territories. Again, aeroplanes will be loaned for distributing propaganda materials within the Japanese sphere of influence."[62] This MOU between Japan and the little known organization IIL was an important landmark in the relationship of India and Japan. Before this event, India did not figure prominently in Japanese foreign policy. Later a liaison agency headed by Fujiwara Iwaichi of Japanese Imperial Army was formed to supervise and guide the activities of the IIL. Both Indian and Japanese were given bands with the letter F written on them as an identification mark.[63]

It may be noted that MOU between Pritam Singh and Col. Tamura had agreed for an identification mark "so that Japanese troops in the operational area could recognize the members of the IIL and not interfere with their free movement in the area."[64] Besides being the initial letter Fujiwara as code word, F also stood for 'Friendship' and 'Freedom'. The F Kikan also took care of providing proper treatment to the surrendered soldiers. True to its commitment, IIL prepared anti-British propaganda leaflet in various Indian languages, asking the Indian soldiers to desert the British Army. When Japanese army was moving towards Singapore and Malaya, in December 1941, the propaganda material prepared by IIL did result in surrender of Indian soldiers to Japanese army. The slogans included: "Asia for the Asiatics," "Keep out the white devils from the East," "We have come out to liberate Asia from the clutches of the Anglo-Saxons," and "No Asiatic is our Enemy."[65] The desertion of soldiers from the British Army made the Japanese task easier and on many fronts they started retreating. While the British Army was retreating, Mohan Singh along with his trusted colleague captain Mohammed Akram surrendered before the Japanese authorities in Alor Star.[66]

Mohan Singh later became an important link between India and Japan, and a point of reference in the history of Indian freedom movement. The Japanese side tried to win support of Mohan Singh to achieve its objectives by arguing that war had given the Indians the best opportunity to win freedom.[67] In his conversations with Mohan Singh, Fujiwara cited reasons for supporting India's independence; first, Japan and India had a common enemy to fight to achieve their objective; secondly, Japan's historical relations with India which was motherland of Japan's religion and culture; thirdly, geographical and ethnic ties in Asia and fourthly, the Japanese people's angry indignation at the subservience and indignity which the Indians were suffering under the British.[68] Mohan Singh offered conditional support to Fujiwara and presented six point proposals before Fujiwara in exchange of this support. These were: a) the Indians would organize an Indian peoples army (it was later named Indian National Army), b) the Japanese army would give it whole-hearted aid, c) the Indian army and the IIL would co-operate for the time being, d) the Japanese Army would recognize Mohan Singh as leader of the Indian captives, e) the Japanese army would treat Indian captives as friends and liberate those who wished to join the Indian army, and f) the Indian army would be recognized as a friendly allied army by the Japanese army.[69]

Fujiwara gave Mohan Singh his personal consent but at the same time, he reminded that recognizing INA as Japan's ally would create technical difficulties with the Japanese.[70] This demand indeed created lots of difficulties between Japanese administration and the INA, which will be discussed later in this chapter. The INA was born following an understanding between Fujiwara and Mohan Singh. Mohan Singh decided to raise the Indian National Army consisting of Indian prisoners of war. INA was considered the military wing of the IIL.

Consequent upon the formation of INA, Mohan Singh started cooperating Pritam Singh in his propaganda war and printed the leaflets. The Japanese army threw these leaflets along battle lines in Malaya.[71] A combination of strategies; an aggressive war backed by propaganda, helped Japan win Malaya war without much resistance from the British Army. A large number of soldiers were taken as Prisoner of War (POW) by the Japanese Army. When the INA was formed, F. Kikan has agreed to expand the INA by recruiting the surrendered soldiers into the INA. Fujiwara tried to impress upon Japanese military authorities, especially Major Ozeki of the 8th section of Imperial headquarters, who visited him at the fall of Kuala Lumpur. T.R. Sareen notes that Fujiwara argued that independence of India with the Japanese cooperation was essential for the successful conclusion of the East Asian war and the realization of Japan's cherished objective of establishing the greater East Asia Co-prosperity sphere. Lebra adds that Fujiwara impressed upon Ozeki to develop a policy of "cutting India adrift from England"[72] and Japan must clarify a basic policy for "Indian Independence movement"[73] The Japanese official did inspect the INA but were not impressed with the stature of Mohan Singh, as he was not a political figure in India, and were reluctant to approve Fujiwara's plan to support India's freedom movement led by Singh. After quizzing Mohan Singh, the visiting Japanese delegation informed Fujiwara that "Captain Mohan Singh is neither a statesman nor an experienced revolutionary."[74] But Ozeki agreed to strengthen Indian Independence League, and it was decided that F. Kikan would be replaced with a more powerful national organization.[75] He also suggested that the new organization should be given the status of a diplomatic mission or embassy rather than a proxy agency of Japanese policy.[76] Meanwhile, the newly formed INA got major boost following the capture of Singapore on February 15, 1942, and Fujiwara handed some 50,000 Indian POWs to Mohan Singh. In a short speech during the handing-over ceremony, Fujiwara told the POWs that "if you make up your mind and fight hand-in-hand with Japan, then it will not be difficult to drive away British from India."[77]

The Iwakuro Kikan and Unification of IIL under Rash Bihari Bose

Following the creation of INA, a military organ of the then IIL, Japan wanted to effectively control the organization to achieve its political objectives. By this time, Japan had replaced Fujiwara Kikan with a newly formed Iwakuro Kikan under the leadership of Colonel Iwakura, a powerful figure in Japanese Army High Command.[78] The Japanese authorities in Tokyo decided to put the leadership of IIL under Rash Behari Bose, who by then had taken Japanese citizenship. An invitation to participate in the meeting to be held in Tokyo was sent under the name of Rash Behari Bose.[79]

It is believed that Iwakuro Kikan with the help of Japanese administration entrusted Bose to take effort to create a single unified organization by bringing various groups active in Japan and Southeast Asia together. A conference held under the leadership of Bose in December 1941 called upon India to rise against the British. The resolution adopted by the conference also urged Japan to help India to achieve its independence.[80] Subsequently, another conference was organized on March 28, 1942 in Tokyo to give proper direction to the question of India's independence.[81] This conference was inaugurated by Iwakuro who in his opening address urged the Indian delegation to fight for the liberation of India asking them to utilize the international situation which has become more favourable to them than ever before.[82]

As expected, the conference elected Rash Behari Bose as President of the IIL. After the conclusion of the conference, premier Tojo invited some of the Malay delegation and held a brief meeting with them assuring them that Japan will assist the Indian Independence movement. But they were not satisfied with the "perfunctory" assurance given by Tojo.[83] The Tokyo conference did lead to the merger of different groups working for Indian independence in East Asia but serious differences emerged between the IIL representative from South East Asia and Japan.

The representatives from Southeast Asia were of the view that Bose was manipulating the conference as per the instructions from the Japanese Government. On the other hand, the Indian representatives based in Japan thought that the Indians living in Southeast Asia had been too loyal to the Britishers and had no experience as revolutionaries.[84] Following this conference, the leadership of the IIL was taken over by "Tokyo Indians."[85] But later, the representatives of the IIL from Southeast Asian nations accepted the leadership of Bose considering that he commanded great respect in Japan and had a very good relationship with the people in the administration.[86]

Following the conference, N.Raghavan one of the participants in the Tokyo conference was of the view that Japan was sincere for India's

Independence and "this sprit was not confined to (the Japanese) statesmen alone. Rich as well as poor, the intellectual as well as the man in the street, almost everyone in the country was actuated with the burning desire to see an India for Indian completely free and Independent."[87] However, contrary to Raghavan, many Indian activists started doubting Japanese intention especially after the Iwakuro Kikan started serving as a liaison agency between INA and the Japanese government.[88] Fujiwara Kikan had built relationship of trust with Indians. Contrary to it, the Iwakuro Kikan failed to earn goodwill from the Indians especially from those living in the Far East.[89]

After taking over the leadership of the IIL, Rash Behari Bose started propaganda activities using Japan Broadcasting Cooperation. At a time when the Japanese army had bombed parts of British bases in Eastern India, in his messages, Bose defended the Japanese bombings of British bases in India and argued that this has been undertaken by the Japanese to strengthen the Indian efforts of freedom and "not to harm the Indian people."[90]

Against this background, Indian Independence League organized a week-long conference at Bangkok on June 15, 1942. The conference was attended by more than 3000 people living outside India and 110 delegation representing two million Indians living in Japan, Manchukuo, Hong Kong, Shanghai, Indo-China, the Philippines, Sumatra, Burma, Borneo, Java, Malaya and Thailand attended it. Apart from the Indian representatives, ambassadors and ministers of Axis powers, including Japan, attended the conference and promised help to India in its independence. Premier Tojo in his message supported India's independence movement and said that "Japan is firmly determined decisively to destroy Britain and she will be compelled to take action so long as British military strength remains in India."[91] Addressing the conference, Rash Behari Bose portrayed Japan as liberator of Asia form the Western Imperialism. He stated:

> We have been working in Japan for decades so that we can see Japan in a position to stand by the oppressed Asiatics and to liberate Asia. We were anxiously awaiting the day when Japan would fully realize the great significance of creating a free and united Asia and would feel convinced that it was in the interest of Japan herself, as also for the

> rest of Asia if not for the world as a whole, that the octopus grip of the Anglo-Saxon in the East must be destroyed route and branch. We all were fully convinced that Japan alone was in the position to take the honour.[92]

As per the resolutions adopted in the Bangkok conference, the INA constituted a Council of Action consisting of Mohan Singh (In Charge of the army), K.P.K. Menon (In charge of Publicity and propaganda), N.Raghavan (In charge of organization), G.A. Gilani (military training).[93] The INA was placed under the Council of Action of the Indian Independence League. Several resolutions were adopted in the Bangkok conference for which an official response was sought from Japan. One of the resolutions demanded: "....immediately on the severance of India from the British empire, the Imperial government of Japan shall respect the territorial integrity and recognize the full sovereignty of India, free of any foreign influence, control or interference of a political, military, or economic nature."[94]

The apparent reason behind this resolution was the apprehension that Japan would treat India at par with Manchukuo or other states which the Imperial Army had occupied.[95] One of the resolutions adopted in the Conference became source of contention between Japan and the IIL. This resolution demanded:

> The imperial government of Japan may be pleased to arrange with the authorities now freed from the domination of the Anglo-Saxons and their Allies by the Imperial forces of Japan to hand over properties owned by Indians (including those owned by Indian companies, firms or partnership) and left behind by them owing to the existence of War to the Council of Action of this movement in trust of their rightful owners, to manage and control the said properties and advance the income thereof for the use of this movement to be paid as and when claimed by the said owners...[96]

More importantly, the resolution demanded Japan to grant status of an allied army to the INA in relation to its Japanese counterpart. Sareen notes that at the end of the conference, on the request of delegates, Rash Behari Bose handed a letter to Iwakuro to pass it on to the Japanese government. The letter asked the Japanese government to make a formal declaration that it will give all possible help to India in its efforts to attain complete independence.[97] The delegation waited to hear the formal response from Japan. However, no formal commitment in this regard was received by the IIL and the delegation returned with an obvious disappointment. The wording of the resolutions, especially demand of parity between INA and the Imperial Army as well as autonomy was not to the liking of Tokyo and hence no response was given by Japan.[98] Iwakuro, conveyed to Bose to keep the Bangkok resolution 'secret':

> I have the honour to inform you that the imperial Japanese government is determined to extend whole-hearted and unstinted support, as evidenced in the repeated statements made by premier Tojo and also in his recent message of felicitation to the Bangkok Conference in regard to the request dated on June the 22nd, 1942, from the Indian Independence League to the Imperial Japanese government with the objective of attaining complete independence for India by supporting the independence movement in India and removing Anglo-American influence. The Imperial Japanese government agrees with your view to keep the resolutions of the Bangkok conference secret, and it is also the wish of the Imperial Japanese government that this reply will be kept under strict secrecy.[99]

The IIL, and especially member of the Council of Action, were not convinced by the response and when they again sought a more detailed explanation, Japan sent a team of Japanese military officials consisting of Col. Kitabe, Tsuchimochi and others and on October 12, 1942 they briefed the members of the Council of Action. A member of the team informed the IIL that it was all right to pass those resolutions but "you will be mistaken that those resolutions are binding on the Japanese government."[100] On the resolution demanding the handover of the properties owned by Indians in the territories liberated by Japanese Army, the Japanese officials categorically rejected this demand citing the reason that "The Council of Action being a body without any territory to rule over and without any financial status, cannot be looked upon as a Government, ...any decision by the Council of Action to be worked upon must be such as to be found acceptable to the Japanese Government."[101]

Lebra notes that when an Indian representative of the IIL asked Japanese delegation to adopt a more conciliatory approach to address the issue, Kitabe responded that "Why not the public be told that IIL works under the leadership of the Japanese Government." Another member, Mr. Yutani intervened by saying that "absentee Indian property according to International Law is enemy property and belongs to the Japanese government," adding that the IIL members are "under the wrong impression that the ownerless Indian properties belongs to them."[102]

Japan's response later created a number of problems within the IIL/INA and created distrust between Japan and the IIL/INA as well.[103] A number of interpretations have been drawn about this problem. Tatsuo Hayashida, a Japanese historian argues that the demand of Imperial response on the Bangkok resolution was "not in good taste." He further argues that "the Imperial Rescript could not be asked for, it had to come as a gift of Emperor as was the Japanese custom. This caused the Indian side to question the sincerity of Japanese leaders and resulted in cooling off the mutual trust between Indian representative and the course of their further dealings."[104] Quite contrary to it, General Kitabe observes that "a point by point reply of their memorandum was not a matter of difficulty. The reason for bungling can be traced to the lack of understanding of the Indian mind by the imperial headquarters and the attitude of Tojo."[105]

Sareen points that unlike Fujiwara, Iwakuro was guided by the policy laid down in Tokyo in 1942. This policy, Sareen argues, was to use INA for "propaganda purposes, particularly to foster anti-British feelings in the British Army and the Indians in the region for controlling the prisoners of war; and maintaining law and order among Indian population."[106] Later, Iwakuro himself explained to the Indian representatives in Malaya that his aim was not to lead the Indian independence movement but to give it a helping hand.[107]

A difference of opinion also emerged between Captain Mohan Singh and Iwakuro over the reorganization of INA. Mohan Singh wanted to raise an army of 2,50,000 personnel as many civilians had shown eagerness to join the army,[108] but Iwakuro favoured raising of small force. Iwakuro allowed raising one division when the liaison agency came to know about the aim of Imperial headquarters to opening a new front in Northeast India for the defense of Burma.[109] The differences between Iwakuro and INA deepened further by the late half of 1942. Sareen points that it was "due more to the mishandling of the situation to Iwakuro than to any other factor."[110] Instead of resolving the problems, both sides became suspicious of one another.[111]

The Bangkok resolution became a source of contention not only between the INA and Iwakuro Kikan but also between the INA and its political organ the IIL, especially between the President of IIL Rash Behari Bose and Mohan Singh. Mohan Singh considered Bose a Japanese puppet who never mustered enough courage to confront the Japanese on many issues.[112] As mentioned earlier, Mohan Singh wanted expansion of the INA and was waiting for Japanese approval. But when he got no indication from Iwakuro Kikan, the liaison agency between Japan and the IIL, he concluded that Japan "wanted a puppet army only for propaganda."[113]

Meanwhile, on July 10, 1942, Iwakuro received a response from Tokyo and passed it on to Rash Behari Bose. However, it was a general response, not a point by point response which was demanded by the IIL in response to Bangkok resolutions. The Council of Action discussed the response of Japan in September 1942 and expressed its dissatisfaction over the Japanese response. On the request of the Council of Action, Rash Behari Bose sent another letter to Iwakuro asking the specific response but the letter was later withdrawn when Iwakuro pointed that it would be construed as a challenge to the Japanese authority.[114] Mohan Singh considered this development as delaying tactics to retard INA's progress.

Iwakuro Kikan decided that the "surplus volunteers" of INA who had not yet joined the INA will be treated as Prisoners' of War. Mohan Singh complained that Japan is not keeping to its word as when the INA was formed, Fujiwara Kikakan, predecessor of the present liaison agency between INA and Japan, had handed over all the POWs of Indian origin to Mohan Singh. Raghavan also took similar line and argued that "if the Japanese were really serious about India's fighting for their independence, then the initiation of expansion (of INA) should have come from the Japanese side."[115]

By this time, Japan had decided troops' movement alongside India-Burma border and was asking contingents of the INA to be deployed there. Enraged over these developments, Mohan Singh demanded that the Japanese side give him a free hand to raise an army of not less than 2,00,000 strong and set a deadline of January 1, 1943 of Japan's response.[116] Fujiwara, who had good rapport with Mohan Singh, tried to assuage him by arguing that it was not possible to "create an efficient army out of the defeated soldiers so quickly."[117] However, Mohan Singh did not relent. He along with his colleagues, Menon and Gilani resigned from the Council of Action. Mohan Singh, however, retained the leadership of the INA.

In yet another development, Captain Mahabir Singh Dhillion of INA who had been sent to Indo-Burma border for intelligence work disserted INA and left for India.[118] The Japanese side suspected that another confidante of Mohan Singh, Col. N.S. Gill, was trying to pass over to British.[119] He was charged by the Japanese officials of having sent a letter to British General in India and an arrest was looming over Gill. Mohan Singh opposed his arrest which resulted in Mohan Singh's dismissal and solitary confinement on December 29, 1942. This development led to a serious blow to the INA and it was at the verge of weathering away.

However, Japanese leadership wanted that the INA continues its existence and decided to give the command to a strong leadership. It started negotiating with Germany to hand over Subhash Chandra Bose. Japanese premier Tojo announced in the Japanese Diet on February 4, 1943 that Japan had no territorial ambitions in India and was willing to give assistance to see India free.[120] To fill the vacuum left by Mohan Singh's dismissal and solitary confinement, INA was put under the control of Japanese military bureau, with Lt. Col. J.K. Bhonsle as Director.[121] Though many Indians left the INA and the League but Rash Behari Bose was successful in keeping the structure of the IIL intact till the arrival of Subhash Chandra Bose in East Asia.

Hikari Kikan, Subhash Chandra Bose and the INA

After utilizing the services of various Indian leaders to achieve its objective of "breaking economic ring" surrounding Japan, officials in Tokyo decided to use Subhash Chandra Bose's charismatic leadership. It may be noted here that the Japanese were keen to utilise Subhash's services for their objectives. Japanese Consul General in Kolkata, in a message to Japanese government suggested to help establish contacts with Subhash who was at that time living in exile in Germany on the one hand, and on the other hand invest in strengthening his party; the Forward block by providing large quantity of weapons so that the party could launch a popular revolt against British government in India.[122] This suggests that Japanese had known the worthiness of Subhash much before the leadership crisis broke out in the INA and the IIL. But they did not execute this policy as they were already working through another Indian revolutionary leader—Rash Behari Bose.[123]

Finally, the Japanese cabinet in its meeting in April 1942 decided that Subhash Chandra Bose could be used "according to the prevalent policy" and he was to be invited to Tokyo to judge his utility value from the standpoint of this policy."[124] However, the plan was not executed until the leadership crisis broke out in INA following the suspension of Captain Mohan Singh from the organisation. Following his departure from Germany, Subhash Chandra Bose arrived in Tokyo in June 1943 and held two meetings with Prime Minister Tojo on June 10 and June 14, 1943. Two days after the meeting, Tojo made a speech in the Diet in presence of Subhash where he said, "India has been for centuries under England's cruel rule. We wish to express righteous indignation at their agony and sympathy for their aspirations for complete independence. We firmly resolve that Japan will do everything possible to help Indian Independence. I am convinced that day of Indian freedom and prosperity is not far off..."[125]

Meanwhile, a new liaison agency, the Hikari Kikan under Yamamoto, a friend of Subhash from Germany days, was set up replacing the Iwakuro Kikan. Two days after meeting Subhash, Tojo announced in the Diet that Japan will extend all support to Indians to end the Anglo-Saxon domination and enable them to achieve their full Independence.[126] Subhash took over the leadership of the IIL and gave speeches using the NHK for his propaganda broadcasts. In his first press conference, Subhash stated that "a powerful Japan is necessary today as in the past for recovery of Asia."[127] After uniting the rank and files of the INA anew, he planned to set up a Provisional Government of Azad Hind with the help of the Japanese government. Sareen notes that the Hikari Kikan and a section of Japanese army were hostile to the plan. They were of the view that establishment of a free government would raise a number of political, military and diplomatic issues in the midst of the World War."[128]

It seems, Subhash was able to convince the Japanese government to treat INA as an ally army, a demand the previous leadership of INA has put forward a number of times and that had led to the disputes between Japan and the leadership of the IIL/INA. An instruction to the Japanese army was issued by the Hikari Kikan in this regard in September 1943. It instructed to the Japanese army that "the Indian National Army constituted by the favour of his Imperial Majesty, is the armed forces of the Indian Independence League" and it would be treated as "the army of ally."[129]

As has been mentioned previously, the main objective of allying with Indian revolutionaries was to evict the British forces from India. The instruction issued to Japanese army also noted this fact:

> To achieve the object of the war, laid down in the Imperial rescript on the declaration of war, which is the destruction of the enemies-England and America, we must drive their forces from India. The Indian National Army, whose objective is to overthrow the British Raj in India, is therefore our ally.[130]

While working with the INA and the IIL, Japanese understood that the Indians are "difficult to handle" and a clear instruction was given to the Japanese officers to avoid any misunderstanding between them and the Indians. The instruction to this effect notes:

> Owing to anti-Japanese propaganda by the British, they have very wrong ideas of Japan. They are strong individualists and materialists as well as possessing many customs arising from their religious beliefs-this makes them very difficult to handle. They frequently have quick tempers especially on the battle-field. We Japanese, as leaders in the building of a new world, as being comrades in the destruction of England and America, must treat them with a kindly and tolerant leniency whatever weak points they may have.[131]

The Japanese also understood that the feelings of superiority among the Japanese officers have led to various misunderstanding between the Japanese and the IIL/INA and the instruction was issued to discard this mentality:

> Discard the feeling of superiority and do not look down on them. The thought that white people are a superior race and coloured people an

> inferior one is to be thoroughly eradicated. It is to break down this what we are waging the Great East Asia War. In the bottom of our hearts we have mistaken pride that we Japanese are a superior people. This must be discarded and we must cease to look down on them and show respect for their official powers.[132]

As has been discussed previously, the IIL was demanding to hand over properties vacated by Indians to the IIL and the Iwakuro Kikan rejected this demand citing that since the IIL does not have any territory of its own and this would cause legal problems. But after the arrival of Subhash Chandra Bose in East Asia and taking over of INA's leadership, the Japanese government recognized the provisional Indian government on October 23, 1943 and it was followed by Germany and Italy. All the Japanese supported government in the region including Philippines, Thailand, Burma, Nanking and Korea extended their recognition to Free Indian Provisional Government (FIPG).

Subhash's next plan was to expand the personnel strength of the INA to 50,000 from the existing 13,000. However, the Hikari Kikan, the liaison agency between the IIL and Japanese government did not allow the INA to increase the strength beyond 30,000.[133] While, Subhash was negotiating with the Hikari Kikan about the expansion of the INA, he never left any chance to support Japan's political objective of creating Greater East Asia Co-prosperity Sphere. Therefore, when Japan organized a conference of Greater East Asian Nation in Tokyo on November 5, 1943, Subhash participated as an observer. He stated in his speech that "the establishment of Greater East Asia Co-prosperity Sphere would pave way for a pan-Asiatic federation," adding that the establishment of "a free and prosperous Greater East Asia depends entirely on our ability to achieve victory in this war with the help of axis power."[134]

Through his fiery speeches in the attendance of Tojo, Subhash struck a chord between INA and Japan. Naturally, when during the conference, Bose demanded Tojo to hand over the territory of Andaman and Nicobar, which Japan occupied after overthrowing the Britishers from there, Japan accepted this demand with certain caveats attached. Subhash impressed upon Japan that if the Provisional Indian government would have a territory of its own, it can get recognition under the International Law. A day after Bose's demand, Tojo made this announcement:

> I take this occasion to declare that the Imperial Government of Japan is ready shortly to place the Andaman and Nicobar Islands, now under the occupation of Imperial Japanese forces, under the jurisdiction of the Provisional Government of Azad Hind, as the initial evidence of her readiness to help in India's struggle for independence.[135]

Japan handed over the island to Free Indian Provisional Government (FIPG), and allowed it to handle the civil administration while keeping the defence and military administration of the island under the Japanese naval command considering that the INA is not equipped enough to secure the territory which has strategic significance to Japan.[136] In the next step, Japan allowed the provisional government to close down the Andman Nicobar jail. Since lots of Indian political prisoners were languishing in the jail, it had an emotional impact on Indians and raised awareness in India about Japan's moves to liberate India.

After setting up free government, Subhash prepared ground to the "March on to Delhi" and wanted that the Japanese army should support the INA to launch this march to liberate India. Prior to Subhash's arrival in East Asia, the Japanese army was also suspecting a counter attack from the British Army to recapture Burma from Japan and to foil the attack the Japanese had prepared a blueprint of an offensive operation named "operation 21." They decided to execute this plan in spring 1942 and as per the plan Japanese army wanted to advance up to Tinsukhia (Assam) and Imphal (Manipur).[137] However, the plan due to some technical reasons had to be postponed. When Subhash asked Japanese army's support to help it advanced towards India, Tojo gave his consent for Imphal campaign considering that Bose's presence in India would have great political impact on Indian people and it will also allay their fears about Japan's advancement towards India. It was also decided that "upon the occupation of Imphal, the provisional Government of Free India will be established there in order to accelerate the political campaign in India."[138]

The INA and the Japanese army did succeed in their campaign and reached up to Manipur. The INA established its headquarters at Moriang in the house of a local Manipuri sympathizer.[139] However, after initial success, Japanese army and INA faced enormous difficulties and they had to retreat from the areas they had captured and could not fulfill their dream to reach Kohima. But Subhash did not lose hope to re-launch another campaign to liberate India and to execute his new strategy he left for Tokyo by the end of 1944. He had consultation with the new Japanese Prime Minister General Kaiso who assured him to provide all political and material support for achieving India's Independence. He also sent a Japanese diplomatic representative to the Free Provisional government of India. But in the beginning of 1945, political landscape of Asia was changing again and Japan was also retreating from various war fronts. Subhash was planning to exercise another option that is to seek Russia's support towards India's Independence and while moving towards Russia in a special plane met with an accident in Taipe. Though Subhash's death remained shrouded with mystery, a number of historical accounts suggests that he breathed his last in a hospital in Taikku (Formosa) battling his injuries in the plane crash there.[140]

It is a fact that Japan's policy to advance towards India ended in failure. Various reasons are cited for Japan's policy failures including the timing of invasion towards India. But the dominant opinion among the historians is that the Japanese policy beginning with Fujiwara's mission in 1940 and later creation of the INA was "chiefly for propaganda purposes, particularly to foster anti-British sentiment."[141] Japan was not willing to advance beyond Assam and the advancement too was to secure Burma from a counter invasion by the British to occupy Burma back.

Conclusion

The discussion above suggests that India-Japan relations following the reopening of Japan in 1868 underwent various phases. In the first phase, developments in Japan fascinated many Indians and they started to look Japan as their role model. However, the relationship between the two countries, up to 1930s, was driven by the personalities and the civil societies. In the late 1930s, India started figuring in Japanese foreign policy priorities because of its "geo-strategic location." India's location still remains an important factor for Japanese foreign policy priorities, a factor that will be discussed during the next chapters. In 1930s, Japan considered that to create new order in Asia free from Anglo-American dominance (also described at times as Anglo-Saxon dominance), it is important to drive

British out of India and to achieve this objective they established contacts with Indian revolutionaries in South East Asian countries and worked with them through liaison agencies headed by serving officials of the Japanese Imperial Army.

As has been mentioned above, Japan could not achieve the objectives but this very experiment left deep impact on Indian peoples' mind. History of Indian freedom movement remains incomplete without Japan's reference. The Japanese in the past have not proclaimed their role in India's freedom movement but of late they, especially the Japanese conservatives, have started claiming their role more openly.[142] It cannot be negated that this experiment led to various misunderstandings between India and Japan but it also helped them understand each other and this understanding led to a stronger bonhomie between the two countries.

END NOTES

1. P.A. Narsimhamurthy writes that Princely state of Mysore and Hyderabad sent its emissaries to Japan to study the developments achieved by Japan in the fields of education and science and implement it back home, See P.A. Narasimha Murthy, "India and Japan: Dimensions of their relations," ABC Publishing House, New Delhi, 1986, pp 23-27.
2. Seven Saaler, "Pan-Asianism in modern Japanese history: Overcoming the nation, creating a region, forging and empire," in Seven Saalaer and J. Victor Koschmann (eds) Pan-Asianism in Modern Japanese History: Colonialism, regionalism and borders, Routledge, New York, 2007, p. 3.
3. Quoted in Yasushi Tomiyama, "Japan India partnership based on History of Human Interactions," lecture delivered at India International Centre, New Delhi, and January 5, 2016.
4. Swami Vivekananda, quoted in "Selections from Complete work of Swami Vivekananda," Advaita Ashram Publication, Kolkata, p.378.
5. Ibid, p.457.
6. P.A. Narasimha Murthy, "India and Japan: Dimensions of their relations," ABC Publishing House, New Delhi, 1986, p.40.
7. Brij Tankha (ed), "Okakura Tenshin and Pan-Asianism: Shadow of the Past," Global Oriental, Folkstone, UK, 2009, p.3.
8. Kazuo Okakura, "The Ideals of the East with special reference to the Art of Japan," John Murray, London, 1905, p.1.
9. Stephen Hay, quoted in P.A. Narasimha Murthy, "India and Japan: Dimensions of their relations," p.44.
10. Tagore's letter to Kimura Nikki quoted in Stephen N. Hay, "Asian ideas of East and

West: Tagore and his critics in Japan, China, and India," Harvard University Press, Massachusetts, 1970, p.53.
11. Stephen N. Hay, "Asian ideas of East and West: Tagore and his critics in Japan, China, and India," p.62
12. "The Spirit of Japan, A lecture by Sir Rabindranath Tagore," Indo-Japanese Association, Tokyo, 1916, p.5.
13. Rabindranath Tagore, "A visit to Japan," translation of Japan Jatri by Shakuntala Rao Sastri, East West Institute, New York, 1961, p.78.
14. Ibid, p.85.
15. "The Spirit of Japan, A lecture by Sir Rabindranath Tagore," Indo-Japanese Association, Tokyo, 1916, p.10.
16. Ibid, p.10.
17. Ibid, p.10.
18. Ibid, p.12.
19. Ibid, p.15.
20. Ibid, p.16.
21. Ibid, p.16.
22. Ibid, p.16.
23. Ibid, p.18.
24. Ibid, pp.19-20.
25. Ibid, p.28.
26. Ibid, p.28.
27. Ibid, p.30.
28. "The Message of India to Japan: A lecture by Sir Rabindranath Tagore," Tokyo University Press, Tokyo, 1916, p.13.
29. Ibid, pp.15-16.
30. P.A. Narsimha Murthy, "India and Japan: Dimensions of their relations," p.67.
31. See for details, Richard M. Jaffe, "Seeking Sakyamuni: Travel and the reconstruction of Japanese Buddhism," *Journal of Japanese Studies*, Vol.30, No.1, 2004, p.74.
32. P.A. Narsimha Murthy, "India and Japan: Dimensions of their relations," p.64.
33. Ibid, p.64.
34. Ibid, p.66.
35. Joyce C. Lebra, "Jungle Alliance: Japan and the Indian National Army," Asia Pacific Press, Singapore, 1971, p.48.
36. Quoted in T.R. Sareen, "Japan and the Indian National Army," Mounto Publishing House, New Delhi, 1996, p.7.
37. Sven Saaler, p.3.
38. Takeshi Nakajima, "Bose of Nakamuraya: An Indian Revolutionary in Japan," (translated from Japanese by Prem Motwani), Promilla and Co., New Delhi, 2005, p.70.
39. T.R. Sareen, "Japan and the Indian National Army," Mounto Publishing House, New Delhi, 1996, p.9.

40. Ibid, p.9.
41. Ibid, p.9.
42. P.A. Narsimha Murthy, however, writes that Barkatullah was compelled to leave Japan after the end of his contract, P A Narsimha Murthy, "India and Japan: Dimensions of their relations," p.88.
43. Takeshi Nakajima, "Bose of Nakamuraya: An Indian Revolutionary in Japan," (translated from Japanese by Prem Motwani), Promilla and Co., New Delhi, 2005, p.51.
44. Ibid, p.59.
45. The Berlin Committee of Germany was organized by Hardayal a former President of Gadar Party.
46. Takeshi Nakajima, "Bose of Nakamuraya: An Indian Revolutionary in Japan," p.66.
47. Joyce C. Lebra, "Jungle Alliance: Japan and the Indian National Army," p.39.
48. Takeshi Nakajima, "Bose of Nakamuraya: An Indian Revolutionary in Japan," p.85.
49. Joyce C. Lebra, "Jungle Alliance: Japan and the Indian National Army," p.49.
50. From 1902 to 1921, Japan has signed three alliances with England known as Anglo-Japanese Alliances. The third Anglo-Japanese alliance lapsed in 1921 and it was not renewed later.
51. Tojo's speech quoted in T.R. Sareen, "Japan and the Indian National Army," p.84.
52. Joyce C. Lebra, "Jungle Alliance: Japan and the Indian National Army," Asia Pacific Press, Singapore, 1971, p.xii.
53. T.R. Sareen, "Japan and the Indian National Army," p.40.
54. Ibid, p.40.
55. Joyce C. Lebra, "Jungle Alliance: Japan and the Indian National Army," p.3.
56. Fujiwara quoted in Joyce C. Lebra , "Jungle Alliance: Japan and the Indian National Army," p.3.
57. "Speech of Pritam Singh on the occasion of the opening of the Independence League of India in Bangkok requesting the Indians to refrain from helping the British War efforts," December 9, 1941. For full text of the speech please refer to Appendix 1, T.R. Sareen, "Japan and the Indian National Army," pp.235-236.
58. Ibid.
59. Ibid.
60. "Memorandum of Understanding between Sardar Pritam Singh and Col. Tamura," December 4, 1941. For full text of the MOU, please refer to T.R. Sareen, "Japan and the Indian National Army," appendix III, pp.243-245.
61. Ibid.
62. Ibid.
63. T.R. Sareen, "Japan and the Indian National Army," p.56. Also see, Joyce C. Lebra, "Jungle Alliance: Japan and the Indian National Army," p.7.
64. MOU between Pritam Singh and Tamura, op.cit., n.60.
65. T.R. Sareen, "Japan and the Indian National Army," p.62.
66. Ibid, p.63.

67. Ibid, p.64.
68. T.R. Sareen, "Japan and the Indian National Army," p.64, Also see Joyce C. Lebra, "Jungle Alliance: Japan and the Indian National Army," p.20.
69. Joyce C. Lebra, "Jungle Alliance: Japan and the Indian National Army," p.24.
70. Ibid, p.24.
71. Ibid, p.26.
72. Ibid, p.26
73. Ibid, p.27
74. Ibid, p.31.
75. T.R. Sareen, "Japan and the Indian National Army," p.75.
76. Joyce C. Lebra, "Jungle Alliance: Japan and the Indian National Army," p.45.
77. T.R. Sareen, "Japan and the Indian National Army," p.77.
78. Joyce C. Lebra, "Jungle Alliance: Japan and the Indian National Army," p.43.
79. Ibid, p. 40.
80. T.R. Sareen, "Japan and the Indian National Army," p. 86.
81. Ibid, p.88.
82. Ibid, p.92.
83. Joyce C. Lebra, "Jungle Alliance: Japan and the Indian National Army," p.46.
84. Ibid, 46.
85. Both Lebra and Sareen describe that the representatives of the IIL from Southeast Asia referred the Indian revolutionaries in Japan as Tokyo Indians.
86. T.R. Sareen, "Japan and the Indian National Army," p. 94.
87. Ibid, 97.
88. T.R. Sareen, "Japan and the Indian National Army," p. 97.
89. Ibid, p. 98.
90. Ibid, p.99.
91. Ibid, p.101.
92. Rash Behari Bose quoted in "Jungle Alliance: Japan and the Indian National Army," Joyce C. Lebra, p.76.
93. Ibid, p.77.
94. Ibid, p.78
95. Ibid, p.78
96. Ibid. p.79.
97. T.R. Sareen, "Japan and the Indian National Army," p.102.
98. Ibid, p.110.
99. Joyce C. Lebra, "Jungle Alliance: Japan and the Indian National Army," p.82.
100. Ibid, p.88.
101. Ibid.
102. Ibid, p.89.
103. Ibid, p. 84.
104. Tatsuo Hayashida quoted in T. R. Sareen, "Japan and the Indian National Army," p.122.

105. Kitabe, quoted in "Japan and the Indian National Army," Sareen, p. 123.
106. T.R. Sareen, "Japan and the Indian National Army," p.108.
107. Ibid, p.109.
108. Mohan Singh in his statement issued on 9 October 1945 states that 'I wanted to raise and train a patriotic force of 200,000 to 500,000 strongly united, well disciplined and completely independent." For details see "Statement by Mohan Singh after his release from interment at Sumatra," appendix VII in T.R. Sareen, "Japan and the Indian National Army," pp. 264-287.
109. Ibid, p.113.
110. Ibid, p.118.
111. Ibid, p.118.
112. Ibid, p.121.
113. "Statement by Mohan Singh after his release from interment at Sumatra," For details see, appendix VII in T.R. Sareen, "Japan and the Indian National Army," pp. 264-287.
114. T.R. Sareen, "Japan and the Indian National Army," p.124.
115. Ibid, p.125.
116. Ibid, p.129.
117. Ibid, p.130.
118. Ibid, p.126.
119. Ibid, p.130.
120. Ibid, p.139.
121. T.R. Sareen, "Japan and the Indian National Army," p.139, also see Joyce C. Lebra "Jungle Alliance: Japan and the Indian National Army," p.100.
122. Joyce C. Lebra "Jungle Alliance: Japan and the Indian National Army," p. 61.
123. Ibid, p.66.
124. Ibid, p.12.
125. Ibid, p.116.
126. T.R. Sareen, "Japan and the Indian National Army," p.148.
127. T.R. Sareen, "Japan and the Indian National Army," p.149. Joyce C. Lebra, quotes Subhash as saying that "Indians feel that the existence of a strong Japan is essential for the reconstruction of Asia," Lebra "Jungle Alliance: Japan and the Indian National Army," p.117.
128. T.R. Sareen, "Japan and the Indian National Army," p.153.
129. "Instructions issued by Hikari Kikan outlining the status of the INA, vis-à-vis Japanese Army," September 1943. For full text please refer to T.R. Sareen, "Japan and the Indian National Army," appendix V, pp.253-259.
130. Ibid.
131. Ibid.
132. Ibid.
133. T.R. Sareen, "Japan and the Indian National Army," p.156.
134. T.R. Sareen, "Japan and the Indian National Army," p. 157. Joyce C. Lebra, "Jungle Alliance: Japan and the Indian National Army," p. 132.

135. Joyce C. Lebra, "Jungle Alliance: Japan and the Indian National Army," p.133.
136. T.R. Sareen, "Japan and the Indian National Army," p.158.
137. Ibid, p.172.
138. Ibid, p.177.
139. Ibid, p.184.
140. Joyce C. Lebra gives graphic presentation of circumstances that led to Subahsh's death, See Lebra, "Jungle Alliance: Japan and the Indian National Army," pp.194-199.
141. Joyce C. Lebra, "Jungle Alliance: Japan and the Indian National Army," p.65.
142. Yasushi Tomiyama, notes that "the Independence of India was not achieved solely by the non-violence and civil disobedience movement. The Independence cannot be explained without referring to the armed struggle led by Subhash Chandra Bose and the role of Japan that supported him." For details see Tomiyama, "Japan India partnership based on History of Human Interactions," lecture delivered at India International Centre, New Delhi, January 5, 2016.

3

INDIA AND JAPAN: THE COLD WAR SHADOW ON THE TWO ASIAN DEMOCRATIC CRESCENTS

Background

The end of World War II brought two different results for India and Japan. While the former emerged as an independent nation, the later was facing trial as a vanquished nation before the world. Moreover, in India the leadership which came to power had mixed feelings about Japan. At one point, it had admired the East Asian nation being the first Asian country to triumph over the Europe and became a source of inspiration for them to fight to end their colonial subjugation.[1] The same set of leadership had taken a critical view of Japan's militaristic activities in Asia later. However, the overwhelming mood among the Indian leadership towards Japan soon after Indian independence, as pointed by P.A. Narsimhamurthy, was to "let bygones be bygones and seek an early peace with Japan."[2] But signing a Peace Treaty with Japan was delayed because of "diplomatic duel"[3] between the US and India.

It is interesting to note that while the Japanese leadership considered the terms of US drafted San Francisco Peace treaty as an "advantage for Japan,"[4] Indian leadership has pointed on more than one occasion that they "did not share the premise on which it was based."[5] India's insistence for separate peace treaty with Japan is viewed as "visible and demonstrable evidence" as a "friendly feeling prevailed in India for the great Japanese people."[6] This aspect has been dealt in this chapter to dispel this perception that the same view existed there among the Japanese leadership. Also, this chapter discusses various internal and external factors that acted as push and pull factors in the relationship between the two Asian countries during the Cold War period. This will help the readers deconstruct why despite good beginning, Indo-Japanese relations could not attain the kind of closeness which was expected following summit level meetings between Japanese Prime Minister Kishi Nobusuke and his Indian counterpart Jawaharlal Nehru.

Introduction

As has been discussed in the previous chapter, the stated goal of Japan to support Indian freedom movement during the World War II, was to help India gain liberation from the British yoke. But this goal was not achieved through the Japanese support to the Indian National Army. The end of the World War II though paved way for India's independence. For Japan, the World War II brought catastrophic defeat and it came under the Allied Forces' occupation led by the US. The military was stripped off and a new transition government was put in place by the occupying authority which continued till 1951 when sovereignty was restored to Japan following a Peace Treaty in San Francisco.

India's Reservation on San Francisco Peace Treaty

As Japan was under the US administration, India started a new framework of cooperation with Japan. It may be noted that as agreed by the Potsdam declaration which resulted into Japan's surrender, the Japanese government was required to sign a Peace Treaty with the nations and states, including India, with which it came into conflict during the World War II. The content of the treaty, however, was largely influenced by the US which was administering Japan at that time. The then Indian political dispensation found it problematic. Yoshida Shigeru, Prime Minister of Japan during the occupation period, also confirms in his memoirs that "terms of the treaty"[7] was made by John Foster Dulles, then advisor to the US Secretary of State. India was not satisfied with the development and when it was asked by the US to join the signing of San Francisco Peace treaty, its response was categorical and it raised two basic questions before joining the signing ceremony of the treaty:

(i) The terms of the treaty should concede to Japan a position of honour, equality and contentment among the community of free nations;

(ii) They should be framed as to enable all countries especially interested in the maintenance of a stable peace in the Far East to subscribe to the treaty sooner or later.[8]

India also conveyed to the US that the treaty does not satisfy either of these two criteria. The communications between India and the US and between India and Japan, suggest that apart from the terms of the treaty, India has three major concerns regarding the San Francisco treaty: (a) Transfer of sovereignty of Japan including Okinawa and Bonin islands, (b) Territories occupied by Japan during its expansion to be transferred to the respective countries, and (c) A security treaty between the US and Japan should be signed when it becomes a truly sovereign nation. The US addressed only the last concern raised by India. It did sign a security treaty with a sovereign Japan but the duration between granting the sovereignty and signing security treaty was barely five to six hours.[9]

By 1950s, it was clear that the US wanted to retain administrative control on certain parts of Japan including Okinawa (Ryuku) for a longer period for strategic purposes. India, however, was opposed to this idea and asked the US to restore the sovereignty over the territory with which the Japanese people have a "historical affinity" and which Japan has not acquired by "aggression" from any other country.[10] This position largely influenced by the idea of Asianism, was generally welcomed by Japan. Noting this position, Japan stated:

> This question is understandable; knowing that she (India) herself was under British domination for more than a century. And we, as Japanese, feel that nothing should be neglected to ensure full enjoyment of the privileges of independence.[11]

Peace Treaty and Disagreements between India and Japan

Position taken by India on the sovereignty of Kurile Islands and Formosa became a point of contention between India and the transitional government of Japan. India wanted that the Kurile Islands and Formosa should be reverted to Russia and China respectively and the Peace Treaty should also mention in clear terms the transfer of sovereignty of these islands to respective countries. In the second letter addressed to the US, India reiterated its position on the sovereignty of Kurile Islands based on Yalta agreement. It stated that "the Yalta agreement provided, without any reservation, that 'the Kurile Island be handed over to the Soviet Union.'"[12] It added that the "Government of India cannot be held responsible for an inconsistency which is the result of the Yalata Agreement."[13] Japan was obviously upset with India's insistence to include such provisions in the San Francisco treaty and especially the transfer of Kurile Islands. The Japanese side conveyed to India that "with the disposition of the Kuriles and South Sakhalin, the Japanese find it impossible to agree."[14] They felt that India is taking this position because of its closeness with the Soviet Union. It noted, "it may be that India, lying almost within the sphere of Soviet influence, has felt it necessary to humour the Kremlin. If this be the case, we cannot but voice our feeling of regret."[15]

It seems, Indian political elite did not had a clear understanding about what transpired in the Yalta Conference participated by soon-to-be victorious powers;—the US, Britain and the Soviet Union. It is widely believed that Soviet Union, with which Japan had a neutrality treaty, consented to join the war against Japan "as a result of persistent lobbying by the US"[16] and it joined the war on August 8, 1945. The Yalta agreement did mention that "(T)he Kurile Islands shall be handed over to the Soviet Union."[17] It also mentioned that "(T)he southern part of Sakhalin as well as the islands adjacent to it shall be returned to the Soviet Union."[18] It is apparent that by offering the sovereignty of the Southern Sakhalin and Kurile islands, the USSR was lured to break the 'neutrality treaty' that existed between Japan and Russia. In the neutrality treaty signed on April 13, 1941, Japan and the USSR agreed that "(B)oth Contracting Parties undertake to maintain peaceful and friendly relations between them and mutually respect the territorial integrity and inviolability of the other Contracting Party."[19]

Indian leadership misconstrued that the entire Kurile Island was occupied by Japan during its militarist expansion. It is well documented in the history that there existed a settled border between Russia and Japan and the two countries had signed three treaties; Treaty of commerce and Navigation in 1855, Treaty of 1875 on the exchange of territory and Treaty of Portsmouth in 1905, a peace treaty following the end of Russo-Japanese war. The treaty signed in 1855 was basically a boundary delimitation treaty in which the two parties settled their boundaries agreeing that the boundary between the two "lay between the Island of Etorofu and Uruppu"[20] in the Pacific Ocean. The two parties signed another treaty in 1875 which was basically a treaty of land swap. Japan "ceded all of Sakhalin Island to Russia in exchange for the Kurile Island"[21] as was agreed in the treaty. The Treaty of Portsmouth was signed in 1905 following Russia's defeat in the Russo-Japanese war and Japan "acquired southern half of the Sakhalin"[22] which it has already ceded to Russia in a bilateral treaty signed in 1875.

However, as the World War II was getting over, Russia broke the neutrality pact and occupied the territories and put it under its administrative control. Therefore, it can be said that the then Indian leadership did not had clear historical background of the treaties that had been signed between the USSR and Japan. Japan did mention about Kurile and Sakhalin in the open letter it wrote to Nehru, but did not specify the historical backgrounds of the territories that were mentioned by India in its letter to the US citing its opposition to the San Francisco Peace treaty. Japan maintained ambiguity and blamed India for siding with the USSR. This led to misunderstandings between the two, and delayed the signing of the peace treaty.

Apart from the issue of sovereignty of Formosa and Kurile Islands, India also had certain reservations as regards the security treaty that was being discussed between Japan and the US. India recognised that Japan has the right to "make arrangement for her defense"[23] but this should be exercised when "Japan has become a truly sovereign nation."[24] In a communication to the US, India argued:

> A provision in the treaty, which suggests that the present occupation forces may stay on in Japan as part of such a defensive agreement, is bound to give rise to the impression that the agreement does not represent a decision taken by Japan in the full enjoyment of her freedom as a sovereign nation.[25]

However, the Japanese side has a different take on this issue. Japan conveyed to India that adequate US forces stationed in the Japanese island is "absolutely essential"[26] for peace and security of Japan and East Asia and "there is no power in the Far East" other than the US which is capable of maintaining peace in the region.[27]

Raising concerns about the terms of the San Francisco Peace Treaty India wrote to the US that the sovereignty of contested territories between Japan and its neighbours should be addressed in the San Francisco Peace Treaty. But it made it clear that it had no objection, if any other country was ready to sign the treaty. In the second letter written to the US, New Delhi showed some flexibility and stated that "the government of India does not wish to come in the way of any nation which is satisfied with the terms of the present treaty and is prepared to sign it."[28]

Few months after signing of the San Francisco Peace Treaty, India announced that the "state of war between India and Japan shall cease to exist."[29] India also stated that it proposes to conclude "a separate bilateral Treaty of Peace with Japan" to bring the amity back in their relationship that "existed between them before the declaration of war with Japan."[30] This was followed by signing of a peace treaty between the two countries on June 9, 1952. Both the countries agreed that there shall be "firm and perpetual peace and amity"[31] between the two countries and their people. They also agreed to accord "most favoured nation treatment"[32] to each others with respect to air traffic rights, custom duties and charges, shipping, navigations and imported goods and in so many other areas. It agreed to waive off "all reparation claims against Japan."[33]

However, not all pre-war claims were waived off between Japan and India. The two parties took two successive attempts to resolve this issue in 1958 and 1963. In 1958, they initiated a negotiation to settle India's pre-war claims against Japan. The government of Japan paid Rs. 20,70,000 to Indian government in pre-war claims. India on its part, returned the properties to their Japanese owners which it has taken as part of "enemy property" following the outbreak of war with Japan.[34] Additionally, Japan paid US Dollar 25,000 to India in 1963 against the damage sustained by Indian nationals during the Sino-Japanese war.[35] By 1963, India and Japan settled all outstanding issues that resulted due to hostilities that broke out between the two during the World War II.

Radha Binod Pal and his Role in Forging People-to-People Ties

Before proceeding further, it is important to discuss Justice Radha Binod Pal's dissenting judgment at the International War Crime Tribunal, which finds vivid references in India-Japan post war relationship. It may be noted that following the end of World War II, the allied powers had constituted an International Tribunal to fix responsibilities of the war which they called war of "aggression." While the majority of the judges considered Japan's attack on Pearl Harbour on December 7, 1941 as "sudden, unexpected, treacherous and unprovoked attack," and found various Japanese guilty for the aggression, Justice Pal argued that Japan's action against the US naval base at Pearl Harbour was the consequence of American deteriorating relations over China. Justice Pal's observation was based on his own studies of the incidences and developments in the Far East starting from the World War I. He was of the view that the judges were taking the recourse of the laws made after 1945. He argued that the allied powers could not rewrite any part of law and put it into action retroactively. He argued:

> Whatever view of the legality or otherwise of a war may be taken, victory does not invest a victor with unlimited and undefined power now. International laws of war define and regulate the right and duties of the victor over the individuals of the vanquished nationality. In my judgment, therefore, it is beyond the competence of any victor nation to go beyond the rules of international law as they exist, give new definitions of crimes and then punish the prisoners for having committed offense according to this new definition.[36]

Pal was of the view that the objective of the tribunal was "essentially political." In his concluding remarks, he observed: "as a judicial tribunal we cannot behave in any manner which may justify the feeling that the setting up of the tribunal was only for the attainment of an objective which was essentially political, though cloaked by a judicial appearance."[37] He also added that "the name of justice should not be allowed to be invoked only for the prolongation of the pursuit of vindictive retaliation."[38]

His observations, however, could not change the verdict of the judicial tribunal. But Pal's dissenting note had a great influence on the Japanese people. Pal, commonly known as *Pal Hanji,* remains one of the revered personalities to a section of the Japanese society. A plaque erected of Pal in Tokyo's Yasukuni shrine and Kyoto's Ryozen Gokoku Shrine and a monument of him in Atami, Kanagawa is a reminder of this fact. Pal's name finds vivid mention in the speeches of Japanese leaders delivered in the context of India-Japan relations. For example, Prime Minister Nakasone Yasuhiro while addressing the Indian Parliament in 1984 observed:

> After World War II, when India achieved its independence, Japan was on trial before the world as a vanquished nation. However, at the Tokyo Tribunal, the eminent Indian jurist Radhabinod Pal displayed a sympathetic understanding toward Japan's past deeds, and the Japanese people, in the depths of their despair and remorse, were grateful.[39]

India and Japan: Beginning of a Political Interaction

As mentioned in the previous sections, while the two governments were engaged in conversations over peace treaty and it did create some distrust at the political level, Pal's dissenting judgment struck a chord between the Japanese and Indian people. Despite initial misunderstanding over the terms and the text of the San Francisco Peace treaty, India and Japan resolved their outstanding disputes. The signing of a separate Peace treaty led to political warmth between the two Asian democracies. Soon after the signing of India-Japan Peace treaty, Prime Minister Shigeru Yoshida, the first postwar Japanese Prime Minister, wanted to undertake a visit to India to strengthen the bilateral relationship. In his memoirs, he writes:

> It has been my original intention to include India and the countries of Southeast Asia in my itinerary, but, because of the prevailing political situation in Japan, the whole trip first had to be postponed, and when

> I finally set forth, it was found that time did not permit me to include Asia in my travels.[40]

However, one of his successors, Nobusuke Kishi became the first Japanese Prime Minister to visit India in 1957. The visit was followed by other two Japanese Prime Ministers Ikeda Hayato and Nakasone Yasuhiro. From Indian side, Prime Minister Jawaharlal Nehru, Indira Gandhi and Rajiv Gandhi visited Japan during the Cold War period.

The joint statements signed during these visits, hint that both the countries had two clear agenda;—at the international level, they wanted to create a new order free from weapons of mass destruction and nuclear weapon and at the bilateral level; they wanted to forge complimentary economic relations. These two issues would be discussed below in the two separate sections.

India-Japan and the Agenda of a Nuclear Free World

The joint statements issued by Prime Minister Kishi and Nehru suggest that concerned over the incidents of nuclear proliferation, they wanted to create a postwar order free of nuclear weapons. India and Japan made an appeal for the "immediate suspension of nuclear and thermo nuclear test"[41] and hoped that the big powers will reach an agreement on "eventual abandonment of these tests and prohibition of all kind of nuclear and thermo-nuclear weapons."[42] Both the countries reiterated the similar stance when Nehru visited Japan in 1957. The joint statement issued by Kishi and Nehru stated that "the piling of arms, especially weapons of mass destruction by the major powers, spells grave danger for the peace of the world"[43] and asked the UN and the big powers to "re-double their efforts"[44] to abandon weapon of mass destruction.

The call of a nuclear free world was being raised by other states and the organisations too, and later it turned into a demand of a universal treaty to abandon nuclear weapon. When Indian Prime Minister Indira Gandhi visited Japan in 1966, the two countries agreed in their joint statement that the "conclusion of a treaty on general and complete disarmament under strict and effective international control would be a lasting contribution to maintenance of world peace and security."[45]

However, with the coming of Nuclear Proliferation Treaty into force, the two countries took different positions. Japan signed the nuclear treaty and expected India also to do so. Against Japan's expectations, India conducted a nuclear test in May 1974. The development not only led to the severe criticism from Japan but also ended its dream to partner with India to eliminate the nuclear weapons and create a global security order not dependent on the nuclear weapons. India on its part tried to assuage Japanese concerns on nuclear proliferation issue but Japan continued on its demand to sign the NPT.

In a statement laid before the parliament, Indian Foreign Minister Atal Behari Vajpayee stated that "the Japanese government had from time to time expressed the hope that all countries including India would accede to the NPT."[46] India, however, did not sign the treaty and considered it discriminatory as it was of the view that the treaty imposes "severe constraints on the non-nuclear weapon states, it left the nuclear weapon states free to conduct their activities in the nuclear field without any outside constraints."[47] India, ever since this statement, has maintained this stance vis-à-vis the NPT. The nuclear question, thereafter, became a thorny issue in the bilateral relations of the two countries and hampered the diplomatic relations as well. This issue has been discussed in chapter 7 in this book.

After India's nuclear test, the bilateral relationship between India and Japan touched the lowest ebb. The engagement between the political leadership also remained limited for the next few years. Japanese Prime Minister Nakasone Yasuhiro took a bold step to break the impasse by visiting India in 1984. In his address to the Indian Parliament, he expressed his personal "determination to take step towards creating a new India-Japan relationship."[48] He had been frank in admitting differences between two Asian countries' foreign policies. He stated that "although we differ in our foreign policies, ..., I believe there is great potential for us to cooperate in maintaining peace and promoting disarmament."[49] Though Japanese political leadership has rejected the idea of a non-aligned world, Nakasone admitted the importance of "Third world and non-aligned countries" and said that Japan is "anxious to strengthen friendly relations"[50] with these countries. From his vision, it was clear that he wanted to use India as a pivot to reach out to the Non-Alignment Movement countries apparently to increase Japan's clout in the United Nations. In his speech he stated:

> On the opportunity of my visit to India, an influential leader in the Non-Aligned Movement, I am hoping to embark upon a new direction in Japan's foreign policy, to further strengthen our dialogue and cooperation with the countries of the Non-Aligned Movement—a force which constitutes nearly two thirds of the United Nations membership.[51]

Nakasone's overture to reach out to NAM countries was apparently aimed at gaining support to increase its political weight in UN led diplomacy and for securing UN Security Council seat as a permanent member and this later resulted into formation of Group of 4 nations (India, Japan, Brazil and Germany) who are jointly vying for securing much coveted seat at the UN.

At the bilateral level, Nakasone showed keen interest to strengthen the economic relations between the two countries. He was keen to start "industrial collaboration projects"[52] between Indian and Japanese industries. The relationship, however, could not take shape into a "new India-Japan relationship"[53] as Nakasone has wished because of political assassination of his Indian counterpart, Indira Gandhi. Hiroshi Sato, a senior Japanese Indologist, believe that had Indira lived for another few years, India could have become one of the important partners of Japan during the Nakasone era itself. He strongly feels that the present India-Japan relations are premised on Naksone's vision.[54] Rajiv Gandhi, who became Prime Minister after Indira Gandhi's assassination made a reciprocal visit in 1985 and then two successive visits to Japan. However, the visits did not result in warmth in the ties at the political level.

India and Japan: The Quest for Complementary Economic Relations

In the postwar period, which coincided with India's liberation, both India and Japan wanted to establish a complimentary economic relationship. Their joint statement reflected that India was eager to establish "long term arrangements for stabilized supply of iron ore."[55] Since India, before the wars, was a supplier of goods as well as raw materials to Japan, it welcomed recovery of Japanese economy for its own economic development. Prime Minister Nehru while meeting a Japanese trade mission remarked that "the economies of both the countries should be complementary."[56] He assured them that India would assist as much as possible in sending "raw materials to Japan."[57] Japan on its part was willing to establish technical training centers in India to promote small and medium scale enterprises.

Japan offered financial help to India in realizing the goals of its five year plans. Japan was the founder member of Aid-India programme of the World Bank starting from 1958. The Indian leadership has acknowledged that Japan's assistance in its development plans have been "crucial."[58] Both Japanese and Indian leadership were keen to establish "mutually beneficial economic relationship." During Prime Minister Nehru's visit to Japan, Tokyo offered to "establish technical training centres in India for the purpose of helping the development of medium and small scale Industries."[59] The joint statements signed between India and Japan during the postwar period, suggests that issues dominating the international affairs gained prominence and the economic cooperation found little priorities. However, during Indira Gandhi's regime effort was made to put economic cooperation at the forefront. This is evident from the fact that during Nehru's period, global concerns were placed in the beginning of the joint statements while during Indira's years, commitments to forge closer economic relations were placed in the beginning of the joint statements. In the joint statement, signed by Indira Gandhi and Eisako Sato both the countries agreed "to hold close consultations at various levels to ensure long term development of trade relations between the two countries on the basis of greater diversification and complementarities."[60]

However, some of the domestic policies adopted by Indira Gandhi such as nationalization and restriction imposed on export of raw materials was not liked by the Japanese business community. But this did not impede the flow of trade and goods between the two countries and gradually, Japan became one of the leading trade partners of India. It was keen to deepen this partnership further. Indian leadership expressed this desire when Ichiro Hatoyama visited Delhi in 1977. The then Indian Foreign Minister Atal Behari Vajpayee stated that "for us in India, Japan is one of our leading partners in trade. However, in the context of Japan's global trading patterns, it is our endeavour in terms of mutual benefit, to become a more significant partner."[61]

Nevertheless, the bilateral relations, especially in the economic field, could not move beyond a certain level, apparently because of the emergence of the Cold War which pushed Japan to US led free world while India chose to remain non-aligned. In the Japanese perception, India, however, was considered closer to the USSR with which the free world had very limited trade and technological cooperation. Thus, the Cold War political equations also impacted the overall India-Japan relations.

Conclusion

As has been discussed above, Indian and Japanese leadership in the postwar period started the bilateral relationship with a commitment to create a world without nuclear weapons at the international level and at the bilateral level tried to forge a complementary relationship in the fields of economics and trade. But they could not achieve these goals due to various domestic and external factors that impacted their bilateral relations. These factors include India's decision to choose to remain non-aligned, strengthening state's control on its economy and conducting a nuclear test. These were the issues on which the positions of the two governments' were not in agreements with each others. They also had different expectations from each others. An Indian observer describes the postwar India-Japan relations as a "victim of unfulfilled relationship."[62]

Despite the factors mentioned above that hindered their overall bilateral relations, India and Japan during the Cold War period had institutionalized a foreign ministerial level dialogue and a separate business cooperation dialogue. Through these two dialogues, both the countries discussed ways to enhance cooperation despite differences in political and economic fields. The dialogues paved way for signing of a number of Memorandum of Understanding and agreements in the fields of trade and commerce. The agreements include; agreements on resuming air services, agreements on double taxation avoidance, agreements on deepening of Cultural relations, and agreements on training of small scale industries. The dialogues between the leadership of the two countries also helped prevent a complete deadlock between the political leadership of the two countries and proved a stepping stone to strengthen relations after the end of Cold War period which coincided with India's economic liberalisation. These issues would be discussed in the next chapter of this book.

END NOTES

1. Jawaharlal Nehru who later became the first Prime Minister of India recalls in his autography that Japanese victories stirred up his enthusiasm and the Japanese victories over Europe inspired him to "fight for India." For details see, Jawaharlal Nehru, "An Autobiography," The Bodley Head, London 1945, p.6.
2. P.A. Narsimha Murthy, "India and Japan: Dimensions of their Relations," ABC Publishing House, New Delhi, 1986, p.276.
3. Ibid, p.275.
4. Prime Minister Yoshida Shigeru in his memoirs describing the San Francisco Treaty writes that "We Japanese must remember with gratitude General McArthur for his consistent advocacy of an early peace treaty, and Mr. Dulles for making the terms of the treaty of such advantage for Japan, and thus producing treaty based, in Mr. Dulles's own words-upon trust and understanding. Yoshida Shigeru, "The Yoshida Memoirs: The story of Japan in crisis," Greenwood Press, Publishers, Westport, Connecticut, 1962, p.243.
5. Reference made by Prime Minister Indira Gandhi at the Banquet held in honour of the Prime Minister of Japan, in New Delhi on May 4, 1984. For details see, P.A. Narsimha Murthy, "India and Japan Dimension of their Relations (Documents)," ABC Publishing House, New Delhi, 1986, pp. 433-435. Here after referred as P.A. Narsimha Murthy, "Documents."
6. Reference made by External Affairs Minister Atal Behari Vajpayee during a speech at banquet given in honour of his counterpart Ichiro Hatoyama in New Delhi July 19, 1977. For details see P.A. Narsimha Murthy, "Documents," pp.376-380.
7. Yoshida Shigeru, "The Yoshida Memoirs: The story of Japan in crisis," Greenwood Press Publishers, Westport, Connecticut, 1962, p.243.
8. Communication from the Government of India to the Government of the United States on Japanese Peace Treaty, August 23, 1951. For details please see, P.A. Narsimhamurthy, "Documents," pp 1-3.
9. Yoshida Shigeru writes that "the San Francisco peace treaty was signed on the morning of 8 September 1951 and at 5 PM the same evening we met the delegates to sign the US-Japan security treaty." Yoshida Shigeru, The Yoshida Memoirs: The story of Japan in crisis, Greenwood Press, Publishers, Westport, Connecticut, 1962, p.263.
10. Ibid.
11. Open letter addressed to the Prime Minister of India on the question of Japanese Peace Treaty, September 15, 1951. For detailed text see, P.A. Narsimhamurthy, "Documents," pp. 7-9.

12. Second communication from the Government of India to the Government of the United States of America on Japanese Peace Treaty, August 28th, 1951. For the text of the communication see, P.A. Narsimhamurthy, "Documents," pp. 3-7.
13. Ibid.
14. Open letter addressed to the Prime Minister of India on the question of Japanese Peace Treaty, September 15, 1951. For the text of open letter see, P.A. Narsimhamurthy, "Documents," pp. 3-7.
15. Ibid.
16. Paul De Vries, "U.S. sees wars' end through the prism of Hiroshima," *The Japan Times*, May 25, 2016.
17. See for details "Text of the Yalta agreement," available online at http://avalon.law.yale.edu/wwii/yalta.asp (Accessed on September 5, 2016).
18. Ibid.
19. See for details, the text of "Soviet-Japanese Neutrality Pact April 13, 1941," available at http://avalon.law.yale.edu/wwii/s1.asp (Accessed on September 5, 2016).
20. For details, "Japan's Northern Territories: For A Relationship of Genuine Trust," Ministry of Foreign Affairs, Government of Japan, available on http://www.mofa.go.jp/region/europe/russia/territory/pamphlet.pdf (Accessed on September 5, 2016).
21. Ibid.
22. Morinosuke Kajima, "A brief Diplomatic History of Japan," CE Tuttle Company, Tokyo, 1969, p.39.
23. Communication from the Government of India to the Government of the United States on Japanese Peace Treaty, August 23, 1951. For the text of communication please see, P. A. Narsimhamurthy, "Documents," pp 1-3.
24. Ibid.
25. Ibid.
26. Open letter addressed to the Prime Minister of India on the question of Japanese Peace Treaty, September 15, 1951. For the text of open letter see, P.A. Narsimhamurthy, "Documents," pp. 3-7.
27. Ibid.
28. Second communication from the Government of India to the Government of the United States of America on Japanese Peace Treaty, August 28th, 1951. For the text of communication see, P.A. Narsimhamurthy, "Documents," pp. 3-7.
29. Government of India notification terminating the state of War with Japan, April 28, 1952. For the text see, P.A. Narsimhamurthy, "Documents," pp. 9-10.
30. Ibid.
31. Treaty of Peace between the Governments of India and Japan, June 9, 1952, Tokyo. For the text of the treaty refer to Tokyo University data base on South Asia, available online at http://www.ioc.u-tokyo.ac.jp/~worldjpn/documents/texts/JPSA/19520609.T1E.html (Accessed on September 7, 2016)
32. Ibid.
33. Ibid.

34. Press Release on India's pre-war claims settlement in Tokyo, February, 1959. For the text, please see, P.A. Narsimha Murthy, "Documents," p.16.
35. Press release on settlement of War damages, December 14, 1963. For the text, please see, P.A. Narsimha Murthy, "Documents," pp.16-17.
36. Pal quoted in Ashish Nandy, "The other within: The Strange case of Radha Binod Pal's judgment on culpability," *New Literary History*, Vol. 23, No.21, 1992.
37. For detailed analysis of the judgment see, P.A. Narsimhamurthy, "India and Japan: dimensions and their Relations Historical and Political," especially chapter 6, *India and the International Military Tribunal for the Far East,* ABC Publishing House, New Delhi, 1986, pp.221-273.
38. Ibid.
39. Japanese Prime Minister Nakasone Yasuhiro's address in the Japanese Parliament, for the text of address, please refer to P. A. Narsimha Murthy, "Documents," pp.423-433.
40. Yoshida Shigeru, The Yoshida Memoirs: The story of Japan in crisis, Greenwood Press, Publishers, Westport, Connecticut, 1962, p.100.
41. Joint statement signed by India and Japan during Prime Minister Nubusuke Kishi's visit to India, May 25, 1957, New Delhi. For the text of the statement please refer to, P.A. Narsimha Murthy, "Documents," pp.318-319.
42. Ibid.
43. Joint statement signed by India and Japan during Prime Minister Nehru's visit to Japan, October 13, 1957, Tokyo. For the text of the statement please refer to, P.A. Narsimha Murthy, "Documents," pp.319-322.
44. Ibid.
45. Joint statement signed by India and Japan during Prime Minister Indira Gandhi's visit to Japan, June 20, 1969, New Delhi. For the text of the statement please refer to, P.A. Narsimha Murthy, "Documents," pp.324-327.
46. Text of statement of the External Affairs Minister laid before the Parliament of India on the visit of the Foreign Minister of Japan to India, July 28, 1977. For the text of the statement please refer to, P.A. Narsimha Murthy, "Documents," pp.338-339.
47. Ibid.
48. Japanese Prime Minister Nakasone Yasuhiro's address in the Japanese Parliament, for the text of address, please refer to P. A. Narsimha Murthy, "Documents," pp.423-433.
49. Ibid.
50. Ibid.
51. Ibid.
52. Ibid.
53. Ibid.
54. Author's interview with Hiroshi Sato, Professor (retired) Tokyo University, on June 9, 2016, Tokyo.
55. Joint statement signed by India and Japan during Prime Minister Nubusuke Kishi's visit to India, May 25, 1957, New Delhi. For the text of the statement please refer

to, P.A. Narsimha Murthy, "Documents," pp.318-319.

56. Hiroshi Sato, "India Japan Peace Treaty in Japan's Post-War Asian Diplomacy," *Journal of the Japanese Association for South Asian Studies*, Vol. 17, 2005, p.9.
57. Ibid.
58. Deputy Prime Minister Morarji Desai's Speech at Luncheon Given in his honour by the Foreign Correspondents' Club, August 21, 1967, Tokyo. For the text of speech refer to, P.A. Narsimha Murthy, "Documents," pp.361-368.
59. "Japan and Asia" (Editorial), *The Economic and Political Weekly*, October 19, 1960.
60. Joint statement signed between India Prime Minister Indira Gandhi and Japanese Prime Minister Eisako Sato during Indira's visit to Japan, June 1969, Tokyo. For the text of statement please refer to P.A. Narsimha Murthy, "Documents," pp.324-327.
61. External Affairs Minister Atal Behari Vajpayee's Speech at Banquet Given in honour of Ichiro Hatoyama, July 19, 1977. For the text of speech please refer to P.A. Narsimha Murthy, "Documents," pp.367-384.
62. S.B. Singh, "India-Japan Relation: An overview," in Dharmadasani, *Indo-Japan Relations: Challenges and opportunities*, Kanishka Publishers and Distributors, New Delhi, 2004, p.122.

4

India-Japan Relations: Evaluating the Impact of Strategic Partnership

Introduction

Indo-Japan economic engagement touched a new landmark following India's adoption of an open economic system and passed through various phases thereafter. Soon the economic interaction transformed into a strategic partnership[1] which consists of not only an Economic Partnership Agreement but also makes commitments to cooperate with each other in the evolving security order both at the regional and international level. The strategic partnership has blossomed over the years as the leadership of both countries have held a series of bilateral ministerial-level talks, but not without causing suspicion and drawing criticism from neigbouring countries as well as at home. This chapter tries to analyse the factors which led both countries to think about such cooperation. A section of this Chapter analyses the issues which are on both governments' agenda and the challenges that lie ahead.

Beginning of the India-Japan Strategic Partnership

At the dawn of the 21st century, Japan was crafting a new strategic policy and found India as a new partner, the foundation of which was laid down by Tokyo's strategic planners. Japan started the initiative at the end of the Cold War to respond to new challenges to its security and foreign policies.

With the end of the Cold War and with the political demise of the hypothetical enemy—the USSR—, the primary goal of the US-Japan Security Treaty which was to contain the spread of communism by providing strategic and logistic support to the US, was achieved. Thus, the Treaty became uni-dimensional as the US still had to contribute to Japan by providing a defense shield from emerging threats from its two neigbours—North Korea and China—with which Japan has had unresolved historical and territorial disputes. Japan on the other hand, had nothing much to contribute from its part to the US. Japan feared a possible "abandonment"[2]from its sole security ally.

Amid the debate of abandonment, Japan began to search for "other friends around the world." Around that time Japanese Prime Minister Takeshi Kaifu visited Asian countries including India, becoming only the fourth Japanese prime minister to visit New Delhi. During his visit, Kaifu stated that "peace and stability in Asia is a matter of great concern for Japan... we must be engaged with multifaceted efforts that suits the region."[3] His announcement was in sync with his policy of making Japan a 'bridge' between the East and the West. His predecessors on the contrary, had tried to project Japan as an international country (*kokusai kokka Nippon*) and a member of the West. In a clear departure from the policy of his predecessors, Kaifu announced a policy for Japan's re-association with Asia and stated that he would like to "pronounce Japan's intent to continue vigorous support for the economic redevelopment and stability of South Asia by engaging in dialogue and cooperation."[4] He announced a South Asia initiative which was based on three pillars: a) promotion of political and economic dialogue, b) expansion of ODA, and c) increased cultural exchange with South Asian countries.[5]

An Indian strategic thinker commenting on Kaifu's visit noted: "With the end of the Cold War, both India and Japan made efforts to reappraise the potential of their relations. Prime Minister Kaifu's visit to India was part of his sojourn to the South Asian region as he projected a new vision of his country in this 'period of rapid transformation in the world'."[6] She also noted that there was a "growing Japanese consciousness of the importance of a 're-association' with Asia not only in economic terms, but also increasingly in political and strategic terms."[7]

India was most forthright in welcoming Japan's support to the region enunciated by Kaifu. In an apparent reference to Japan's desire to contribute to regional peace and stability, Prime Minister Narsimha Rao during his visit to Japan stated:

> We (India and Japan) share a common interest in Asian peace and security which will enable India and other countries to concentrate on economic development. India has welcomed Japan's constructive engagement in the world because we see this buttressing India's own peace, stability and development.[8]

It may be noted that Japan has banked upon India to draw strength and "political capital"[9] whenever it felt the need to bargain with big powers. Prime Minister Shinzo Abe notes that when Kishi Nobusuke, his grandfather was to review the US-Japan security treaty, he "chose to come to India before setting foot on the soil of America."[10] For Nobusuke, America was the first, second and the third most important country for Japan, notes Abe. But why did he choose to visit India before going to the US? An explanation can be found in Shinzo Abe's remarks. Abe explains that "India indeed gave my grandfather a great deal. When he met later in Washington, D.C. with Dwight Eisenhower and Richard Nixon, he was more confident knowing that Japan was not alone but backed by India, already the biggest democracy in the world."[11] Tomohiko Taniguchi, an advisor to Abe Cabinet, believes it was because of India's strategic location, Kishi Nobusuke, opted to visit India. He emphasises that it is "L, (location) word that decides and will decide Japan's foreign policy vis-à-vis India."[12]

Apart from India's geo-strategic location, India's economic liberalisation was one of the factors which cannot be discounted when analyzing new beginning of the bilateral relationship. With the economic liberalization and the end of License Raj, a number of Japanese companies viewed India as a potential market. As has been discussed in the previous chapter, despite a good beginning in the 1950s, political relations between the two countries entered into a recalcitrant phase. The obvious reason behind the political chill was India's tilt towards the Soviet Union including campaigns for a Non-Alignment Movement (NAM). Japan, on the other hand, found itself comfortable with the US led free world. The psychological barriers which were created between the two, however, started disappearing when NAM of which India was a leading member, lost its relevance at the end of the Cold War as the world became uni-polar. India adopted an open economic model with which Japan and members of other free world were comfortable with. The end of Cold War paved the way for the two countries to re-establish their centuries old civilisational ties which were disrupted during the lost decades.

Blossoming of Indo-Japan Relationship

In the post-Cold War period, political and economic interaction between the two countries increased many folds and proved a cornerstone in the diplomatic relations between the two countries. However, diplomatic relations between the two again touched the lowest ebb following India's 1998 Pokhran nuclear test. But it was India's economic recovery that led to many nations to remove sanctions and Japan also followed the suit. Another incident around that time that acted as an intervening variable was the Indian Coast Guards' rescue mission of a Japanese flagship merchant vessel which was hijacked by the pirates in the Indian Ocean. (This issue has been discussed as part of the case study in this chapter in a separate section). Japan for the first time officially acknowledged India's indispensability in securing Japanese national interest. Prime Minister Yoshiro Mori's visit to India in 2000 was a stepping stone in the bilateral relationship of the two Asian nations. He envisaged a "global partnership" between the two countries and announced that the "relations between the two nations, which offer great possibilities for both parties, would be further strengthened, not just bilaterally but also by playing a role together regionally and internationally."[13]

During the visit, Prime Minister Mori announced a series of measures to strengthen Indo-Japan bilateral relations including, regular meetings at the prime ministerial and foreign ministerial levels, opening talks on national security between foreign and defence officials, bilateral conferences for promoting IT cooperation.

The relationship, however, acquired a "strategic dimension" when Prime Minister Manmohan Singh and Prime Minister Junichiro Koizumi signed a global and strategic partnership agreement in 2006. The two prime ministers for the first time in their joint statement confirmed that: "The global partnership between India and Japan reflects a broad convergence of their long-term political, economic and strategic interests, aspirations, objectives and concerns. India and Japan view each other as partners that have responsibility for, and are capable of, responding to global and regional challenges in keeping with their global partnership. A strong, prosperous and dynamic India is, therefore, in the interest of Japan and vice a versa."[14]

To reinforce the strategic focus of the partnership both the countries identified an "eight fold initiative" which included (a) an enhanced and upgraded dialogue architecture, including the launching of a high level strategic dialogue and full utilization of the existing dialogue mechanisms; (b) comprehensive economic engagement; (c) enhanced security dialogue and cooperation; (d) science and technology initiative; (e) cultural and academic initiatives and strengthening of people-to-people contacts; (f) cooperation in ushering a new Asian era; (g) cooperation in the United Nations and other international organizations, including cooperation for the early realization of UN reforms, particularly Security Council reform; and (h) cooperation in responding to global challenges and opportunities.[15]

Koizumi's successor, Shinzo Abe added his personal touch to the blossoming Indo-Japan ties by identifying India as a pivotal partner in his book, *Towards a Beautiful Country* which he wrote before assuming Japan's premiership. In his book, he describes how Japan could advance its "national interests" by strengthening "ties with India." He speculated that "it will not be a surprise if in another decade Japan-India relations overtake Japan-US and Japan-China ties."[16] The high priority Abe gave to India is reflective of the fact that when Prime Minister Manmohan Singh visited Tokyo, Abe honoured him by giving the stage to address the joint session of the Japanese Diet, a rare opportunity provided to any Indian prime minister.

New Delhi also gave Abe a similar welcome when he visited India in 2007.[17] In his address to a joint session of the Indian Parliament Abe stated that he had grown up with a dream to strengthen a tie that his grandfather, Kishi Nobusuke, had initiated. In the same address, he mooted the idea of a "broader Asia" at the confluence of the two seas of the Indian and Pacific Oceans and urged that the democratic nations located at opposite edges of these seas deepen the friendship among their citizens at every possible level. He highlighted that "this 'broader Asia' will evolve into an immense network spanning the entirety of the Pacific Ocean, incorporating the United States of America and Australia."[18] Abe urged the security and diplomatic personnel of both countries to consider future India-Japan cooperation when he commented that "what Japan and India should do cooperatively in the area of security in the years to come is one that the officials in charge of diplomacy and defence in our countries must consider jointly."[19]

It is interesting to note that at this stage of relationship, both the leadership of Japan and India were speaking in same tone and tenor. If Abe floated the idea of a "broader Asia," based on the "Arc of freedom and Prosperity," Manmohan Singh talked of creating "an 'arc of advantage and prosperity' across Asia, laying the foundation for the creation of an Asian Economic Community."[20]

But what caught much more attention during Abe-Manmohan commitment, was two lines in their 2006 joint statement which stated that "the two leaders share the view on the usefulness of having dialogue among India, Japan and other like-minded countries in the Asia-Pacific region on themes of mutual interest. The two governments will consult on the modalities."[21] The statement was construed by some analysts as India joining the group that believes in China's containment. "New Delhi—which had been resisting the idea of a quadrilateral security meeting for more than a year because of its 'encirclement of China' connotations-finally committed itself to a dialogue with Japan 'and other like-minded countries in the Asia-Pacific region on themes of mutual interest' during Prime Minister Manmohan Singh's visit to Tokyo last December," noted an strategic thinker in a column in an Indian daily.[22] However, India has continuously repeated that this security framework was not aimed at containing any particular country, a statement which has only few takers.

Notwithstanding the concern expressed in certain quarters, both countries firmly established annual prime ministerial talks. When Indian Prime Minister Manmohan Singh met his lame-duck Japanese counterpart Taro Aso, they "pledged to continue their efforts to broaden and deepen the relationship on the basis of the shared congruence of interests in order to develop it as an essential pillar for the future architecture of the region."[23]

The political scene in Japan appeared shaky in 2009 as well as the future of Indo-Japan relations. The Democratic Party of Japan (DPJ) which was poised to wrest power sought to forge close ties with the region in its manifesto but India was not specifically mentioned. The manifesto stated that the DPJ led government would "develop relation of mutual trust with China, South Korea and other Asian countries."[24] The ambiguity in DPJ's manifesto over whether India fits in DPJ's strategy generated concern in New Delhi that whether the DPJ would chalk out a new strategy for regional integration leaving aside India? This could have jeopardized the existing strategic relationship that was laid during the successive LDP governments.

But when the entire Japan was observing the year-end holidays, Japanese Prime Minister Yukio Hatoyama made a visit to New Delhi on December 29, 2009 and signed yet another joint statement in which both the leaders "reaffirmed that India and Japan as partners which share common values and strategic interests, will develop the Strategic and Global Partnership further for the deepening of their bilateral relations as well as peace and prosperity of the region and the world."[25]

The Indo-Japan strategic relationship reached a new height when Prime Minister Naoto Kan and his Indian counterpart Manmohan Singh decided to "steadily expand security and defence cooperation between India and Japan" and pledged to "cooperate to enhance their capacity in responding to security challenges such as maritime security which entails the safety and freedom of navigation and counter piracy, humanitarian assistance and disaster relief and response, *inter alia*, through bilateral and multilateral exercises, information sharing, training and dialogue."[26] The developments at the Indo-Japanese strategic fronts during the two successive DPJ prime ministers suggest that support for the bilateral relationship between the two countries is bipartisan and a regime change will not affect the relationship.

The domestic politics in Japan forced Prime Minister Yoshihiko Noda to call for a snap general elections in December 2012. The result did not go in its favour and the LDP headed by Shinzo Abe, took back the reins of Japanese government. The Abe government took a decision to engage Emperor in diplomacy to convey its citizens as well as Indian people that the bilateral relationship has reached to a new height. Following cabinet approval, Japanese Emperor Akihito visited India in December 2013.

It is generally believed that visits by the Emperor and Empress are meant to improve ties with a particular country following Japanese Cabinet's approval. Whenever, the Japanese Emperor visits abroad, the Japanese media shifts its focus on the imperial couple's engagements abroad. Similarly, when Japanese emperor made his visit to India in 2013, both electronics and print media gave unprecedented coverage to his visit and in this process the Japanese people got to know about the prominence India gained in Japan's Foreign Policy.

India made another diplomatic overture by inviting Abe, an ardent friend of India, as a Chief Guest of India's Republic Day ceremony in January 2014. Seen from Indian perspective, the decision to host Abe as a Chief Guest was to convey to both Indian and Japanese people that the relationship between the two countries has reached to the highest peak. During the visit, Abe showed his commitment to further deepen cooperation with India in the fields of security, education, economy and trade.

India-Japan Relations and the Modi Era

As mentioned earlier, change of powers in Japan in 2009 did not impact the bilateral relationship because it enjoyed bipartisan support. Similarly, when a transition of power took place in India in 2014, it did not have any adverse impact on India-Japan relations. Prime Minister Narendra Modi's visit to Japan in September 2014 and his interactions with Japanese counterpart Shinzo Abe was the continuation of a prime ministerial level engagement institutionalised in 2006. It may be reminded that while signing the strategic partnership in 2006, India and Japan agreed to hold summit-level talks annually, alternating between New Delhi and Tokyo. Since 2006 the annual prime ministerial level summit talks has continued barring once in 2012 when the talks could not take place because of announcement of snap general elections in Japan by Prime Minister Noda.

When the change of government took place in New Delhi, Japan from its part was eager to continue and intensify this complementary relationship with India. It lost no time in extending an invitation to the new Indian

Prime Minister. Tokyo was keen to become Modi's first foreign host soon after his assumption of the office. Nonetheless, Indian Prime Minster chose neighbouring countries, including Bhutan and Nepal for his foreign visits. After rescheduling his Japan visit twice because of domestic engagements, Indian Prime Minister visited Japan in August 2014, which was his first bilateral visit outside South Asia. Notably, Japanese Prime Minister "expressed his deep appreciation"[27] for choosing Japan as his "first destination for a bilateral visit outside India's immediate neighbourhood."[28] The statement is reflection of Japan's sense of satisfaction towards deepening India–Japan relations.

During the visit, the old issues in India–Japan bilateral relations: expansion of trade and economic ties; foreign direct investment, cooperation in infrastructure sector; development of rail, road and port facilities as well as civil nuclear cooperation etc., dominated the agenda.[29] Since some of the issues identified previously have not reached to fruition, it was a wise strategy of the present political dispensation to carry forward the consultations on these issues and take it to a logical conclusion. However, the new agenda, especially some of the dream projects of Prime Minister Modi, also surfaced during the visit and became the part of bilateral cooperation. Some of these agenda have been discussed below.

Giving New Dimension to Bilateral Strategic Partnership

One of the important outcomes of Prime Minister Narendra Modi's Japan visit was elevation of existing strategic partnership to a "special" strategic and global partnership.[30] As of now, India has signed strategic partnerships with 29 countries and regional groups. However, the terminologies used are slightly different. Before this summit meeting, India had accorded this "special" status only to Russia, with which it has traditional and time-tested ties. Granting Japan a similar status at par with Russia is an indication that India attaches utmost importance to its ties with the East Asian country and in the coming decades Tokyo will remain on the top of New Delhi's foreign policy priorities. Japan was also eager to upgrade the existing 2 plus 2 dialogues between Japanese foreign and defense ministries and their Indian counterparts to the defense and foreign ministers' level. The 2 plus 2 dialogues between India and Japan at present takes place at the levels of top bureaucrats of the two governments. The joint statement issued at the end of the summit meeting between Indian and Japanese Prime Ministers notes the two leaders "underlined the importance of the 2 plus 2 dialogues, involving Foreign and Defence Secretaries, for their growing strategic partnership, and decided to seek ways to intensify this dialogue."[31] However, the statement stopped short of announcing the up-gradation of this dialogue.

The statements signed by the two countries and commitments made during these years is indicative of the fact that both countries see each other as an important nation to safeguard for each country's national security. In Japanese strategic thinking India figures as an important partner as it realizes that its security ally—the US—is overstretched with military missions in Iraq, Syria and Afghanistan and thus it is not focusing much on East Asian regional security. Japanese defence planners have also noted that with the rise of China, there has been a relative decline of the US power in the region. Thus they need someone to fill the void. India certainly fits in that calculation. However, China factor in India-Japan relations needs much more focus and it has been discussed below in a separate heading.

India-Japan Strategic Cooperation: Assessing the China Factor

A section of scholars, both in China and India, have viewed strategic ties between India and Japan as a 'containment strategy' to a rising China. To assume that China has been the prime factor behind growing partnership between India and Japan and analysing their relationship with this hypothesis would lead to a wrong conclusion. India's present strategic partnership with Japan as well as institutionalisation of an annual prime ministerial dialogue has reached to this stage after a sustained political engagement between the leaders of the two countries. The annual summit level meetings between two prime ministers are part of that institutional mechanism which started in 2006 onwards. It was not triggered by a Sino-Japanese standoff over East China Sea or a "rising tension" in East Asian region as has been interpreted in certain section of media and strategic circles.

History suggests that China was nowhere in the minds of the Indian strategic planners who envisaged a closer relations with Japan. India's developmental priorities, post 1991, pushed India to forge a "complementary" relationship with Japan, which was number one Asian economy at that time.[32] J.N. Dixit, a former Foreign Secretary of India, in his memoirs notes that Japan was identified as "one of the most important source of both investment and technology"[33] by India. The then Finance Minister of India, Manmohan Singh laid the foundation for "increasing the content of Indo-Japanese relations."[34] Also, Japan's interest in India was largely economic. It saw opportunities in a newly liberalised Indian economy. Dixit's observation, which he made in 1996, was prophetic:

> Japan's interest in India is primarily economic. In other spheres, India does not form a primary focus of attention yet. This is the backdrop against which Indo-Japanese relations will evolve in the future.[35]

Till 2006, India-Japan relations were driven by economic factor. A "strategic" factor crept in the relationship when the two countries signed a "strategic Partnership." Since then the Prime Ministers of the two countries have held an annual interaction and have discussed issues concerning both the countries' bilateral interests, including the security issues. However, the agenda of their cooperation have been dominated by the economic issues; signing a Comprehensive Economic Partnership Agreement, trade and investment, infrastructure developments, cooperation in the field of energy etc. Though they have cooperated in maritime security and Sea Lanes of Communications, it has been driven more by Japan's economic interest than the traditional security interests. By enhancing maritime cooperation with India, Japan wants to secure passage of its inbound and outbound goods which has been lifeline of its economy. India has participated in naval exercises with Japan including the bilateral naval exercise since 2012 that has been viewed as aimed at China. But the fact that India and China have established a military to military cooperation should not be omitted in an academic debate. They held hand-in-hand military exercise in 2006 and have established various military-to-military contacts. Most recently, India and China conducted first military exercise in the state of Jammu and Kashmir in October 2016. This was a follow up exercise of a similar exercise that the militaries of the countries held on the

Chinese side in February 2016.[36] As regards India-Japan naval exercise of June 2012 is concerned, the facts remains that the same Indian naval fleet which had naval exercise with Japan left for China for another exercise, though the nature of the exercise was different.

However, it would be difficult to negate that China was totally absent from the Indian strategic thinking when it signed strategic partnership with Japan in 2006. The joint statement signed during Abe-Singh summit meeting in 2006 stated the "usefulness of having dialogue among India, Japan and other likeminded countries"[37] on the issues of "mutual interest." This was interpreted by the strategic analysts as India and Japan are attempting to create an exclusive security architecture in Asia-Pacific (also being termed as Indo-Pacific) excluding China. Talks of quadrilateral mechanism among the US, Japan, Australia and India emboldened their speculations. This led them to opine that India is entering into a security arrangement aimed at encircling China. But the quad did not take a concrete shape because of concerns expressed by China and due to various reasons including change of government in Australia.

Since then India has tried to dispel the perception that it is bandwagoning with any power to counterbalance other power. At many occasions, Indian leadership has stated that New Delhi has "no intention" of allowing itself to be "utilised by any power to contain any other power."[38] In fact, when Abe mooted a proposal of a security framework (consisting of US, Japan, Australia and India) to safeguard "maritime commons," New Delhi merely stated that India and Japan need an open, rule based international trading system to prosper and they have "shared interest in maritime security." The statement made by Manmohan Singh during his Tokyo visit in May 2013 suggests that India was not eager to extend the existing bilateral maritime cooperation to a multilateral arrangement. Although Japan has tried hard that India takes a clear stand on various issues that concerns Japanese security including China's recently enacted Air Defense Identification Zone (ADIZ) encompassing Senkaku (known as Diaoyu in China) over which both the countries have contested claims, New Delhi's position has been ambiguous. In their joint statement after Abe's New Delhi visit the statement noted that the two prime ministers underscored the "importance of freedom of over-flight and civil aviation safety in accordance with the recognised principles of international law"[39] but stopped short of taking position over China's ADIZ.

There is a tendency, in both Indian and Chinese media, to overplay the China factor in India-Japan relations, but sufficient attention has not been paid to India's engagement with China and a fine balance its foreign policy planners are trying to maintain vis-à-vis China and Japan. Selective portrayal of facts by media has lead readers and researchers to draw a wrong assumption. An analysis of India-Japan relations should not be independent of India-China relations. A sections of strategic thinkers have used selective contents from India-Japan joint statements signed over the seven eight years to support their China containment theory. But it should be noted that if India has identified certain areas in which both India and Japan can complement each other it has also identified complementarities with China. The then Indian Prime Minister Manmohan Singh during his speech at China's Central Party School in October 2013 highlighted eight specific areas where he saw opportunity of cooperation between India and China including in the field of manufacturing, energy, infrastructure developments. Interestingly, some of these areas of cooperation overlap with that of ongoing cooperation between India and Japan. Also he outlined "seven practical principles of engagement."[40] Welcoming the emergence of China, he reiterated that "old theories of alliances and containment are no longer relevant."[41]

Then what the two countries want to achieve by forging strategic partnership? China's assertive behaviour and identifying a number of core interests, one after the other, as well as making resolves to use force to secure those interests has caused apprehensions regarding Beijing's motives. Therefore, both New Delhi and Tokyo have come closer and have been using international fora to set a norm to moderate China's assertive behaviours and they have been partly successful in their objectives.

China Factor and Indo-Japan Strategic Relations: How it is being viewed in China, India and Japan?

Notwithstanding the fact that India has clarified that it does not want to balance one country against the other, the ongoing Indo-Japan strategic cooperation has drawn reactions and criticism from China. Experts in the Chinese academia, especially those working on strategic issues, have viewed the strategic relationship between the two countries as an alliance aimed at containing China. For example, The *Beijing Review* quoted Li Yan, a scholar at the China Institutes of Contemporary International Relations (CICIR), as opining that Abe's attempts to promote 'value-oriented diplomacy' and construct a 'four-nation alliance' are apparently directed at China. Japan is concerned that its status in East Asia would decline in the wake of China's development. Abe's vision of a "quadrilateral grouping" comprising Japan, the United States, India and Australia aims to expand Japan's diplomatic frontiers and to marginalize China by citing "common democratic values" and besiege the country geopolitically. The *Beijing Review* also quoted yet another Chinese scholar, Liu Jiangyong, a professor at the Institute of International Studies of Tsinghua University, as saying that "by proposing the 'broader Asia' concept, Japan is taking a step toward implementing its 'value-oriented diplomacy'...It is obviously not a geographic concept but a political one, because Japan does not put its relations with China on a par with its relations with the other three countries (the US, Australia and India)."[42]

Others in the Chinese media are equally fueling the fire by interpreting the ongoing relationship in their own way. Against the backdrop of a joint drill by the US, Australia, Japan and Indian navies, China's official newspaper the *People's Daily* observed that "it is absolutely not new for Japan and the US to sit down and plot conspiracies together but it is rather intriguing to get India involved."[43]

Similarly, India's growing interaction with Japan and ASEAN countries has also caused alarm among few strategic circles in China. In an opinion column in the *People's Daily*, Li Hongmei wrote that "India is viewed by Japan as an ideal partner to establish the strategic cooperation in security, based on the assumption that both of them are being threatened by China's military assertiveness in East China Sea as well as in the Indian Ocean. On this basis, Japan and India have both placed high expectations upon each others in combining strengths to counterbalance China." She further added that "by taking advantage of the face-off between China and Japan, India still cannot relax its spasm of worries about China, nor can it brush aside the fear that China might nip its ambitions in the bud."[44] Yet another scholar observes that "...China is quite perplexed that two countries such as India, which has traditionally been seen as the leader of the non-alignment, and Japan, traditionally acknowledged to pursue an economic-oriented foreign policy, were able to engage in security cooperation measures."[45]

However, in Chinese strategic community there are voices, though in minority, which see the India-Japan relations in a different perspective. For example, Liang Jun argues "What is involved in China-India relations denotes much more than the display of the blossoming personal friendship between Modi and Abe."[46] He believes the intimacy between the two leaders will only bring "psychological comfort"[47] to the two countries adding that "Sino-Indian ties can in no way be counterbalanced by the Japan-India friendship."[48] Similarly, yet another strategic observer suggest China not to feel "excessively nervous"[49] because of increasing intimacy between Tokyo and New Delhi. He is of the view that India is not likely to give up its "strategic autonomy." He argues:

> India has long been cherishing strategic autonomy as the standard of its foreign policy, and it has no reason to give it up now. New Delhi will strike a balance between Tokyo and Beijing.[50]

Echoing the similar sentiments, an editorial that appeared in the *Global Times* just after Prime Minister Modi's visit to Japan in November 2016, stated that "China and India have many problems between them, however, Sino-Indian relations are improving. National leaders frequently meet and are securing the right direction in bilateral ties. Even if India signs the "Indian Ocean-Pacific Pact," it won't have as much strength to contain China as Abe expects."[51] The Daily also asserted that "India will not become a pawn for Japan to contain China, as it wants to become a power on par with China and Japan and benefit from both sides. India will get closer to Japan but will not enter into a "brotherhood" relationship."[52]

China, at the official level, however, expressed its apprehension about the emerging quadrilateral alliance consisting of the US, Japan, Australia and India and issued separate demarches to each country days before the first-ever official level security consultation among them. It sought to know the purpose behind their meeting.[53] On the other hand, China has time and again expressed that both China and India have enough space to grow and prosper together. Chinese authorities have made no explicit comment at the official level about the Indo-Japan strategic relations which could be construed as its wariness about the bilateral relationship. While analysing India-Japan relations-keeping China as a factor, one must not omit the "strategic assurance" the Indian and Chinese leadership has given to each other about their bilateral relationship with another country. It must be noted that when the then Indian Prime Minister Manmohan Singh visited China, a bilateral statement issued by the two countries noted that "We agreed that, as large neighbours following independent foreign policies, the relationships pursued by India and China with other countries must not become a source of concern for each other. This will be our strategic reassurance."[54]

Unlike Chinese strategic thinkers who believe that an strengthening Indo-Japan strategic cooperation aimed at containing China, the opinion among Indian strategic thinkers are diverse on this issue. As regards the ongoing strategic cooperation, Brahama Chellaney, notes that "concerned over China's lengthening shadow, Japan and India are bracing for a strategic challenge in the Asian heartland, not to gain preeminence but to thwart preeminence" and observes that "in this distinct strategic triangle, if China were A, and India and Japan were B and C, the sum of B plus C will always be greater than A. That is why India and Japan are bound to become close strategic buddies, even as they attempt to ensure that their relations with Beijing do not sour." Against this backdrop, Chellaney emphatically argues that "the balance of power in Asia will be determined by events as much in the Indian Ocean as in East Asia, India and Japan have to work together to promote peace and stability, protect critical sea lanes and stem the incipient Asian power disequilibrium."[55]

In yet another column Chellaney termed the ongoing burgeoning relationship between India and Japan as a significant milestone in building "Asian power equilibrium." He notes that Japan and India are natural allies, with no negative historical legacy and no conflict of strategic interest. He observes that "never before in history have China, India and Japan been all strong at the same time" and advises that the three powers "need to find ways to reconcile their interests in Asia so that they can peacefully coexist and prosper." But he opines that only "India and Japan desire a multipolar Asia and multipolar world." The other two have "different playbooks: the US wants a unipolar world but a multipolar Asia; China seeks a multipolar world but a unipolar Asia."[56]

Harsh V. Pant, echoing a similar line, observes that "the rise of China in the Asia-Pacific and beyond has altered the strategic calculus of India and Japan, forcing them to rethink their attitudes toward each other." He notes further that Japan is "reassessing its role as a security provider in the region and beyond, and of all its neighbors, India seems most willing to acknowledge Japan's centrality in shaping the evolving Asia-Pacific security architecture."[57] Similarly, Rajaram Panda, another Indian strategic thinker, presently Visiting Professor and India Chair at Reitaku University, Japan, also considers that Japan can be an important country to be considered for an Asian equilibrium. He believes that growing Indo-Japan ties "can keep China in check." He observes that China's assertive posture over territorial disputes with its neighbours, including India and Japan, coupled with its military modernization "does not augur well for peace and stability in Asia." Against this context, he opines that "for India, Japan as a partner in development vis-à-vis China, would serve a twin purpose: to help engage China, and also keep China under check."[58]

Indian strategic thinker and President Carnegie India, C. Raja Mohan, observes that the rise of India has changed the "template of Asian balance of power." He is of the view that "until recently, the triangular relationship between the US, Japan and China defined the terms of the regional security order. The rise of India...has altered the power politics of the region. Washington was quick to see the implications of a rising India and has rapidly transformed its relations with New Delhi. Abe's India sojourn (in 2007) has signaled that Japan is following suit." He also speculated that "as Japan and India move from an indifferent relationship of the last many decades to an all encompassing strategic partnership, Asia's geopolitics is bound to alter irrevocably."[59]

However, there is yet another emerging view among the Indian strategic thinking. This school of thought believes that both Japan and China are equally important. Most prominent voice representing this view is Srinath

Raghavan, a Senior Fellow at Delhi based think tank, the Centre for Policy Research. He believes that China is important for both India and Japan. He argues that "from a strategic standpoint, it would be unwise to convey an impression to China that our relationship with Japan is primarily directed against it." He believes that both India and Japan has to cope with the rise of China "without stoking insecurity." However, Raghavan, adds that India's closer ties with Japan may also provide "strategic pay-offs" vis-à-vis China. "At a minimum, it will indicate to China that India has an important role in the emerging Asian security landscape. This, in turn, will strengthen India's hand in dealing with China on bilateral matters. Nevertheless, India should not overestimate the importance of that aspect. Nor should we underestimate negative fall outs," Raghavan says.[60]

Siddharth Varadarajan, who has similar views, argues that leaders of India and Japan "need to realise is that the Indo-Japanese relationship will prosper and scale new heights only if it has intrinsic value. Treating the relationship with India as a derivative product of, say, Japan's relations with China, may give a temporary boost to bilateral ties but that boost will not endure."[61]

Finally, how India-Japan relations are viewed within Japan? The Japanese domestic constituency, especially the Japanese mainstream media, has a mixed view about India-Japan relations and they do not necessarily see the Rise of China as a driving factor. For example, the *Japan Times* through its editorials have argued that Japan should not use India as a "means of checking China." The Daily suggests that "Japan should refrain from using its ties with India merely for political expediency. Instead, it should cultivate cooperative ties with India with a wider perspective and a long-range view."[62] The *Yomiuri Shimbun*, yet another influential daily has a different take. It argues to bolster Japan-India relations to check China. In an editorial it opined that China's maritime expansion is a "matter of concern common to Japan and India" and stated that "we want to see Japan-India cooperation in maritime security steadily bolstered."[63]

A section of Japanese observers also believe that China is a major factor "nudging the two countries to come closer."[64] Takenori Horimoto opines that "coping with China" would be a "challenge for Japan-India relations in the coming decades."[65] Similarly, Toru Ito argues that most Japanese people evaluate India in terms of its value as a "card to be played against China."[66] He emphasizes that "Japan would not have realized the diplomatic importance of India without a China factor."[67] The arguments by Horimoto and Ito gets vindicated when one comes across the Japanese strategic narratives on Japan's post Cold War grand strategy. Hiroshi Kaihara, a proclaimed Japanese conservative states that "if China's strategy of 'necklace of pearl' is completed, the Sea lane between the Middle East and Japan will come under China's control."[68] To overcome this problem, Kaihara suggests that Japan should help India to become technologically and economically powerful country. He hopes that Indian will become a "cornerstone for Japan's security."[69]

Japan's New National Security Strategy: India Gains Prominence

It is not surprising that the concerns expressed in the Japanese strategic circles about the China threat have influenced the strategic view of the Japanese establishment as well. Japan in its new strategic doctrines unveiled in 2014, have identified India among the countries that are "primary drivers" of change in global "balance of power." Japan has adopted two strategic documents (National Security Strategy and National Defense Guidelines 2014) under the leadership of Prime Minister Shinzo Abe, which will guide country's security and diplomatic policies for the next decade.

The security doctrines identify a number of areas in which Japan would like to strengthen cooperation with India in the near future. Despite the fact that India and Japan signed a strategic partnership agreement way back in 2006 and the successive bilateral statements urged the need to enhance "strategic" partnership, India did not find primacy in Japan's official strategic doctrines including the National Defense Programme Guidelines (NDPG) adopted before 2010. The NDPG adopted by the Democratic Party of Japan (DPJ) government did mention India, but for a different reason. It identified India for enhancing cooperation in securing "maritime navigation." To "complement" Japan-US security arrangements; NDPG had identified new regional powers including Australia, Republic of Korea, and ASEAN countries. The official document listed these countries with which Tokyo wanted to "enhance security cooperation."[70] But India's reference was missing in the defence policy doctrine. It was clear that the DPJ government wanted not to affront Beijing by mentioning India among the group of countries with which it wanted to strengthen security cooperation. Previously Beijing had voiced its concerns about these moves and had in fact viewed these efforts as ganging up against China.

With the change of government in 2012, the LDP discarded the NDPG adopted by the DPJ government. It adopted a new guidelines in 2014 which will remain effective up to 2023. The new defense guidelines as well as first ever National Security Strategy (NSS), also adopted in 2014, by Shinzo Abe government has made a departure from the previous stance. It attaches importance to India for its security and diplomatic policies. After assuming office in 2012, Abe has stated that the existing defence Guidelines does not reflect the changing security realities and his government will announce new guidelines taking an assessment of regional security situation. Japan in the Abe led administration created a National Security Council (NSC) in 2013 headed by the prime minister of Japan to formulate diplomatic and security policies. The National Security Strategy, a doctrine that clubs security and diplomacy, has been adopted by the new NSC and will remain effective for the next ten years. It identifies challenges faced by Japan in both security and diplomatic areas and reflects changing strategic thinking of Japan.

The revised defense guidelines, recognises India's ascendance among the security players. It notes that "as a result of change in the balance of power due to the development of countries such as China and India...multipolarisation of the international community is progressing."[71] The NSS doctrine puts this issue more strongly and argues that India and China are the "primary drivers" of change in the "balance of power."[72] As regards the security cooperation with India is concerned, the defence Guidelines states that "Japan will strengthen its relationship with India in a broad range of fields, including maritime security, through joint training and exercises as well as joint implementation of international peace cooperation activities."[73] Japan's enunciation that it will strengthen relationship with India in "broad range of fields" is reflective of the fact that it does not want to limit its security cooperation in maritime field only, as was envisioned in defense guidelines adopted by the previous DPJ government. More importantly, the NSS document clubs India among the countries with which Japan wants to strengthen its "cooperative relations." The strategic doctrine, stipulates that Japan will strengthen its "cooperative relations" with countries including India, with which it "shares universal values and strategic interests."[74] The other countries mentioned in the documents are: Australia, South Korea and ASEAN countries. It further notes that "India is becoming increasingly influential" among the international community. It recognises that India because of its "geographic location" remains "important for Japan" and to secure its maritime interest it will strengthen cooperation with India.[75]

By boldly positioning India in its security and diplomatic strategy, Japan has sent a clear signal that New Delhi remains important not only for its maritime security but for its overall security. India which has forged strategic partnership with Japan and has set up an annual bilateral maritime dialogue also accords greater importance to Japan in its diplomatic and security strategy. The shift in Japanese strategic thinking has helped cement the ties further. However, it has also created some unease for New Delhi, which so far has maintained ambiguity over certain issues that impacts Japanese security including developments in East China Sea. When Tokyo says that both India and Japan share "universal values and strategic interests" it also expects unified response on various issues impacting Japanese security. A section of Japanese strategic thinkers have expressed surprise over New Delhi's studied silence over China's ADIZ announced in December 2013 that encompasses the Senkaku/Diaoyu Islands, a contested territory between Japan and China.[76] They expect that India, like other democratic countries denounce China's move to unilaterally change the status quo in the East China Sea.

Beijing had viewed Tokyo's security partnership with New Delhi, as a mechanism to 'encircle' China and had expressed its concerns at few occasions regarding the two countries coming strategically closer. The strategic doctrine which gives lots of importance to India for its diplomatic and security policies has deepened Chinese doubts further.

India-Japan Strategic Partnership: Assessing the Impact

The impact on the deepening of India-Japan relations can be clearly witnessed on two fronts; regionally it has resulted in deepening of India-Japan maritime cooperation and internationally it has resulted in the two countries seeking for an adequate representation in the United Nation's Security Council (UNSC) as permanent members. By seeking role commensurate with their economic and global stature, both are trying to enhance their say in the international security. The next section of this chapter examines the two issues as case studies in details.

Case Study I

Maritime Security Cooperation: Strategic and Economic Aspects

The maritime security cooperation between India and Japan is driven by two factors: the strategic factor and the economic factor. It will not be an exaggeration to say that Indo-Japan maritime cooperation is driven more by economic concerns than the security concerns. In fact, the hijacking incident of Alondra Rainbow—a Japanese freight ship which was rescued by Indian coastguards in 1999 triggered this cooperation.[77] (For the location of the hijack see the map below)

Map 1: Alondra Rainbow Incident

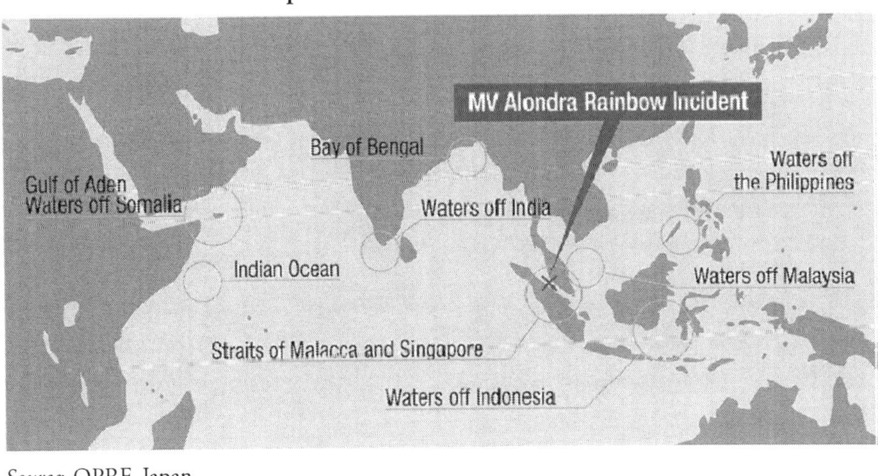

Source: OPRF, Japan.

It was an act that threatened Japan's economic security since its 98 per cent of inbound and outbound trade takes place through the sea. For the first time, the then Japanese Vice Transport Minister Toshihiro Nikai in a letter to Indian Defense Minister underscored the need of combating piracy and sought India's cooperation.[78] Prabhakaran Paleri, a former Director General of Indian Coast Guard, also believes that the Alondra Rainbow hijacking "opened a new chapter in Indo-Japan relations" and both the countries are collaborating "to eliminate the bane of piracy."[79]

A year after Alondra Rainbows hijack, the then Indian Defence Minister George Fernandes visited Tokyo in 2000. He announced that both the countries will held annual high level defence consultation and noted that "...the Japanese coastguard ships and Indian vessels will conduct joint training in tackling piracy. The issue, though, is not piracy alone."[80] While referring to the unresolved territorial disputes in the South China Sea region, he further stated, "a strong India, economically and militarily well endowed, will be a very solid agent to see that the sea lanes are not disturbed and that conflict situations are contained."[81] The statement by Fernandese, clearly suggests that India was not looking maritime cooperation from an "economic security" prism only. He saw the issue from a strategic angle as well. Interestingly, the then Japanese Foreign Minister, Yoriko Kawaguchi, during India visit in 2003 stated that maintenance of maritime traffic between Indian Oceana and the Straits of Malacca are among the "security and defense issues which deserves our increased attention."[82]

Similarly, the then Japan's Defense Agency Chief, Shigeru Ishiba who later became Defense Minister, referring the need of a stronger maritime cooperation in the region observed:

> The most important thing for this region is to have a good collaboration between Australia, the US, India and Japan. These four countries should have a candid exchange of views and then try to make a contribution to formulate rules for international society.[83]

These statements suggest that Japan wanted to extend existing maritime cooperation—, which it started with India to ensure the safety of Sea-Lane of Communication (SLOC)—beyond the present commitments.

Against this background, India, Japan, the US and Singapore participated in a joint naval exercise in the Bay of Bengal in 2007. Though the participating countries claimed that the exercise was aimed at responding a regional disaster, it was construed in strategic circles that this is aimed at containing China which by that time had started naval expansion in the Indian Ocean.[84] Gradually, this maritime cooperation from multilateral exercise has been transformed into a bilateral naval exercise. In June 2012, navies of both the countries held bilateral naval exercise in Japanese waters. Since then, India and Japan have had maritime exercises in each others' waters which some time has been joined by other naval powers including the US. A veteran strategic thinker in India saw these exercises as "expanding engagement" between the two navies. He opined:

> The expanding engagement with the Japanese navy, one of the strongest in the world, should give boost to India's maritime diplomacy in Asia. If New Delhi's interests in Pacific are growing, Tokyo's naval profile in the Indian Ocean has begun to expand.[85]

The maritime cooperation between India and Japan reached to a new height as they held first maritime dialogue in January 2013. In the dialogue they discussed issues of "maritime security including non-traditional threats, cooperation in shipping, marine science and technology, marine biodiversity and cooperation at various multi-lateral forums."[86] Institutionalisation of the dialogue between New Delhi and Tokyo would mean that they will meet alternately in the two capitals and will discuss issues pertaining to maritime interest.

In future also, maritime security would remain one of the driving factors of India-Japan relation as China's "first island" and "second island chain" strategy have generated wariness in Japan's strategic community. It must be mentioned here that in 1982 Chinese strategic planners under the leadership of Liu Huaqing, then Vice Chairman of the Central Military Commission had envisioned a "three stage scenario"[87] for its maritime expansion planning. For their first stage scenario from 2000 to 2010, they had identified naval expansion through "first Island Chain." The Senkaku Islands in East China Sea and various contested islands in South China Sea fall within the "first island chain." For the second stage scenario from 2010 to 2020, the Chinese maritime planners have identified its naval expansion along "Second Island Chain" that links to Japan's Ogasawara Island, Guam and Indonesia. In the third and final stage from 2020 to 2040, China envisages to put an end to US domination over the Pacific and Indian Ocean through its naval expansion.

The recent naval expansion and repeated intrusion by Chinese vassals in Japanese waters, off Senkaku, has been interpreted in Japan as a Chinese plan to control the "first island chain." They are also increasingly worried about China's "second island chain" strategy that seeks to control the waters around Ogasawara Island—600 km south of Tokyo—in the next 10 years.[88]

In case China aggressively pushes its maritime strategy, there are strong possibilities that it will impact on free flow of Japanese in-bound and out-bound goods. In the foreseeable scenario, Japan wants to ensure freedom of navigation and looks for partners. India, being one of the regional players, is one of the hopes for Japan. Yuriko Koike, Japan's former Defense Minister and presently the Governor of Tokyo, in an opinion piece has opined that "... fear of provoking China should not stop Asia's leaders from seeking a regional security consensus, such as the proposed code of conduct for disputes in the South China Sea."[89] She adds that "America alone cannot construct a viable security structure for the region. From India to Japan, every Asian country must play its part."[90] In the backdrop of increasing conflicts in the Pacific involving China, India has ensured that it will stand by Japan to ensure freedom of navigation. India's the then Foreign Minister Salman Khurshid while visiting Tokyo in March 2013 stated:

> Countries like India and Japan must cooperate in ensuring the security of global commons including freedom of navigation on the high seas that is critical to both our countries which imports large amounts of oil and gas.[91]

Freedom of Navigation in the South China Sea

The statement above, reflects the fact that both Japan and India want that China abide by the internationally-accepted laws and norms on the freedom of navigation. Nevertheless, India was a little cautious about forcefully raising this issue. But, it has started raising the issue of a rule-based maritime order more emphatically since China objected to India's hydrocarbon exploration and exploitation projects in the South China Sea off the coast of Vietnam in 2011. It was reported widely in the Indian media that a Chinese warship confronted the Indian Navy vessel INS *Airavat* shortly after it left a Vietnamese port in the South China Sea in late July 2011. Breaking its silence over this issue, India stated that "it supports the freedom of navigation in international waters including the South China Sea, the right of passage and unimpeded commerce in accordance with accepted principles of international law, and peaceful settlement of maritime disputes. These principles should be respected by all."[92] Since this episode, India has been consistently making statements about developments in the South China Sea, maintaining that it is not a "party to the dispute," and that its interest in the South China Sea, is "purely commercial."

However, whenever the situation in the South China Sea has escalated, India has made statements on the developments in the region. Expressing concern over a stand-off between China and the Philippines in May 2014, India observed that the "maintenance of peace, stability, growth and prosperity in the region is of vital interest to the international community." India's Ministry of External Affairs also maintained that the "freedom of navigation in the South China Sea should not be impeded and calls for cooperation in ensuring the security of sea-lanes and the strengthening of maritime security."[93]

Finally, the South China Sea issue also surfaced in India-Japan joint statement signed during Shinzo Abe's Delhi visit in December 2015. The joint statement stated that "the two Prime Ministers noting the developments in the South China Sea called upon all States to avoid unilateral actions that could lead to tensions in the region."[94] India has been reiterating a similar stance on the freedom of navigation in its bilateral and multilateral engagements with Japan and the US. For example, in the first-ever trilateral meeting attended by the US Secretary of State and its Japanese and Indian counterparts, the three democratic countries "underscored the importance of international law and peaceful settlement of disputes; freedom of navigation and over-flight; and unimpeded lawful commerce, including in the South China Sea."[95]

The case study above, suggest that though India-Japan maritime cooperation initially was aimed at safeguarding economic interest, gradually it has transformed into a security cooperation. Both the countries have been raising the issue of freedom of navigation in the bilateral, regional and international fora. However, securing economic interest of both the countries' remains one of the essential elements of the bilateral maritime cooperation.

Case Study II

India-Japan and the UN Reform

United Nations reform, specially the expansion of permanent membership of the UN Security Council (UNSC) and cooperation in UN Peacekeeping Operations (UNPKO), is yet another issue on the bilateral agenda of both the governments. It may be mentioned that when Japan decided to forge a new relationship with India, it identified few global agenda for its "global and strategic partnership."[96] Partnering with India to seek for UN reform and expansion of Security Council was part of this global partnership. From Asia, both Japan and India are aspirants of acquiring a permanent seat on the UNSC. But instead of lobbying for the high table alone, which could have led to some bickering between the two, both decided to join hands with other aspirants—Germany and Brazil. They formed Goup-4 to realize their quest for UNSC seats. This gave a new push to India-Japan bilateral relationship. In 2004, they reaffirmed that they "will work together towards realizing a meaningful reform of the United Nations, including that of the Security Council, together with other Member States" and pledged to "support each other's candidature."[97]

In 2005, the G-4 countries compiled a draft resolution calling for the council membership to be expanded. And argued that "the Security Council must be reformed to represent today's global realities, not the world of 60 years ago" and demanded that "the Security Council must be expanded in both permanent and non-permanent categories, on the basis of equitable representation, with the inclusion of both developed and developing countries."[98] However, after the term of Kofi Annan as Secretary General of UN (who was one of the strong proponents of UN reform) ended, the issue has not been debated vigorously.

Nonetheless the issue remains on the agenda of both the governments as they keep reiterating the need for UN reform and expansion of the Security Council. Both Japan and India reiterated their commitment in a joint statement when Prime Minister Hatoyama visited India in 2009. Both "decided to accelerate their efforts, in close cooperation with the G-4 and other like-minded countries...to make the Security Council more representative, credible and effective for meeting the challenges of the new century."[99] Japan on its part, has made concerted efforts and has also shown flexibility to gain the much coveted seat. In 2012, Japanese representative in the UN Tsuneo Nishida presented a flexible formula which included "establishing a longer-term category with the possibility of its conversion to the permanent category after a certain period of time."[100] Apart from regularly raising the issue related to the UN reform on different forum, the aspirants have set up permanent representative to the UN of the G-4 countries and have been aggressively lobbying to achieve this goal. This body once again issued a call on the UN to reform the UNSC as "the current Security Council does not reflect the geopolitical realities of the 21st century."[101] It demanded that the UNSC "should be reformed to make it more representative, legitimate and effective." The body consisting of the G-4 nations has started diplomatic initiative identifying the countries amenable to expansion of the UNSC and reform of the UN.

Despite the hectic diplomatic parleys and call for the UN reform by G-4 leaders, the Japanese academia seems pessimistic about the achieving the goal. Professor Toshitaka Takeuchi cites two biggest hurdles; first gaining two-third majority in the General Assembly and the G-4 failed measurably in 2005 when it tried to gain support from the African Union and Second, overcoming the China's veto. He points, "Japan's strategy is to garner an overwhelming majority in the General Assembly so that China would be reluctant to use its veto power. But China may be determined to veto any reform push that would enable Japan to gain a permanent seat on the UNSC no matter how much support Japan has in the General Assembly given the tense relations between the two countries."[102] Since China opposes Japan's entry into the UN and G-4 nations are presenting their joint bid to the much coveted seat, China's veto will also scuttle the chances of other three countries. However, how the UNSC reforms pans out in the future would be an interesting phenomenon to be observed. Antonio Guterres, who previously served as UN high commissioner for refugees, has taken over as the new UN Secretary-General. Though, he is an insider in the UN system, his stance on the UN reform is not known. Much will depend whether he, like Annan, will push for the UNSC expansion or will maintain silence like Ban Ki-moon.

Conclusion

As has been discussed above, Japan and India have firmly established strategic partnerships. Despite US's renewed interest in the Asia-Pacific following its "pivot to Asia," policy, Japan still wants to strengthen its relationship with India. India will remain an important partner for Japan's national interest is evident from Japan's new defence guidelines. Japan has stated that it will "enhance cooperation with India and other countries that share common interests in ensuring the security of maritime navigation from Africa and the Middle East to East Asia."[103]

India's swift dispatch of a team of its National Disaster Response Force to lend its help in relief missions in tsunami and radiation affected areas[104] has enhanced Japan's faith in India's capability, and it believes, it will remain a key nation for Japan's overall national security. The ten-day Indian mission, according to the then Prime Minister Naoto Kan demonstrated "India's true friendship and feeling of goodwill towards Japan."[105] The special mention of Indian assistance following March 11 crisis by Prime Minister Kan is indicative of the fact that India is seen as a responsible player in Japan's security.

Maritime security will continue to bring both the countries closer together in the next few decades because maritime security in East Asia and beyond seems shaky. The East Asian region is likely to witness more unpleasant incidents in the future following the nationalization of Senkaku islands by Japan and China's imposition of ADIZ encompassing the Senkakus. Reports suggests that China after completing the "first stage strategy" to strengthen its naval presence near the *Senkaku* Islands will embark on its "second stage strategy" during the period 2010 to 2020 and would seek to establish control of waters within the "second island chain" that links Japan's Ogasawara island chain, Guam and Indonesia. In the third and "final stage" from 2020 to 2040 China envisages to put an end to the US's domination over the Pacific Ocean and Indian Ocean.[106] India will certainly seek the help of Japan and other countries to overcome the planned domination by China. However, there are other factors such as the interdependent nature of the countries' economies as well as their shared democratic values that will bind the two countries closer in the near future. These issues would be discussed in the next few chapters.

END NOTES

1. The canvas of a "strategic relationship" is much larger than a mere "political relationship." While a political relationship means maintaining periodic dialogue on bilateral, regional and global issues, a strategic relationship goes beyond mere political dialogue and encompasses defence, economic and security dimensions impinging in the bilateral ties, in the region and in the world," writes Rajaram Panda. For details see Rajaram Panda, "India and Japan: Exploring Strategic Potential," *Journal of Defence Studies*, Vol. 4, No. 4, October 2010.
2. Recalling a conversation with US Congressmen around 1987 Shintaro Ishihara, the Governor of Tokyo and a member of the LDP notes in his book that a Congressman told him—"US-Soviet ties have dramatically improved and it is quite possible that the partnership between Washington and Tokyo might be dissolved... The United States may even abandon Japan." Ishihara notes that he replied "....if the United States no longer wants Japan an ally, then we will have a free hand to look for other friends around the world." See, Shintaro Ishihara, "*The Japan that can say No,*" Simon & Schuster, New York, 1991, pp.77-78.
3. Toshiki Kaifu, "Japan and South Asia: In pursuit of dialogue and co-operation," April 30, 1990, Text of Prime Minister Kishi's address to Indian Parliament. For details see, P.A. Narsimha Murthy, "India and Japan: Dimension of their relations, Appendix II, pp. 434-448, Lancer Book , New Delhi, 1992.
4. Ibid.
5. Ibid.
6. Sanjana Joshi, "Prospect for Security Cooperation Between India and Japan," *Strategic Analyses*, Vol. XXV, No.2, Routledge/Institute for Defence Studies and Analyses, May 2001.
7. Ibid.
8. P.V. Narsimha Rao, "Towards an India-Japan partnership in the Twenty-first Century," *Japan Review of International Affairs*, Vol. 6, No.2, 1992, pp.195-202.
9. Shinzo Abe, "Two democracy meet at Sea: For a Better and Safer Asia," in India-

Japan Joint Study: Strategic Partnership in the face of Chinese assertiveness, The JINF Review, Volume 2, *Japan Institute of National Fundamentals*, Tokyo, 2012, p.218.

10. Ibid.
11. Ibid.
12. Author's interview with Tomohiko Taniguchi, February 5, 2015 at Raiosha, Keio University Hiyoshi Campus, Kanagawa.
13. "Japan India summit meeting," summary available at http://www.mofa.go.jp/region/asia-paci/pmv0008/india_s.html (Accessed on September 10, 2016).
14. "Joint Statement, India-Japan Partnership in a New Asian Era: Strategic Orientation of India-Japan Global Partnership," available at http://meaindia.nic.in/mystart.php?id=10059479 (Accessed on September 10, 2016).
15. The detailed of the eight fold initiative is available at http://meaindia.nic.in/mystart.php?id=10059479 (Accessed on September 11, 2016).
16. As quoted in Brahma Chellaney, "India, Japan: natural allies," *The Japan Times*, August 16, 2007.
17. For a comprehensive analyses of Shinzo Abe's India visit please see, Naidu, GVC, "New Dimensions to the India-Japan Strategic Partnership: Shinzo Abe Visit," *Strategic Analysis*, Vol.31,No.6, November 2007.
18. "Confluence of the two Seas," speech by Prime Minister Shinzo Abe at the joint session of the Indian Parliament, available at http://www.mofa.go.jp/region/asia-paci/pmv0708/speech-2.html (Accessed on September 10, 2016).
19. Ibid.
20. "(Indian) PM's address to the joint session of the Diet," December 14, 2006. The text of address available at http://pmindia.nic.in/visits/content.asp?id=142 (Accessed on September 11, 2016)
21. "Joint Statement Towards India-Japan Strategic and Global Partnership," December 15, 2006, available at http://meaindia.nic.in/mystart.php?id=100512192 (Accessed on September 11, 2016).
22. Siddharth Vardarajan, "Four-power meeting drew Chinese demarche," *The Hindu*, June 14, 2007.
23. "Joint statement on the Advancement of the Strategic and Global Partnership between India and Japan," October 22, 2008, available at http://www.mea.gov.in/mystart.php?id=100514278 (Accessed on September 12, 2016).
24. The Democratic Party of Japan's Platform for Government (Election manifesto, 2009), p.28, issued on August 18, 2009.
25. "New Stage of India-Japan Strategic and Global Partnership," December 29, 2009, available at http://www.mea.gov.in/mystart.php?id=100515441 (Accessed on September 12, 2016).
26. "Joint statement: Vision for India-Japan Strategic and Global Partnership in the Next Decade," available at http://www.mea.gov.in/mystart.php?id=100516597 (Accessed on September 13, 2016).
27. "Tokyo Declaration for India-Japan Special Strategic and Global Partnership,"

September 1, 2014, *Ministry of External Affairs of India*, available at http://www.mea.gov.in/bilateral-documents.htm?dtl/23965/Tokyo+Declaration+for+India++Japan+Special+Strategic+and+Global+Partnership. (Accessed on September 13, 2016).

28. Ibid.
29. For Detailed analysis of Indian Prime Minister Narendra Modi's Japan visit see, Shamshad A. Khan, "Deconstructing "Tokyo Declaration" 2014: Takeaways from Indian Prime Minister's Japan visit," *ICWA Issue Brief*, September 24, 2014, available online at http://www.icwa.in/pdfs/IB/2014/DeconstructingTokyoDeclaration2014.pdf (Accessed on September 14, 2016).
30. Ibid.
31. Ibid.
32. For a detailed analysis of China factor in India-Japan relations see, Shamshad A. Khan, "Assessing Japan-India Relations: An Indian Perspective," March 7, 2014, Institute of Peace and Conflict Studies, New Delhi.
33. J.N.Dixit, "My South Block Years: Memoirs of a Foreign Secretary," *UBS Publishers and distributors*, New Delhi, 1966, pp.262-263.
34. Ibid.
35. Ibid.
36. Dinakar Peri, "India, China conduct first military exercise in J&K," *The Hindu*, October 20, 2016.
37. "Joint Statement Towards India-Japan Strategic and Global Partnership," December 15, 2006, available at http://meaindia.nic.in/mystart.php?id=100512192 (Accessed on September 15, 2016).
38. India's (the then) External Minister Pranab Mukherjee quoted in P. Surya Narayana, "We do not believe in containing any country," *The Hindu*, June 21, 2007.
39. For complete text see, "Joint Statement on the occasion of Official Visit of the Prime Minister of Japan to India (January 25-27, 2014)," Ministry of External Affairs, Government of India, available at http://mea.gov.in/bilateral-documents.htm?dtl/22772 (Accessed on September 15, 2016).
40. Prime Minister Manmohan Singh's speech at the Central Party School in Beijing-India and China in the New Era, October 24, 2013, http://pib.nic.in/newsite/PrintRelease.aspx?relid=100218 (Accessed on September 15, 2016).
41. Ibid.
42. "A Broader Asia without China?," *Beijing Review*, No.38, 20 September 2007, available at http://www.bjreview.com.cn/quotes/txt/2007-09/25/content_77617.htm (Accessed on September 15, 2016).
43. "A 'goodwill' joint naval drill?," *Peoples Daily*, April 21, 2007, available at http://english.people.com.cn/200704/21/print20070421_368521.html (Accessed on September 15, 2016).
44. Li Hongmei, "India's Look East Policy means Look to encircle China?," *The Peoples Daily*, October 27, 2010, available at http://english.peopledaily.com.cn/90002/96417/7179404.html (Accessed on September 16, 2016).

45. Hayoun Ryou, "India-Japan Security Cooperation: Chinese Perception," *IPCS Issue Brief*, No. 89, available at http://www.ipcs.org/search_result.php?keyword=Hayoun+Ryou (Accessed on September 15, 2016).
46. Liang Jun, "Modi-Abe diplomacy bring scant comfort," *Global Times*, September 02, 2014.
47. Ibid.
48. Ibid.
49. Zhao Minghou, "Mutual Great power ambition brings Japan-India closer," *Global Times*, September 1, 2014.
50. Ibid.
51. "India Will not become a pawn of Japan," (Editorial), *The Global Times*, November 12, 2016.
52. Ibid.
53. Siddharth Vardharajan, "Four-power meeting drew Chinese demarche," *The Hindu*, June 14, 2007.
54. "Prime Minister (Manmohan Singh)'s statement to media after delegation level talks to the Chinese Premier," October 23, 2013.
55. Brahma Chellaney, "Japan, India: natural allies," *The Japan Times*, August 16, 2007.
56. Brahma Challaney, "Towards Asian power equilibrium," *The Hindu*, November 1, 2008.
57. Harsh V Pant, "India aims to raise its profile vis-a-vis China by 'looking east'," *The Japan Times*, January 31, 2011.
58. Rajaram Panda, "Indo-Japanese ties can keep China in Check," *The Economic Times*, October 29, 2010.
59. C Raja Mohan, "Japan and India: The making of a new alliance?," Commentary, *Rajaratnam School of International Studies*, August 27, 2007, available at http://www.rsis.edu.sg/publications/Perspective/RSIS0912007.pdf (Accessed on September 17, 2016).
60. Srinath Raghavan, "China is most important for India and Japan," *The Economic Times*, October 29, 2010.
61. Siddharth Varadarajan, "Calibrating India's term of engagement with Japan," *Business Standards*, August 30, 2014.
62. "Japan's Future path with India," *The Japan Times* (Editorial), December 11, 2013.
63. "Bolster Japan-India Security tie-up to help keep regional maritime order," *The Yomiuri Shimbun* (Editorial) July 16, 2016.
64. Takenori Horimoto, "Strategic Convergence of Japan-India Relations and China's emergence," in Takenori Horimoto and Lalima Varma, (eds), India-Japan Relations in Emerging Asia, Manohar 2013, p.19.
65. Ibid.
66. Toru Ito, "China threat theory in Indo-Japan Relations," in Takenori Horimoto and Lalima Varma, (eds), India-Japan Relations in Emerging Asia, Manohar 2013, p.117.
67. Ibid.
68. Hiroshi Kaihara, "Japanese Conservatives and Foreign Affairs: Grand Strategy After

the Cold War," Nova Science Publishers, New York, 2010, p.70.

69. Ibid.
70. For a detailed analysis of Japan's 2010 defense guidelines adopted by Democratic Party of Japan government please refer to Shamshad A. Khan, "Japan's New Defense Guidelines: An Analysis," *Strategic Analysis*, Vol. 35, No.3, May 2011, pp. 391-395.
71. National Defense Programmes Guidelines for 2014 and beyond (summary), Ministry of Defense, Government of Japan, 2014, p.1.
72. National Security Strategy, Ministry of Foreign Affairs, Government of Japan, 2013, p.6.
73. Ibid, p.24.
74. Ibid, p.23
75. Ibid, p.24.
76. Jayant Jacob, "India refuses to take side in China's Air Defense Row," *Hindustan Times*, December 3, 2013.
77. Vijay Shakuja, "Indo-Japanese maritime cooperation," *Strategic Analysis*, Vol. 24, No.1, p.187.
78. Ibid.
79. Prabhkaran Paleri, "The Pirates and Indo-Japanese Relations," *Ship and Ocean Newsletter*, No. 198, November 5, 2008, pp. 7-8.
80. Nayan Chandra, "After the Bomb, India is forging ties with Japan and Vietnam as it seeks to establish itself as a player in Regional Security," *Far Eastern Review*, April 13, 2000.
81. Ibid.
82. Madhuchanda Ghosh, "India and Japan's Growing Synergy: From a Political to a strategic Focus," *Asian Survey*, Vol. XLVIII, No. 2, March/April 2008, p. 287.
83. Indo-Japan Dialogue on Ocean Security, Keynote Address by Hon'ble Mr. Shigeru Ishiba, *Journal of Indian Ocean Studies* (Delhi), Vol.13, No.1, April 2005, pp. 6-10.
84. Sandeep Dixit, "Biggest joint naval exercise in Bay of Bengal in September," *The Hindu*, July 13, 2007.
85. C. Raja Mohan, "Japanese Navy," *The Indian Express*, June 13, 2012.
86. Kenji Menemura, Island a base for South China Sea push, *The Asahi Shimbun*, October 1, 2010.
87. Ibid.
88. For details see, Michishita Narushige, "The Future of Sino-Japanese competition at Sea" *The Nippon.com* available at http://www.nippon.com/en/in-depth/a00504/. (Accessed on September 18, 2016).
89. Yuriko Koike, "To kowtow or cooperate in Asia," *The Japan Times*, November 29, 2012.
90. Ibid.
91. "We stand by Japan on freedom of navigation: Khurshid," *The Hindu*, March 27, 2013.
92. This statement was made by the then Minister of State for External Affairs Praneet Kaur in the lower house of the Indian Parliament in response to a question raised

by a member of the parliament; details available online at http://www.mea.gov.in/lok-sabha.htm?dtl/19800/Q5353+Exploration+in+south+china+Sea (Accessed on September 18, 2016).

93. Full text of the statement is available at http://www.mea.gov.in/media-briefings.htm?dtl/23312/Official+Spokespersons+response+to+a+media+ query + on +the+South+China+Sea (Accessed on September 19, 2016).
94. "Japan India vision 2025 Special Strategic and Global Partnership Working Together for Peace and Prosperity of the Indo-Pacific region and the World," (joint statement), Ministry of Foreign Affairs, Government of Japan, December 12, 2015, available at http://www.mofa.go.jp/s_sa/sw/in/page3e_000432.html (Accessed on September 19, 2016).
95. The full statement is available at "Inaugural US-Japan-India Trilateral," September 29, 2015, available at http://www.state.gov/r/pa/prs/ps/2015/09/247483.htm (Accessed on September 20, 2016).
96. Author's Interview with Ambassador Hiroshi Hirabayashi, December 25, 2015, Tokyo, Japan.
97. Joint Press statement India, Brazil, Japan and Germany Meeting on UN Reforms, September 21, 2004, available on http://meaindia.nic.in/mystart.php?id=10058464 (Accessed on September 20, 2016).
98. Joint Press statement India, Brazil, Japan and Germany Meeting on UN Reforms, June 22, 2005, available on http://meaindia.nic.in/mystart.php?id=10059811 (Accessed on September 22, 2016).
99. "New Stage of Japan-India Strategic and Global partnership," Joint statement between Indian Prime Minister Manmohan Singh and Japanese Prime Minister Yukio Hatoyama, December 29, 2010 available at http://www.mofa.go.jp/region/asia-paci/india/pmv0912/joint.html (Accessed on September 22, 2016).
100. "Japan make more flexible attempt at permanent Security Council Seat," *The Japan Times*, July 5, 2012.
101. Joint Statement on the meeting of Directors General on United Nations Affairs and Permanent Representatives to the United Nations, June 6, 2016, available at http://www.mofa.go.jp/files/000163155.pdf (Accessed on September 22, 2016).
102. Toshitaka Takeuchi, "Japan's quest for UN Security Council reform going nowhere," *East Asia Forum*, February 26, 2016.
103. "National Defense Program Guidelines for FY 2011 and beyond," Ministry of Defence, Government of Japan, p. 9.
104. "Indian relief team begins work in Japan," *The Hindu*, March 29, 2011.
105. Naoto Kan, "Japan: the road to recovery and rebirth," *The Hindu*, April 29, 2011.
106. For Chinese aggressive naval strategy see "Island a base for South China Sea push," *Asahi Shimbun*, January 1, 2011 and also "China's scenario to seize isles in South China Sea," *Asahi Shimbun*, December 31, 2010.

5

INDIA-JAPAN POLITICO-ECONOMIC ENGAGEMENTS

Introduction

Up to the end of the Cold War period, trade and economic ties between Japan and India—the number two and number three economies in Asia has not been as strong as was expected. Though bilateral economic ties are improving gradually, it has not achieved its optimal level. Statistics suggest that Japan's two-way trade with India is only one percent of its total trade. The scholars have argued that this is mainly because of the minimal political interactions between the two countries during the Cold War period. It is argued that during the Cold War period, India tilted towards the Soviet Union and adopted a socialist economy with which Japan—a member of free world—was not comfortable with. New Delhi took steps to engage with Japan both politically and economically following the end of the Cold War which coincided with India's economic liberalization.

Japan welcomed the new initiatives taken by New Delhi but was not satisfied with the pace of its reform. Therefore, during the next few years, India-Japan economic relations did not witness a quantum jump. New Delhi, however, made consistent efforts to attract Japanese investment and took various initiatives including signing of a Comprehensive Economic Partnership Agreement (CEPA) referred as Economic Partnership

Agreement (EPA) in Japanese literatures. The agreement signed in 2011 promises gradual elimination of tariffs and offers “national treatment” to each others’ investors.

This chapter, against this context, looks at various aspects of India-Japan economic engagement from the perspectives of political economy. It has tried to capture the political and economic interactions between the two countries especially after 1950s. It discusses various factors that drives India-Japan economic relations and speculates on the emerging contours of the bilateral economic and trade relations. Since there is a debate in the academia and the media that the India-Japan economic engagement has some strategic intent in it, the researcher, in a separate section, has tried to capture the debate. There is a greater concern among the Japanese investors that India’s infrastructure does not meet their expectations and standards, the researcher has tried to look into these aspects as well. This chapter also examines two case studies; India-Japan CEPA, its objectives and impacts as well as India-Japan infrastructure cooperation. These are the two areas in the realm of economic partnership that has gained wider attention among the academia as well as the strategic community and therefore the author thought it important to analyze these two issues as part of the case studies.

India-Japan Economic Relations in Retrospect

India and Japan will complete 65th years of their diplomatic ties in 2017. But over more than six decades of their diplomatic history, this relationship has witnessed some intermittent phases during which the interactions between the two Asian democracies had been minimal. However, one binding factor between them all through the years has been economic and trade relations, even though it was marginal. Certainly, it was economy and trade upon which India and Japan’s relations have evolved over the years. In 1894, when India was still under British Empire, Japan signed a trade convention which gave fillip to the cotton trade. The trade convention also paved the way for the opening of the regular ocean transport between India and Japan.[1] By the mid 1910s, India became third leading partner for Japan after the United Kingdom and the United States.

In terms of Japanese exports, India by 1920s became the fifth largest market after China, the United States, Hong Kong and the United Kingdom.[2]

With no regular bank facilities for transactions, both the countries were using barter system in lieu of the present system of their trade settlements. Toshio Yamanouchi, one of the Japanese businessmen, notes that in exchange of first shipment of "10,000 tons of iron ore" from a mine in Goa, Japan sent "a small carton of Japanese pearls."[3] Apart from the iron ore, other raw materials included supply of raw jute and raw cotton to Japan.[4] It was because of the interdependent nature of Indian and Japanese economies that developed during pre-war years, India wanted to see an economically resurgent Japan following the World War II. A senior Japanese observer notes:

> India's position clearly contrasted with that of the UK and Australia, which showed extreme caution against Japan's post-war recovery as a revival of competitive economic power....Independent India, on the contrary, envisaged the Japanese economic recovery not in a competitive but in a more complementary perspective.[5]

Since India, before the wars, was a supplier of capital goods as well as raw materials to Japan, it welcomed recovery of Japanese economy for its own economic development. Prime Minister Nehru while meeting a Japanese trade mission remarked that "the economies of both the countries should be complementary." He assured them that India would assist as much as possible in sending "raw materials to Japan."[6]

Despite good beginning, both the countries could not take their relations to an upper trajectory. Many Indian scholars as well as bureaucrats believe that it was because of the perception in Japan that India has tilted towards the Soviet Union and has adopted a socialist economy.[7] Japanese businessmen were not comfortable with socialist system and they favoured US-led free world. They viewed Indian economic policies as "un-realistic and non-pragmatic."[8] Yasukuni Enoki, Japan's former ambassador to India pointed that during the Cold War period, there was a "psychological fence separating Japan from India."[9] Similarly, Sakutaro Tanino, yet another Japanese ambassador to New Delhi noted that India's special relationship with the USSR and Japan's security engagement with the US "eventually resulted in the cooling-off of the great enthusiasm of the 50s."[10] A retired senior Indian bureaucrat, however, believes that India was equally responsible for ignoring Japan. He notes:

> If India was guilty of dismissing Japan as a camp follower of the US, the Japanese in turn, perceived India as a chaotic, dysfunctional, desperately poor country and not as a potential partner.[11]

Despite the low economic exchange between India and Japan during the Cold War period, India remained a resource supplier for Japan. Yoichi Funabashi, a veteran Japanese journalist and presently Chairman of Rebuild Japan Foundation, acknowledges that when Japan "still found itself surrounded by hostile nations, India offered it an olive branch, giving Japan coal and steel when others would not and reaching out the hands of friendship."[12] Similarly, a Japanese businessman writes that newly independent India "extended maximum cooperation" to Japan. As a result, "the Japanese steel industry could make a start in the direction of reconstruction and expansion."[13] However, he divides India-Japan relations into a "bright" and a "dark" periods. According to him, the dividing lines between the two periods was "end of Nehru era." By 1956, India has started to nationalise mines and restricted export of iron ores and minerals for the needs of its domestic industries. A similar strategy was adopted by other resource suppliers such as Australia. Toshio Yamanouchi, was so upset with the Indian nationalization process that he went on to suggest that the tourism and trade are the two sectors from which the "government should keep itself away and leave them to the private sector."[14]

Despite the nationalization of mines, India continued export of iron ores to Japan. Yamonouchi acknowledges that till late 1950s "India accounted for approximately 31 to 32 per cent of total iron ore by Japan."[15] In 1960s Australia replaced India as number one iron ore supplier to Japan when it opened iron ore exports. However, till 1980s, iron ore remained the biggest item of India-Japan trade composition. In 1980, diamond became number one item in their bilateral trade.[16] Recent statistics suggest that presently Japan imports only 3 per cent of iron ores of its total steel production from India. Bulk of its raw material for steel industries comes from Australia (62%) and Brazil (28%).[17] India, however, once again has identified that steel should be the pillar of India-Japan economic cooperation. India has signed an agreement with Japan to export 2.1 million tonnes (mt) of Iron ore to Japan over three years.[18]

The sad part of India Japan economic relations during the Cold War period was that it remained a "resource driven" relationship. The Japanese companies and investors did not show much interest in investing in India. Sakutaro Tanino notes that the only "strong pillar" which sustained economic relationship between the two countries during this period was Japan's Official Development Assistance (ODA). The ODA has played an important role in India's infrastructure development. Highlighting the significance of Japanese ODA to Indian economic development, Arjun Asrani, a former Indian ambassador to Japan notes that "the most outstanding" ODA contribution to India was the Bombay High Deep Sea Drilling Project which "greatly reduced India's dependence on expensive imported oil."[19] He enumerates other projects such as Vishakhapatnam Outer Hrabour Project in Andhra Pradesh and Cochin Shipyard in Kerala which played an important role in India's infrastructure development. He also lauds Japan's role in "making India self-sufficient in food grains production" by establishing several fertilizer projects through the ODA.[20]

A fact cannot be negated that during the Cold War period, India adopted a restrictive private investment policy, especially for foreign investors, and this is attributed as the main reason for the absence of Japanese companies in the Indian market. As per Indian law a foreign company could have equity holdings of only up to 40 per cent. However, Japanese companies were not totally absent from the Indian market altogether. Srabani Roy Choudhury points that few Japanese companies had circumvented the Licence Raj system. For example, Honda was operating with its Indian Partner Hero and was doing business in India.[21]

By the 1980s, some relaxation was made in the foreign investment policy, and this resulted in the setting up of Maruti, a central government joint venture with Suzuki Motors of Japan, in 1982. Maruti's joint venture with Suzuki has an interesting background. It was Sanjay Gandhi, son of the serving Prime Minister Indira Gandhi who dreamt of manufacturing of peoples' car and "sought and obtained a license from Government of India for the manufacture of a technologically efficient smaller car that would call for no foreign collaboration or foreign exchanged outlay."[22]

Many high profile people invested in Sanjay Gandhi's project but the company could not produce a single car. After the death of Sanjay in an aircraft accident, Indian government enacted Maruti Limited (Acquisition and Transfer of Undertaking) Act[23] and sought a foreign partner. Finally, the Suzuki from Japan was identified as a partner to Maruti and the joint project proved a big success in Indian market. A crop of Japanese companies followed, who gained entry through technical collaborations or by getting exemptions. Sanyo and JVC used the technical collaboration route.[24]

Economic and trade cooperation between India and Japan took a new turn in 1991, when India initiated a policy of economic reform and "Japan was identified as one of the most important source of both investment and technology by the government of India."[25] Japanese side also view "economic liberalization" as "return to the inspiring phase" of Indo-Japan relations.[26] From Indian point of view, the decision to engage Japan was a political decision. J.N. Dixit, the then Foreign Secretary of India describes that "the Finance Minister Dr. Manmohan Singh established contacts with his Japanese counterparts, thereby laying the foundation for increasing the content of Indo-Japanese relations."[27] This was the phase during which other industrially advanced countries were also showing interest in Indian economic reforms. But Japan was "the most responsive"[28] to the economic transformations being undertaken by India. However, Japan was not satisfied with the pace of India's economic transformation. Sakutaro Tanino blamed "red tapeism" of Indian bureaucracy in delaying reforms. He noted that many of the Indian officials "still seem to be prisoner of the erstwhile controlled economy and this often leads to bureaucratic high-handedness and questionable practices distorting the system."[29] J.N. Dixit also pointed that Japan was not happy with the pace of Indian economic reforms. He noted:

> Japan remains impatient with regard to the speed and extent of our economic liberalization. Consequently, there has been no quantum jump in Indo-Japanese economic relations. In fact, expansion and growth pattern have been cautious and gradual."[30]

J.N. Dixit, despite these concerns, noted that it is the economy which will drive the relationship between the two countries:

> Japan's interest in India is primarily economic. In other spheres, India does not form a primary focus of attention yet. This is the backdrop against which Indo-Japanese relations will evolve in the foreseeable future.[31]

India-Japan Economic Engagement: The Current Phase

In the post-Cold War period, political and economic interaction between the two countries increased many folds and proved a cornerstone in the diplomatic relations. But the diplomatic relations between the two touched the lowest ebb once again after Japan's reactions following 1998 Pokhran nuclear test. However, Japan resumed the normal relations within a few years. A number of scholars in India believe that the economic stake of Japan in Indian market had become so strong in post-liberalization period that Japanese had to set aside the economic sanctions and Prime Minister Mori envisaged a "global partnership" in which economic relations was an essential component.[32]

As mentioned above, J.N. Dixit had noted that the then Finance Minister Manmohan Singh was instrumental in forging economic ties with Japan. When Dr. Singh became Prime Minister, he took some bold initiatives to strengthen the economic ties further. He announced that the economic ties should be the "bedrock"[33] of Indo-Japan relationship. During his leadership both the countries institutionalised annual Prime Minister level talks and since 2005 Prime Ministers of both the countries have been holding summit level talks alternating between Tokyo and New Delhi. Both the Prime Ministers have signed a series of Memorandum of Understandings (MOUs) during their meetings and have issued statements in which economy and trade relations has been a prime focus.

A joint statement signed by Japanese Prime Minister Koizumi and his Indian counterpart Manmohan Singh noted that "a strong prosperous and dynamic India is in the interest of Japan and vice versa."[34] However, Manmohan Singh acknowledged that economic ties between the two countries remain "well below the potential."[35] As a result of strategic talks, both the Prime Ministers agreed in 2005 to set up a joint study group to study areas in which both the countries could engage in bilateral trade. The group, in 2006, came up with a set of proposals. It concluded that "there is a huge untapped potential to further develop and diversify the economic engagement between India and Japan."[36]

For a "comprehensive expansion of bilateral economic and commercial relations," the joint study group suggested negotiation on a Comprehension Economic Partnership Agreement (CEPA) covering "trade in goods, trade in services, investment inflows" and ways to enhance their trade. Prime Minister Singh considered the CEPA with Japan so important that he visited Tokyo (by preponing his scheduled visit) in October 2010 to announce that negotiations between the two had been completed. Indian Prime Minister termed the conclusion of CEPA as a "historic agreement"[37] The reason why he termed the conclusion of CEPA as a historic one as it was his personal wish to forge a "complementary relationship" between India and Japan. In his view "India's buoyant economy, young population and large market combine well with Japan's technological prowess, manufacturing skills and financial sources to create a win-win situation for both the countries."[38] He added that both the countries must synergise their "complementary strengths" to impart momentum to Asian as well as global economic growth and prosperity.[39]

Manmohan Singh's view on achieving complementary relationship with Japan was coincidently similar with that of Prime Minister Nehru's vision. There was only one difference; Nehru wanted to maximize economic benefits by providing raw materials to the Japanese industry and wanted to see a re-emergence of an industrial Japan. Prime Minister Singh wanted to take the relationship beyond a resource provider and wanted to maximize benefit from Japan's technological prowess, manufacturing skills and financial sources. The then Indian Foreign Secretary, Nirupama Rao termed the agreement as "an alliance between Japanese technology and capital and a young Indian labour force."[40]

The goal of CEPA, however, was not limited to achieving economic objectives. It also has some strategic intent in it. A joint declaration by India and Japan notes that "the India-Japan CEPA will elevate the strategic and Global Partnership between India and Japan to a new level."[41] Various scholars have argued, perhaps because of this single sentence, that the CEPA is aimed at challenging China's economic pre-eminence in Asia. Their arguments have been analysed in a separate section in this chapter.

Apart from the CEPA both the countries took series of measures to take their economic relations to a new height. In 2011, India and Japan upgraded their currency swap arrangement from the previous US Dollar 3 billion to US Dollar 15 billion in 2010 and in 2013 from US Dollar 15 billion to US Dollar 60 billion. The swap agreement will help both countries in managing short term liquidity problems.[42] As per the agreement, Japan will accept rupee and give dollars to India for up to 30 billion. Similarly India will take yen and send dollars for the corresponding amount to Japan if speculators seek to thrash down respective currencies.[43]

India on its part is doing its best at the political and economic level to keep Japanese economy unharmed. China had restricted exports of rare-earth materials—key component for manufacturing high-tech products—following a spat between Chinese fishing trawler and Japanese coast guards in September 2010. This move by China was construed in Japan as a strategic move by Beijing to squeeze Japan economically. The shortage of rare-earth minerals, used in manufacturing of high-tech products had some negative impact on production and export of electronic goods. Against this backdrop, India offered cooperation in rare-earth minerals to Japan. After one and half year discussion at the political level on the possibility of exporting rare-earth minerals, both the countries agreed in May 2012 to jointly extract rare earth minerals in India. Japan's Toyota Toshu Corp. and Indian Rare Earths Limited are collaborating in rare-earth extraction project. The project will provide 4000 tons of rare earth to Japan annually accounting for about 14 per cent of Japan's annual demand of the strategic elements.[44] This helped Japan in mitigating shortage of rare earth minerals. This move was seen in Indian strategic circles as a strategy to break China's monopoly in rare earth materials.[45]

India-Japan Engagement under Modi Government

After assuming office in 2014, Prime Minister Narendra Modi has also kept the momentum going in the trade and economic fields. His main focus seems to seize the opportunity to attract Japanese investment in India. During his two successive visits to Japan in September 2014 and November 2016, he has assured the Japanese investors that India is replacing 'red tape' with 'red carpet' for Japanese businessmen. Addressing a gathering of Japanese entrepreneurs in Tokyo, Indian Prime Minister informed them that India has adopted an "ease of business" policy.[46] Explaining his "three D Mantra," he said that India is not only the biggest *Democracy* in the world but also has large *Demography* and *Demand.* Since, India has a young population; demand for goods will remain high domestically for a longer time and thus India can be a place where the Japanese investors can make their fortune. Elaborating on India's geostrategic location on the world map, he informed them that if they make India their manufacturing hub not only can they sell their finished products to Indian market but also export it to different Asian and African countries through its ports situated alongside India's Eastern and Western coasts.

During his 2014 visit, Japan has also agreed to earmark 35 billion US dollars through "loans and investments" to India during the next five years. Undoubtedly, this will help India improve its infrastructure, which observers believe, has been one of the impediments in attracting foreign direct investment within the country. Additionally, India agreed to introduce bullet train technology between Mumbai and Ahmadabad and the Japanese side has expressed its "readiness to provide financial, technical and operational support to introduce *Shinkansen* system."[47] Finally, in December 2015 during Prime Minister Abe's visit to India both the countries inked the deal to introduce first bullet train in India. The project is estimated to cost 980 billion rupees (about 1.8 trillion yen). The Japanese government is planning to provide about yen one trillion in loans for the project. However, it will take a little more time to introduce this technology and the first bullet train can run between Mumbai and Ahmedabad by 2023. The success of the bullet train between Mumbai and Ahmadabad will certainly pave the way for introducing this technology between different major cities of India.

Some breakthrough was also achieved for joint collaboration in the field of defence technology. Most importantly, Japan has also delisted some of the Indian defense enterprises from its "End Users List" which will pave the way for joint defense production among Japanese and Indian companies and thus will help decrease defense spending. India has been willing to partner with Japan in the field of defense technology. However, Japan owing to its decade-long self-imposed ban on exporting defense and defense related technology, had been showing reluctance. Shinzo Abe's cabinet, eased these restrictions in 2014.

Stalemate, however, continues over India's procurement of US-2 amphibious aircraft, the only of its kind available in the world for advanced air–sea search and rescue operations, which can land on rough sea surface as well as land. Tokyo wants to sell US-2 aircraft to New Delhi, but New Delhi wants to produce them jointly since the cost of a single US-2 aircraft is roughly $109 million. There were speculations that Japan will give green signal to its companies to go for a joint production of the US-2 given the changes in domestic laws that allow them for joint collaboration but the two counties could not reach an agreement. The joint statement, however, "welcomed progress made in discussions in the Joint Working Group on cooperation in US-2 amphibian aircraft and its technology, and directed their officials to accelerate their discussions."[48]

To attract Japanese investment in India, the new political dispensation has announced some new measures during this visit including a plan to establish a new unit under the Prime Minister's Office that will facilitate Japanese investment in India. But the political commitment can only be realised when it is backed by its entrepreneurs and investors. It is yet to be seen how the Japanese entrepreneurs respond to Prime Minister Modi's call.

During September 2014 visit, the Indian Prime Minister also exhorted Japanese leadership to adopt a new political vision to deepen the ties between the two countries. He impressed upon Japanese leadership to establish a "Look at India" policy on the similar lines of India's "Look East Policy"[49] to further deepen economic and political relationship between the two countries. He also observed that "India is incomplete without Japan and Japan is incomplete without India."[50] This statement is akin to the 2006 commitment in which both the countries identified that a strong and prosperous India and Japan are in each other's interests.

As a result of consistent political and economic interactions between the two governments, Japanese investors are also showing interest in the Indian market. A survey by the Japan Bank of International Cooperation (JBIC) conducted in 2013 suggests that 74.9 percent of the 605 Japanese manufacturers selected India as their investment destination over the next

10 years, compared with 71.7 percent that chose China. A previous survey conducted by JBIC in 2009 found that China was first and India second.[51] Here territorial disputes with China over Senkaku is acting as a factor as more and more Japanese investors want to reduce their dependence on China and wants to diversify investment risk. They are looking at India and Vietnam. However, China remains the top favourite for short term investment for Japanese entrepreneurs. The 2012 JBIC Survey suggest that though China remains number one country among the most favourite destination for the Japanese companies, India has narrowed the gap. The percentage gap among the respondent companies between China and India was only 2.8 per cent (see table 1). The surveys conducted during the last few years also shows the similar trends as Japanese investors continue to take keen interest in Indian market.

Table 1: Recounted Ranking of Promising Countries/Regions for Japanese Business Operations

Ranking			Country/Region	No. of resopndent companies (Total: 288)			Percentage Share	
Added this time	←	July survey Recounted		Added this time	July survey Recounted	Increase or decrease	Added this time	July survey Recounted
1	—	1	China	172	184	▲ 12	59.7%	63.9%
2	—	2	India	164	163	1	56.9%	56.6%
3	—	3	Indonesia	130	118	12	45.1%	41.0%
4	⬆	5	Thailand	102	97	5	35.4%	33.7%
4	—	4	Vietnam	102	99	3	35.4%	34.4%
6	—	6	Brazil	63	62	1	21.9%	21.5%
7	—	7	Mexico	48	41	7	16.7%	14.2%
8	—	8	Russia	35	35	0	12.2%	12.2%
9	—	9	Myanmar	34	33	1	11.8%	11.5%
10	—	10	USA	30	26	4	10.4%	9.0%
11	—	11	Malaysia	27	23	4	9.4%	8.0%
12	⬆	14	Korea	13	9	4	4.5%	3.1%
13	⬇	12	Turkey	11	11	0	3.8%	3.8%
14	⬆	17	Philippines	10	7	3	3.5%	2.4%
14	⬇	12	Taiwan	10	11	▲ 1	3.5%	3.8%
16	⬇	14	Cambodia	9	9	0	3.1%	3.1%
17	⬇	14	Singapore	8	9	▲ 1	2.8%	3.1%
18	—	18	Australia	7	6	1	2.4%	2.1%
19	⬇	18	Bangladesh	5	6	▲ 1	1.7%	2.1%
20	—	20	Germany	3	4	▲ 1	1.0%	1.4%

Source: JABIC Survey 2013.[52]

India-Japan Economic Cooperation: The Case Studies

To understand the evolution of the India-Japan economic cooperation and its impact on the bilateral relations, two case studies have been identified in the following sections.

Case Study I

India-Japan Economic Relations: A Case Study of CEPA

India and Japan formally signed a Comprehensive Economic Partnership Agreement (CEPA) in Tokyo on February 16, 2011 which came into effect from August 1, the same year. CEPA covers not only trade in goods but important areas of trade in services, movement of natural persons, investment, intellectual property rights, custom procedure and other trade related issues.[53] The CEPA will gradually lead to a reduction of 10 percent of the tariff; India had been imposing on, over 9,000 imported Japanese industrial products. The official CEPA document has laid down rules for elimination of custom duties in Article 19.[54]

The document has classified goods traded between the two countries in separate schedules and has divided them in total seven categories and have marked them as A, B5, B7, B10, B 15, Pa/Pb and X. Custom duties on goods identified as A has been eliminated from the date of entry into force of the CEPA, while custom duties on goods identified as B5, B7, B10, B15, will be eliminated in six years, eight years, 11 years and 16 years respectively. The custom duties on goods identified as Pa and Pb shall be reduced in accordance with the terms and conditions set out in respective Notes indicated in Schedule of India. However, there would be no duty elimination on goods indicated as X.[55] Some of the goods on which both countries will remove tariff in phases have been indicated in Table 2.

Under the CEPA, some 17.4 percent of the tariff lines have been offered for immediate reduction of tariff to Zero percent by India while Japan has put 87 percent of its tariff lines under immediate reduction to zero.[56] Since CEPA is not only limited to goods but it also covers trades in services and investments, the scholars have identified few areas in which both countries can benefit from each other. (Please refer to figure 1 depicting opportunities CEPA offers to Japan and India)

Table 2: Selected list of goods on which tariff would be eliminated gradually. Source: CEPA pages 105 to 961/CII Study on India-Japan relations

Period over which tariff has to be reduced	Goods Description	
	Schedule of India	Schedule of Japan
Immediate	• Most textile products including yarn and fabric • Computer printers, PCs and other automatic data processing machines • Cell phones and other types of phones, networking equipment and SIM cards • Capacitors, diodes, specified measuring instruments	• Specified petroleum products • Ores, slag and ash • Inorganic chemicals and specified organic chemicals • Machines – mechanical and electrical and parts thereof • Most textile and textile products
Seven years	• Lubricating oil	• Specific types of fish and fish meat
Ten years and above	• Specified petroleum products • Most metals and articles thereof • CDs, DVDs, watches, musical instruments • Arms and ammunition • Certain types of furniture	• Specified iron and steel products • Certain fruits like oranges, apples, grapes

Figure 1: Opportunities for Japan and India under the CEPA

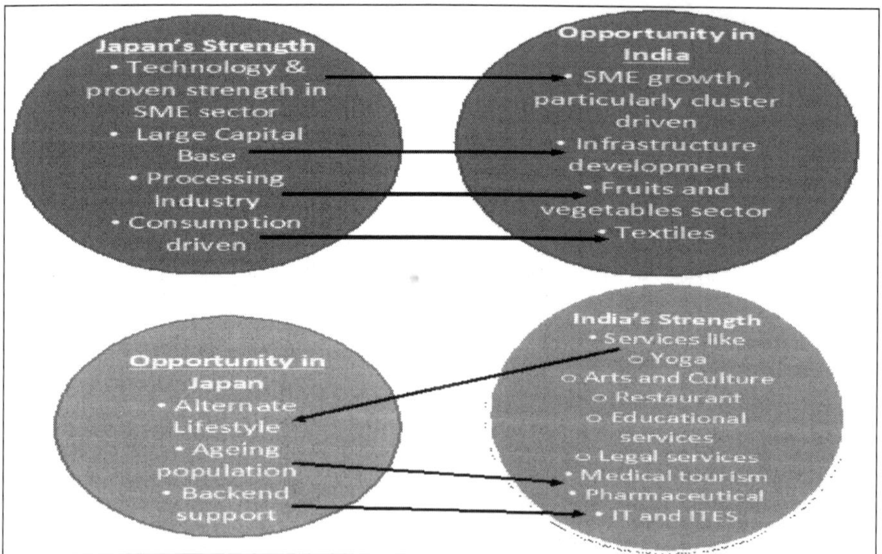

Source: Pinaki Dasgupta, "India and East Asia: Towards a regional economic integration," *Keizai Koho Centre*, Tokyo.

To attract Japanese investment in India, the CEPA has given Japanese investor a kind of "national treatment." One of the provisions in CEPA states:

> Each Party shall accord to investors of the other Party and to their investments treatment no less favourable than that it accords like circumstances to its own investors and to their investments with respect to investment activities in its Area.[57]

Both the countries have granted Most Favorite Nation treatment under the CEPA. It seems, it is a calibrated move by the two governments, to give this status given the fact that Japanese investors had largely been confined to East Asian countries. Ranja Sengupta points that "countries usually impose performance requirements on foreign investment such as limits on ownership, board membership, and on exports; compulsory local content etc. But under CEPA these restrictions are no longer permissible."[58] The CEPA also provides investor, investment protection and also allows foreign investor to sue the government if their rights and profit are infringed upon.[59]

India had been demanding from a long from Japan to allow its Basmati Rice to Japan but during the negotiations, New Delhi agreed to put rice sector under the "exclusion" list. However, in a similar FTA signed with Malaysia, India has successfully bargained for allowing rice imports into Malaysian market. It seems, India considered the sensitivities of Japanese farmers who have also been opposing Japan's participation in Trans Pacific Partnership as they are wary that the preferential trade agreement will allow inflow of cheaper rice from the TPP member countries.

India was expecting that Japan will allow entry to its nurses and caregivers to Japan with a long term work permit. New Delhi was demanding treatment to its caregivers at par with Indonesia and Philippines, with whom Japan has also signed Economic Partnership Agreements. However, Japan has asked India to wait as it is facing some problems as the nurses from these countries have not been able to pass the necessary language tests after two years of their probations. However, some media sections in Japan have urged their government to make "concessions" to India on this point. The *Yomiuri Shimbun* in its editorial demanded that "to deepen economic partnership between this country and India, Japan should make concessions."[60]

Despite the CEPA easing the duties on the goods, Indian export will continue to face some non-tariff barriers such as standards and technical barriers. The Indian producers will have to match with standards set by Japanese importers.[61] Geethanjali Nataraj, points that "Japan's Sanitary and Phytosanitary Measeures (SPS) standards are major barriers of Indian exports of poultry, meat, tuna, shrimp, mine products and fruits." She suggests that both the countries should share and facilitate "the underlying technology" to help improve Indian products sanitary standards.[62]

India-Japan CEPA has generated wider interest in Indian media and academic circles. B.S. Raghavan, a columnist of *Business Line*, argues that "there is a great responsibility cast on both India and Japan to make a success of it so that it becomes a path setter for CEPAs with other developed countries."[63] He cites a simulated computer study to suggest that India's GDP can grow by as much as 3.45 percent if New Delhi signs similar agreements with the ASEAN countries and its dialogue partners.[64] C.P. Ravindaran, however, believes that the gains from India-Japan CEPA "will come eventually through competition with more efficient producers on the one hand and in demanding markets, on the other." He adds that the CEPA through its free trade provisions, hold such possibilities for India.[65] Ambassador Arjun Asrani, who was part of 50 member India-Japan study group which recommended negotiation on CEPA between the two countries, however, believes that the inclusion of a large number of goods in the negative list would remain an impediment in the wider trade flows between the two countries.[66] The Japanese expert participating in the deliberation that suggested CEPA to be signed says that we pointed that India is imposing high rate of import duty for auto parts and "recommended that the tax reduction for auto parts is needed." But it was not reflected in the final draft of the CEPA.[67]

The CEPA has certainly boosted bilateral trade. In 2010-11 fiscal, trade between the two countries stood around USD 13.4 billion. However, in fiscal 2011-12, within months of CEPA coming into effect it touched USD 18.3 billion. But, after two consecutive years of touching new heights, the bilateral trade has decelerated (See graph 1). After touching US dollar

18.51 billion in fiscal year 2012-13, bilateral trade between India and Japan came down to US dollar 16.29 billion in fiscal year 2013-14. It slid further down to US dollar 15.51 billion in fiscal year 2014-15 and to US Dollar 14.51 billion in fiscal 2015-16. If the trend continues, it may reach the level of 2010, in another few years, defeating the purpose of the CEPA.

Graph 1: India-Japan Bilateral Trade

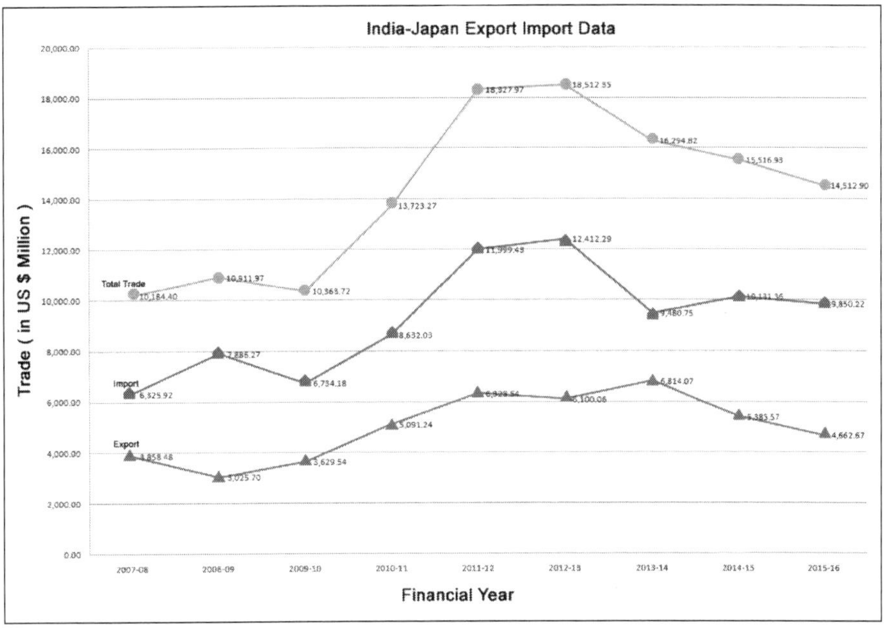

The CEPA had few negative fall outs too. Following signing of the CEPA, the trade gap between India and Japan has widened. Trade balance which was in Japan's favour has grown exponentially in its favour (see graph 1). Concerns about growing trade balance in Japan's favour have also started surfacing in India. Indian media reports suggest that India-Japan merchandise trade grew 38 percent from August 2011 to March 2012. Japanese exports to India grew by 40.96 percent while India's export to Japan managed to grow only 18.39 percent. A year before CEPA Indian exports to Japan had grown by 43 percent and imports had grown by only 28 percent. Concern in Indian business circles that CEPA has increased the trade balance in Japan's favour has started surfacing.[68]

Some concerns of growing trade imbalance also came to the fore at the political level. Indian media quoted Commerce, Industry and Textile Minister conveying his Japanese counterpart that India's generic medicines' share in Japanese markets is less than 1 percent of the total Japanese market and urged Japan to remove "non-tariff barriers" on the Indian drug companies. The then Commerce Minister Anand Sharma requested Japanese government to start negotiations on nursing and healthcare.[69] Sharma's successor, Nirmala Sitharaman has similar concerns. In a seminar organized by New Delhi based think tank; the RIS, the Commerce Minister expressed satisfaction over growth in bilateral trade post-CEPA. However, she expressed concern over growing trade deficit between India and Japan post-CEPA. In her words, "trade deficit of India with respect to Japan has also increased from 3.1 USD billion pre CEPA to 5.2 USD billion post-CEPA." She was of the view that both the countries must look at ways and means to address this "skewed trade." She suggested that this problem can be addressed by increasing India's exports to Japan and increasing the pharmaceutical export to Japan could be one option adding that "the share of India in the Japanese drug market continues to be below par."[70]

The CEPA also failed to push bilateral trade to the expected level. Despite consistent efforts by both the governments, bilateral trade which was projected to touch US Dollar 20 billion by 2010, missed the target.[71] Trade between India and China touched around US Dollar 75 billion despite no FTAs with the neighbour and no visible political backing to improve trade relations. By signing the CEPA with Japan, India wants to attract more Foreign Direct Investment (FDI) in India and increase its trade volume from its current level. The statements by the Indian leadership suggest that they want to see "Japan become the largest FDI investor in India, in addition to being the largest development partner of India." One of the Indian External Affairs Ministers noted that "Japanese investment is still insignificant compared to its total FDI, and very low compared to levels of China, and even in South East Asian countries."[72] But since China is registering high growth, for the Japanese investor it will remain a favourite destination for the next two to three years. So how to wean Japan away from China is a biggest puzzle for the Indian leadership and economic community?

There is another expectation from India in terms of trade relations. India wants to achieve complementarities when it comes to trade. But finding such complementarities with Japan is difficult since Japan is an ageing society and consumerism there remains low. India on the other hand has a growing economy and a society with a large consumer base. So in this scenario, it would be difficult to find complementarities and a trade balance which remains in Japan's favour is likely to grow further. Thus, it will be a challenge for both economies to achieve a balance in trade. But surely, a trade conflict between India and Japan is not likely to emerge as was seen between the US and Japan during the late 80s because India is offering trade relaxation to Japan with an objective that goes beyond the economic dividend.

India-Japan CEPA: The Strategic Aspects

There is a general perception among the academia and the media that the unstated purpose of India-Japan economic engagement is to achieve some strategic objective. Yazuru Takano, New Delhi based correspondent of *Asahi Shimbun* notes in an opinion column that CEPA will bring "huge economic benefits to Japan" but it is unlikely to "offer new benefits to India."[73] His argument that the trade pact is not going to bring huge benefits to Indian is based on the fact that Japan's tariffs on imports of industrial products were already low. He adds that during the negotiations, India made no major demand concerning agricultural products such as rice. Then why India offered a bigger market to Japan? To substantiate his arguments, Takano quotes Rahul Khullar, the then Secretary in Indian Commerce ministry as saying that the CEPA is aimed at sending a "signal of bilateral cooperation to the world." Takano has ably interpreted that "Khullar's message would become clearer if "the world" here is replaced by 'China'."

A section of Indian scholars also believe that the CEPA between India and Japan would act as a "counterbalance" to China. Geethanjali Nataraj, for example, argues that "for many countries in the region, enhanced trade and investment relations between Japan and India would act [as] a counterbalance to the growing influence of China."[74] She adds that "stronger economic ties with Japan would also help India establish its presence in East Asia and get market access for its exports through Japan's bilateral agreements with other countries in the region."[75]

Harsh V. Pant elaborating on India's economic engagement with East Asia and ASEAN countries points that India's FTAs "allows India to challenge China's growing penetration of East Asia and prevents India's growing marginalisation in the most economically dynamic region in the world."[76] Interestingly, he also notes that "smaller states in the region are now looking at India to act as a balancer in view of China's growing powers..."[77] Pravakar Sahoo, a former Visiting Research Fellow at the Institute for Developing Economies also believes that CEPA is a "strategic move given the overdependence of Japan on China for trade in goods." [78] Arjun Asrani, former Indian ambassador to Japan, who was part of India-Japan study group that recommended CEPA negotiations, says that CEPA is not only aimed at challenging China's economic clout in Indian market but it is also a joint effort by India and Japan to thwart China's economic pre-eminence in entire East Asian market.[79]

A somewhat similar observation has also been made by the Japanese experts who closely view India-Japan economic ties. For example, Masanori Kondo, who had been a part of 50 member India-Japan study group which recommended negotiation on a CEPA, believes that India made concessions to Japan during the negotiations "partly in the hope of counterbalancing China's increasing clout by firming its relations with Japan."[80] He explained to this researcher that a high tariff imposed by India on imported machinery has been impacting on profitability of Japanese manufacturers in the Indian market. With tariffs removed, profitability and global competitiveness will increase challenging monopoly of cheaper Chinese goods in Indian market. He added, however, that the Japanese SMEs are still hesitant to go to Indian market because of inadequate infrastructure.[81] He is also of the view that CEPA has a strategic objective. Masanori Kondo opines that "Indian government wanted to show China (its potential enemy but did not want to fight directly as India cannot win) that India and Japan have a very good relationship, which will give China some pressure that if China will fight against India, Japan will back up India. Around the time India and China had several problems like Arunachal Pradesh...etc, and Japan had some problem after Koizumi went to Yasukuni shrine as well. So India wanted Japan to be in its camp as soon as possible so India compromised to make EPA done earlier, to show Japan and India are real friends against China."[82]

India has also signed similar Free Trade agreements with South Korea, Singapore and Malaysia but has showed no indication that it will sign a preferential trade agreement with China. This also deepens doubts of academicians and media that by signing these agreements, India is aiming for a certain kind of economic hedging with China. When Manmohan Singh was to visit Tokyo to announce the conclusion of land mark trade agreement with Japan in October 2010, the Japanese media was curious whether India will sign a similar agreement with China. When the Japanese media posed a pointed question to the then Prime Minister Singh asking him "do you see a need for an EPA with China," he was categorical in his answer: "as regards the economic cooperation agreement, we have not reached to that stage" adding that "there is an imbalance in our trade."[83]

Some Japanese media has also viewed the CEPA as a tool to reduce Japan's "economic dependence on China." The *Japan Times,* for example, has stated in an editorial that "the Japan-India CEPA will not only help Japanese firms catch up with Korean firms but also help Japan reduce its economic dependence on China."[84] The daily reiterated this point in yet another editorial. It stated that "Japan can counter China" by deepening ties with India and "can reduce the excessive economic reliance on China."[85] In a similar tone, *The Yomiuri Daily*, Japan's largest selling daily, observed in its editorial that "enhancement of Japan's economic partnership with India will alleviate the nation's economic dependence on China."[86]

The arguments above, suggest that there is a perception among the academicians and the media that the agreement is not merely "entrepreneurial" in nature. It has a broader objective. Let me refer to Takano again. He argues that behind the economic partnership agreement was "New Delhi's strategic thinking based on a broad diplomatic perspective." He advises Tokyo to "asses the value of its trade pact with India from a broader strategic perspective."[87]

The recent statistics, however, suggests that China remains top trading partners for both India and Japan and the CEPA has not helped lessen their dependence on China. India-China trade hovers around 75 billion US dollars and in few years it is expected to surpass US Dollar 100 billion marks. This suggests that economics work on a different formula and not necessarily could be contained by strategic calculations. It is yet to be seen whether India and Japan succeed in countering China's economic clout in Asia. But one thing is sure that both can ease the economic overdependence on China in their markets by offering preferential treatment to goods from countries other than China.

Case Study II

India-Japan Infrastructure Cooperation

One of the key areas of India-Japan economic cooperation is infrastructure development projects including the rail, roads and transportation sectors. India plans to invest US Dollar 1 trillion on infrastructure during its 12th five year plan, during 2012 to 2017.[88] Japan is helping India through ODA loans and Japan Bank for International Cooperation (JBIC) to finance some of these projects. But one of the projects that have become a landmark of India-Japan cooperation in development project is Delhi-Mumbai Industrial Corridor (DMIC). This dedicated freight corridor is based on Tokyo-Osaka expressway model along which several industrial zones would be set up. This 1483 kilometers long mega project will start from Delhi National Capital Region and will link to Mumbai port in Maharastra crossing through six Indian states viz. Uttar Pradesh, Haryana, Rajasthan, Madhya Pradesh, Gujarat and Maharshtra.[89]

This mega project was institutionalized at the political level. A Memorandum of Understanding was signed in December 2006 between Vice Minister, Ministry of Economy, Trade and Industry (METI) of Government of Japan and Secretary, Department of Industrial Policy & Promotion (DIPP), India. A Final Project Concept was presented to both the Prime Ministers during Prime Minister Shinzo Abe's visit to India in August 2007.[90]

India has floated Delhi-Mumbai Industrial Corridor and Development Cooperation (DMIDC)—a public enterprise to complete this project. The

Map 2: Delhi-Mumbai Industrial Corridor

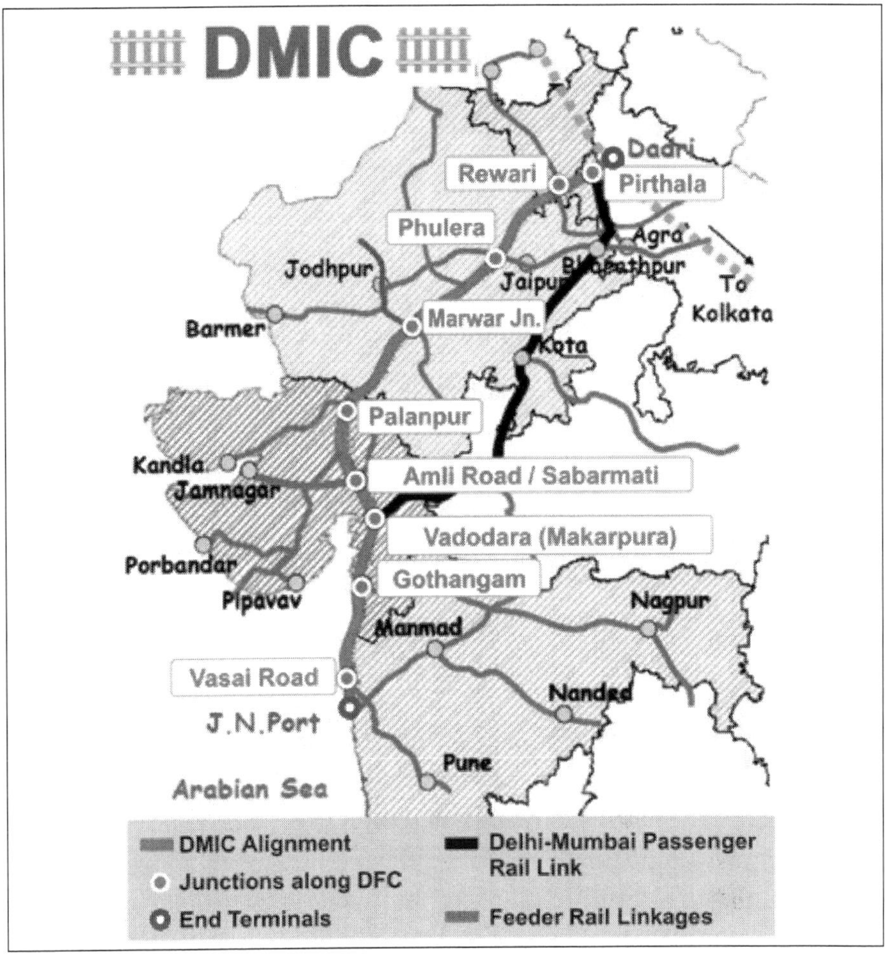

Source: DMIC website.

company has identified a band of 150 km (Influence region) on both sides of the Freight corridor to be developed as the Delhi-Mumbai Industrial Corridor. The vision for DMIC is to create strong economic base in this band with globally competitive environment and state-of-the-art infrastructure to activate local commerce, enhance foreign investments, real-estate investments and attain sustainable development. In addition to the influence region, DMIC would also include development of requisite feeder rail and road connectivity to hinterland and markets and select ports along the western coast. Yet another aim of the project is to ensure faster movement of goods. At present, the goods that arrive at Mumbai port from abroad takes some 40 days to reach to a market in Delhi. The completion of the project will lessen the timing and certain goods can be delivered within 13 to 14 hours after its arrival on Mumbai port.[91]

It has been planned to construct new eco-friendly cities along both the sides of the DMIC, with world class infrastructure including the airports. It will incorporate 11 investment regions and 13 industrial areas. If materialized, it will give new shape to India's landscape.

The cost on the project has been estimated at USD 90 billion, part of which would be covered by Japanese funding and loans. India has cleared political obstacles to provide 26 per cent equity stake to Japan in DMIDC and allowed the participation of the Japanese government in DMIC.[92] Japan has already established a "Japanese Zone" in Neemrana, Rajasthan where Japanese companies have started setting up their industries.

This project has generated huge interest in India including New Delhi's strategic circles. Rajaram Panda, a senior Indian observer on Indo-Japan relations, notes that "this huge project will dramatically transform the character of India-Japan economic relations in few years."[93] Professor K.V. Kesavan, a distinguished fellow at the Observer Research Foundation, believes that the dedicated projects being built with the help of Japan are expected to "bring greater flow of Japanese investment and technology" as well as "change the industrial climate of several states in India."[94] However, a section of people including the farmers, it seems, are unhappy with these moves and they have formed a collective, headed by social activist Medha Patkar, to protest these moves. They claim, that "farmers land has been illegally marked as 'R' (reserved) in land records, fraudulent public hearings being organized, forceful consent being taken and many other illegalities done by the authorities."[95] The protests by farmers have brought development versus displacement paradox to the fore and that needs to be addressed for smooth implementation of the DMIC.

Apart from dedicated corridors that India is building with the help of Japan, Japan's bullet train technology is also fascinating Indians. On the other hand, Japan has been looking at Indian mass transport system including the export of Shinkansen technology for its own economic gains. And with this in mind, Japan in 2009 invited Lalu Prasad, the then India

Railways Minister and gave him a bullet train ride from Tokyo to Kyoto.[96] Lalu also showed interest in linking Indian cities with bullet trains. Japan was willing to start bullet trains on seven routes including between Mumbai and Ahmedabad. But apparently because of finance crunch with the Railways Ministry, the project was not considered viable. Japan, however, kept pushing for the project and it was stated in the joint statements between India and Japan that Japan is interested to cooperate with India in promoting High Speed Train technology. During summit level meeting with Abe and Manmohan Singh, India conveyed to Japan that it will "plan such projects based on its infrastructure priorities, commercial viability and financial resources in India."[97] But they agreed to "co-finance a joint feasibility study of High Speed Railway system on the Mumbai-Ahmedabad route."[98] Japanese media reported the same year that East Japan Railway Company and Kawasaki Heavy Industries Limited bagged the project which is expected to cost some one trillion yen and would be undertaken by Japan.[99] In July 2015, the feasibility study was completed and it reported that "Shinkansen system would be optimal for the project."[100] If completed, the Shinkansen line would shorten the 500-kilometer trip between Mumbai to Ahmedabad to two hours from the current 10 hours. The deal was finally inked between India and Japan during the visit of Japanese Prime Minister Abe in 2015. According to the current plan, the construction of the railway is scheduled to start in 2017 and operations can kick off in 2023.[101]

Japan is not only keen in Mumbai-Ahmedabad line but it is also keen to replicate this project by linking other Indian cities with the similar Shinkaknsen technology. Keeping this in mind, Japan provided bullet train ride to Prime Minister Modi from Tokyo to Kobe during his November 2016 visit. He has visited Kawasaki Hevay Industry's Kobe based site. Since the same company has bagged contract to lay Shinkasen line between Mumbai and Ahmedabad, the visit has rekindled Japan's hope that the high speed train, using Japanese technology, will run between other Indian cities. However, it is yet to be seen who will bear the cost? Since Indian Railways does not have sufficient funds to bear the costs, it will depend on Japan for both technology and project funds. Japan has already provided 15 billion loan to India for Mumbai-Ahmedabad. Whether Japan can afford to offer similar loans for other projects remains an open ended question?

India-Japan Economic Relations: The Challenges and Prospects

Despite all efforts, Japan's two-way trade with Asia's number three economy accounts for only one per cent. This is the biggest challenge as well as impediments in bilateral economic relations. On the contrary, Japan's trade with China—Asia's number one economy accounts for some 20 percent of Japan's total trade. Why this is so? To find the answer, one can compare the number of Japanese companies based in China and India. There are some 14,400 Japanese firms that are operating in China whereas in India the number remains some 1229. If the numbers of all the Japanese establishments are included, the number will reach to 4417 (see Map 3). Also, presence of Japanese companies remains largely concentrated in few selected states. However, there is one positive trend in Japanese investment in India. The number of Japanese companies has grown from 550 in 2008 to 1229 by 2016.

Various factors can be attributed to the Japanese companies' slow pace of flow towards India. An observor has argued that "poor infrastructure, corruption, and a dense Indian bureaucracy as well as the political instability and social unrest prevalent until the end of the 1990s presented many risks to Japanese firms."[102] Japan Chamber of Commerce and Industry in India (JCCII) has also identified infrastructure as one of the "bottlenecks"[103] in enhancing manufacturing and industrial capacity in India. In its suggestion to government of India, the JCCII has suggested "early completion of Bengaluru-Chennai expressway project," "introduction of the efficient operating controlling system for Railways" and introduction of comprehensive port logistic management system."

Other hurdles in flow of Japanese companies and its associate identified by JCCII were VISA procedures. It demanded that Japanese professional dispatched by Japanese companies should be eligible for business visa. Similarly, it requested issuance of stay permit by FRRO as same as the period of validity of Employment Visa. These are not the major hurdles and it could be addressed gradually by the government agencies. However, the major demand by the JCCII is regarding the tax system. Most importantly introduction of Goods and Services Tax (GST) and abolition

Map 3: Presence of Japanese Business Establishments in India

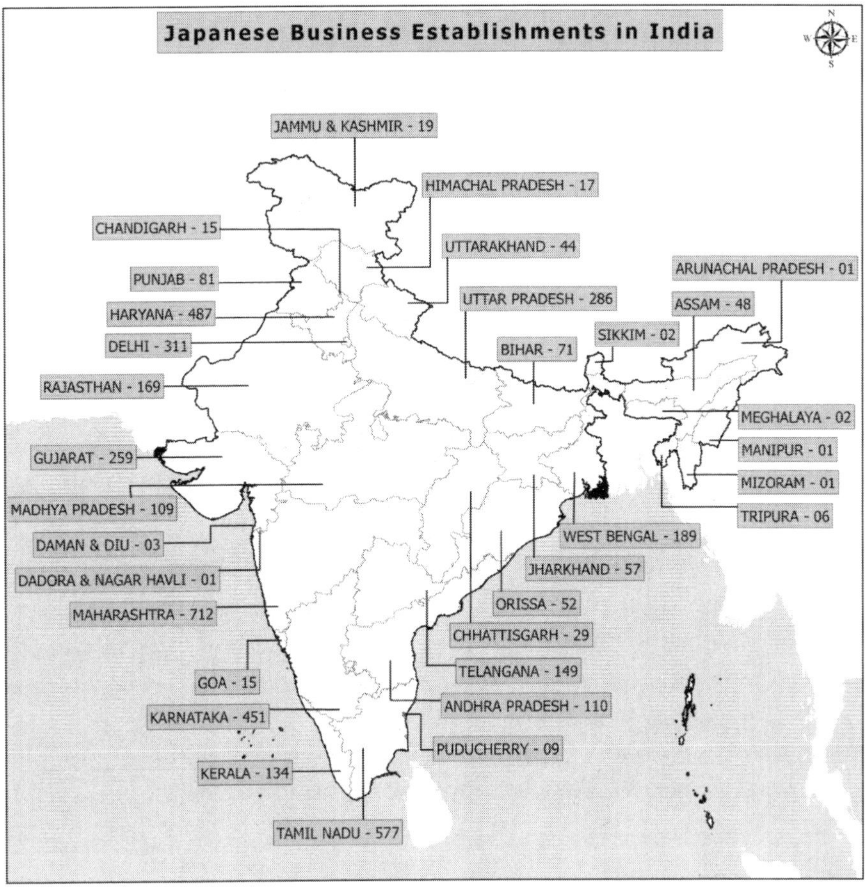

Source: Embassy of Japan, New Delhi.

of the surcharge, education cess and Central Sales Tax remains their major concerns. It also demands exemption of Special Additional Tax for the Completely Built Unit automobile for sale. These demands have not only been raised by the industry bodies but also by the Japanese leadership. Prime Minister Shinzo Abe conveyed similar concern to Indian Finance Minister who visited Tokyo in April 2013. The Japanese media quoted Japanese Foreign Ministry as saying that Abe suggested the visiting Indian minister "to pursue financial sector regulatory reform and improve its tax system in order to increase Japanese investment there."[104]

Some of these demands certainly have some merits and the demand of implementation of the GST has been taken care of by implementing the GST Act in 2016. However, the Japanese company should not make it a pre-requisite in moving towards India. Rather they should look at bigger size of the Indian market, profitability and a long term demand in the country. The Japanese companies should have a bigger strategy to tap Indian market which has 1.3 billion consumers. The Indian market is likely to outstrip China as Chinese society will become an ageing society in the next 20 years and will lose the current purchasing power parity. It should be noted that as per the 2009 estimate the percentage of ageing people (65 and above) in 1.35 billion Chinese population is around 8.1 per cent while this is only 5.2 per cent in 1.18 billion Indian population. India has median age of 25 while China has median age of 34, which means China would become an ageing society faster than India. China would lose appetite for automobile and home appliance product, the Japanese are known for.

Indian census data shows that by 2021 percentage of ageing population (60 and above) will be merely 10.7 per cent while those ranging from 15 to 59 years will constitute 64 per cent. So India will be a relatively young society as compared to other rising powers and consumerism will remain high here for a longer period.

Graph 2: Age Distribution of Population in India

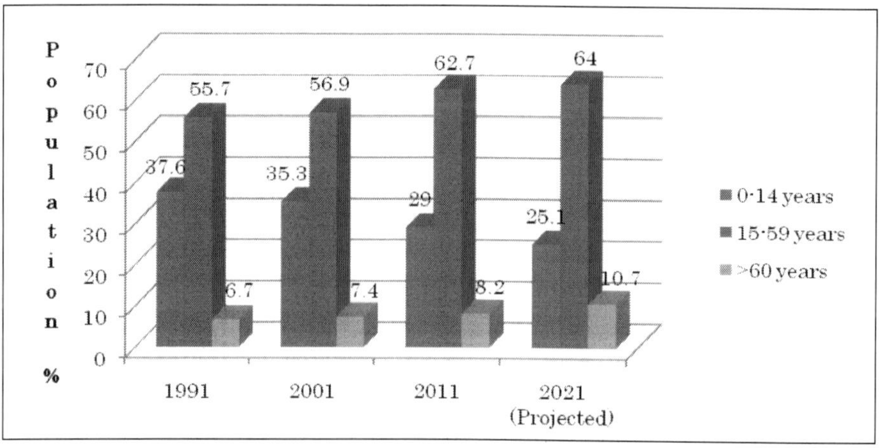

Source: Census of India 2011.

A house hold survey conducted by Census of India suggests that consumption of key entities such as computer, cars, mobile and internet facilities, both in urban and rural India still remains low. However, the demand is growing in these sectors. Some of the facilities including house, gas and electricity connection are still unsaturated and this can be tapped by investors and manufacturers (see graph 3).[105] It remains to be seen whether the Japanese companies who feel that the Japanese market in these fields have saturated at home, sets their eye on Indian market in near future or not.

Graph 3: Household Survey in India-Key Entities (in terms of Percentage)

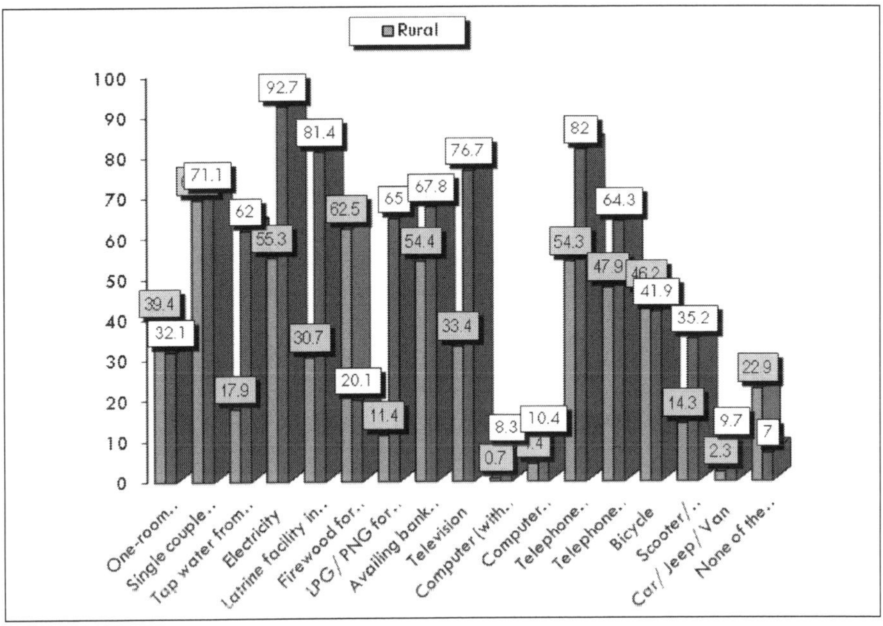

Source: House, Household Amenities and Assets Survey, Census, 2011.

The Japanese companies should also look into the reports of its own ministry which projects that consumer market in India will continue to surge. A study by METI conducted in 2011 also suggest that the consumer markct in India will surge from 660 billion US dollars to 3.06 trillion dollars by 2020.

One of the key concerns, as mentioned above, for Japanese investors is India's poor infrastructure that constrain them to set up their base in

India. The infrastructure development is certainly an issue in India at present. However, India in consultation with Japan is taking efforts not only to enhance infrastructure within the country but it is also taking efforts to re-integrate with its neighbouring countries by laying new rail and road networks and increasing the aviation links to promote people-to-people and trade relations with its neighbours.

As mentioned previously, Japan is already helping six states of India to develop as a global manufacturing and trading hub. Once the Delhi-Mumbai Industrial Corridor (DMIC) completes and Japanese companies set up their industrial bases alongside the DMIC, it will give outlet to Japanese companies to reach out to West Asian countries through the ports. On the other hand, the rail and road networks India is laying to connect itself with its periphery more closely, will also provide new avenues to the Japanese companies to transport their goods to all the land locked countries. Thirdly, India's efforts to develop road and port connectivity with Southeast Asia through Myanmar and Thailand, where the Japanese companies already have their production base, will help Japanese companies extend their supply chain to Indian states.

Conclusion

The analysis above suggests that India-Japan economic relations have transformed from a "resources driven" trade ties to a strategic partnership. Comprehensive Economic Partnership Agreement signed in 2011 has given a new dimension to the relationship. It has pushed trade flows between the two countries and thus bilateral trade between the two countries has registered a 38 per cent jump as compared to 2010 statistics. However, some concerns of growing trade imbalance in Japan's favour have come to the fore. India has demanded to ease the non-Tariff Barriers including the early conclusion of an agreement on nurses and care givers, which was part of CEPA negotiation, but remained inconclusive as Japan demanded more time. These concerns are not likely to hamper the normal economic relations as the objective of CEPA is wider than achieving a trade balance.

The analysis above also suggests that for India at least, one of the objectives is to ease its economic over-dependence on China, whose presence in Indian market is growing. As various scholars have argued,

India has signed various Preferential Trade Agreements with South East Asian countries to allow a level playing field in Indian market and thus wants to minimize dependence on China. Therefore, the trade imbalance will not become a major irritant, as is being witnessed in India-China economic relations. However, conclusion of nursing and caregiver agreements, an inconclusive part of CEPA, will help ease some of these concerns. Japan should give India a similar treatment at par with Indonesia and Philippines, with whom it has signed similar EPAs.

India has helped Japan diversify the need of its rare-earth elements; following China restricted export of these metals and thus tried to stifle production of various electronic items. An estimate suggests that India alone can offer 14 per cent of Japan's rare earth needs. Seen from this perspective, India has become a shock absorber for Japan.

Another expectation from India is to attract investments from Japan. Keeping this in mind the CEPA has given Japanese investor "national treatment" in the trade pact. But the flow of Japanese manufacturers to India remain slow. Statistics suggest that as of March 2016 only little more than 1200 companies have set up their bases in India, while in China their numbers have crossed 8000. There are various factors that checks Japanese companies' influx into India. As discussed above 'poor infrastructure' in India remains one of the major problems for Japanese companies. However, Japanese investors should not ignore the fact that, India is improving its internal infrastructure, with the help of government of Japan. It's western (Delhi-Mumbai Industrial Corridor) and eastern corridor is an example.

Secondly, owing to its strategic concerns, propelled by China, which is integrating with various Asian countries through port and rail networks, it is re-connecting with South Asian and East Asian neighbours by laying, rails and roads as well as developing ports. This can prove a boon for the investors who plan to make India a trade hub for West Asian and Southeast Asian countries. Japan should also take advantage out of it by making India a trade hub for its exports. Thirdly, Japan should not ignore the fact that there is a huge demand of electronic goods and household utilities in India and this will surge in near future. Instead of waiting for India's infrastructure to improve, Japanese investors should grab the opportunity and they should not be the late comers in Indian market.

END NOTES

1. T.R. Sareen, "India and Japan in Historical Perspective" in Rajaram Panda and Yoo Fukuzawa (eds) *India and Japan in Search of Global Roles*, Promila and Company Publishers, New Delhi (2007), p.30.
2. Purnendra C. Jain and Maureen Todhunter, "India and Japan: Newly Tampering Relations," in Purunendra C. Jain (ed.) *Distant Asian Neighbours: Japan and South Asia, Sterling Publishers Private Limited*, New Delhi, 1996, p.87.
3. Toshio Yamanouchi, "India through Japanese eyes," Sterling Publisher pvt limited, New Delhi, 2000, p. 21.
4. For a detail account of items traded between the two countries during the pre-war period, please refer to P.G. Rajamohan, Dil Bahdur Rahut and Jabin T. Jacob, " Changing Paradigm of Indo-Japan Relations: Opportunities and Challenges, Working Paper No.212, Indian Council for Research on Economic Relations, New Delhi, 2008.
5. Hiroshi Sato, "India Japan Peace Treaty in Japan's Post-War Asian Diplomacy," *Journal of the Japanese Association for South Asian Studies*, Vol. 17, 2005, p.9.
6. Selected Work of Jawaharlal Nehru, Vol. 6, p. 481, as quoted in Hiroshi Sato, India Japan Peace Treaty in Japan's Post-War Asian Diplomacy, *Journal of the Japanese Association for South Asian Studies*, Vol. 17, 2005, p.10.
7. Arjun Asrani, "India-Japan Relations in the 21st century," *The Japan Foundation*, New Delhi, Issue No.1, October 1995, p.14.
8. Tarun B. Bhat, "Outlook on Trade, Investment and Technology Transfer," in Rajaram Panda and Kazuo Ando (ed) India and Japan: Multi-dimensional perspective, *The Japan Foundation*, New Delhi, 1997,
9. Yasukuni Enoki, "The Japan-India New Partnership," *Journal of the United Service Institute of India*, Vol. CXXXIV, No. 557, July-September 2004, p.327.
10. Sakutaro Tanino, "Japan-India Relations: A Perspective," *Embassy of Japan*, New Delhi, 1998, p.9.
11. Lalit Man Singh, "India-Japan Relations," Institute of Peace and Conflict Studies, New Delhi, Issue Brief, No. 43, January 2007, p. 1.
12. Yoichi Funabashi, "India and Japan: A new Strategic Affinity," *Journal of the United Service Institute of India*, Vol. CXXXIV, No. 556, April-June 2004, p. 213.
13. Toshio Yamanouchi, "India through Japanese eyes," Sterling Publisher pvt Limited, New Delhi, 2000, p. 49.
14. Toshio Yamanouchi, p. 38.
15. Toshio Yamanouchi, p. 42.
16. Toshio Yamanouchi, p. 42.
17. Data received by the author during company visit to Nippon Steel and Sumitomo Metals at its Kimitsu Plant on December 18, 2012.
18. "India to export 2 MT Iron Ore to Japan over three years," *The Economics Times*, May 1, 2012.
19. Arjun Asrani, "India-Japan Relations: Looking Back, Looking Ahead," *Contemporary India Forum*, No.12, 2012, p.23.

20. Ibid.
21. Srabani Roy Choudhury, "Japan's Foreign Direct Investment in India: Lesson learnt from Firm Level Survey," Working Paper No. 243, Indian Council for Research on Economic Relations, New Delhi, 2009.
22. Raja Venkatramani, "Japan Enters Indian Industry: The Maruti Suzuki Joint Venture," Radiant Publishers, New Delhi, 1990, 16.
23. Ibid.
24. Srabani Roy Choudhury, "Japan's Foreign Direct Investment in India: Lesson learnt from Firm Level Survey," Working Paper No. 243, Indian Council for Research on Economic Relations, New Delhi, 2009.
25. J.N. Dixit, "My South Block Years: Memoirs of a Foreign Secretary," UBS Publishers and Distributors, New Delhi, 1996, p.254.
26. Toshio Yamanouchi, p. 55.
27. J.N. Dixit, p. 254.
28. Ibid.
29. Sakutaro Tanino, p.14.
30. J.N. Dixit, "My South Block Years: Memoirs of a Foreign Secretary," UBS Publishers and Distributors, New Delhi, 1996, p.262.
31. J.N. Dixit, p.263.
32. N. Krishnaswamy, "India and Japan" (opinion), *The Hindu*, April 27, 2002.
33. "(Indian) PM's address to Joint Session of the Diet," December 14, 2006, Press Information Bureau, Government of India, available online at http://www.pib.nic.in/newsite/erelease.aspx?relid=23318. (Accessed on September 23, 2016).
34. "Japan-India Partnership in a New Asian Era: Strategic Orientation of Japan-India Global Partnership," (2005), Ministry of Foreign Affairs, Government of Japan, available online at http://www.mofa.go.jp/region/asia-paci/india/partner0504.html#eight. (Accessed on September 23, 2016).
35. "(Indian) PM's address to Joint Session of the Diet."
36. "Report of the India-Japan joint Study Group," Department of Economic Affairs, Ministry of Finance, Government of India, New Delhi, June 2006, p.2.
37. "Japan, India sign deal to boost trade, investment," *Associated Press/Mainichi Daily*, October 26, 2010.
38. India Japan concludes CEPA talks," *The Indian Express*, October 26, 2010.
39. Ibid.
40. "India, Japan to expand strategic relations," *The Hindu*, October 25, 2010.
41. "Joint Declaration between the Leaders of India and Japan on the Conclusion of Comprehensive Economic Partnership Agreement," October 25, 2010, Ministry of External Affairs, Government of India, available online at http://mea.gov.in/press-releases.htm?dtl/830/Joint+Declaration+between+the+Leaders+of+India+and+Japan+on+the+Conclusion+of+the+Comprehensive+Economic+Partnership+Agreement (Accessed on September 23, 2016).
42. "Japanese PM in Delhi, currency pact soon," *The Hindustan Times*, December 28, 2011.

43. Rajaram Panda and Shamshad A. Khan, "The Implications of Noda's visit to India," IDSA Issue Brief, January 13, 2012, available online at http://idsa.in/system/files/IB_TheImplicationsofNodasVisittoIndia.pdf . (Accessed on September 23, 2016).
44. Tokyo, New Delhi agree to bolster India's infrastructure, *Kyodo news/The Japan Times*, may 1, 2012.
45. Ajay Lele, "India-Japan join hands to challenge China's Rare-earth monopoly," *IDSA Comments*, November 20, 2012 available online at http://idsa.in/idsacomments/IndiaJapanJoinHandstoChallengeChinasREE_AjeyLele_201112 (Accessed on September 23, 2016).
46. Text of PM's keynote address at event organized by Nikkei Inc. and Japan External Trade Organization (JETRO), September 2, 2014, *Prime Minister Office of India*, complete text of speech available at http://pmindia.gov.in/en/news_updates/text-of-pms-keynote-address-at-event-organized-by-nikkei-inc-and-japan-external-trade-organization-jetro-2/ (Accessed on September 23, 2016).
47. "Tokyo Declaration for India-Japan Special Strategic and Global Partnership."
48. Ibid.
49. Text of PM's keynote address at event organized by Nikkei Inc. and Japan External Trade Organization (JETRO).
50. Ibid.
51. India overtakes China as most attractive market for Japanese firms, *The Mainichi Daily*, January 5, 2011.
52. The survey result was sent by Mr. Shin Oya, JBIC's Chief Representative in New Delhi, on the request of the researcher through an email.
53. Arun Goyal, Minister (Economic and Commercial), Embassy of India, Tokyo, interview with *Economics Times*, "CEPA: A way forward," December 28, 2012.
54. Comprehensive Economic Partnership Agreement between Republic of India and Japan, 2011, Ministry of Commerce, Government of India, p.23 available online at http://www.commerce.nic.in/trade/IJCEPA_Basic_Agreement.pdf. (Accessed on September 25, 2016).
55. Ibid, pp.103-104.
56. Pinaki Das Gupta, "India and East Asia: Towards a regional economic integration," Keizai Koho Centre, Tokyo, p.5, available online at http://www.kkc.or.jp/english/activities/indianscholars/KKC_FINAL_PAPER_PDG_.pdf. (Accessed on March 28, 2013).
57. "Comprehensive Economic Partnership Agreement between the Republic of India and Japan", p. 66.
58. Ranja Sengupta, "India's FTA choices get more ambitious," *Economic and Political Weekly*, June 25, 2011. VolXLVI, Nos. 26 & 27, p. 18-22.
59. "Comprehensive Economic Partnership Agreement between the Republic of India and Japan," Article 96, p.73.
60. "Japan-India accord should lead to more EPAs," (Editorial), *The Yomiuri Shimbun*, September 22, 2010.
61. Ranja Sengupta, "India's FTA choices get more ambitious."

62. Geethanjali Nataraj, "India-Japan Economic Partnership Agreement: Gains and Future Prospects," Policy Research Institute, Ministry of Finance, Government of Japan. 2010.
63. B.S. Raghavan, "India-Japan CEPA holds great promise," *Business Line*, September 7, 2011.
64. Ibid.
65. C.P. Ravindranathan, "FTA with Japan holds promise," *Business Line*, June 21, 2011.
66. Author's interview with Arjun Asrani, India's former ambassador to Japan, March 18, 2013, New Delhi.
67. Email interview with Masanori Kondo, Japanese academician who participated in joint study group which suggested to signing of CEPA. Response received on April 23, 2013.
68. Timsy Jaipurya, "It's advantage Tokyo in India-Japan economic pact," *The Financial Express*, May 7, 2012.
69. "India urges Japan to remove non-tariff barriers," *The Times of India*, May 1, 2012.
70. "Commerce Minister Says Steps have been taken to sort out the implementation issues related to CEPA and improve bilateral trade as trade balance with Japan (Press Release), Ministry of Commerce, Textile and Industry, New Delhi, October 6, 2016.
71. Prof. Makoto Kojima of Takushoku University, who was part of 50 member India-Japan joint study group which recommended negotiation of CEPA between the two countries, disagrees that a target to reach a certain trade volume was ever agreed. He says this is creation by the Indian politicians, personal interview, January 23, 2015, Tokyo.
72. Address by External Affairs Minister Shri K. Natwar Singh, at the inauguration of the India-Japan Parliamentary Forum, Federation House, New Delhi, April 29, 2005, full text available at http://meaindia.nic.in/mystart.php?id=10059484. (Accessed on March 28, 2013).
73. Yuzuru Takano, "Japan needs strategic view of EPA with India," Opinion, *The Asahi Shimbun*, October 20, 2010.
74. Geethanjali Nataraj, "India-Japan Economic Partnership agreement: Gains and Future Prospects," *Policy Research Institute*, Ministry of Finance, Government of Japan, November 26, 2010, p.3, available online at http://www.mof.go.jp/pri/international_exchange/visiting_scholar_program/ws2010_b.pdf. (Accessed on September 23, 2016).
75. Ibid.
76. Harsh V. Pant, "India aims to raise its profile vis-à-vis China by 'looking east'," *The Japan Times*, January 31, 2012.
77. Ibid.
78. Pravakar Sahoo, "India-Japan CEPA: a strategic move," East Asia Forum, November 12, 2010.
79. Author's interview with ambassador Arjun Asrani, March 18, 2013, New Delhi.
80. Kondo quoted in Miya Tanaka, "Japan-India pact may help exports," *Kyodo News/The Japan Times*, October 26, 2010.

81. Interview with Prof. Masanori Kondo, International Christian University of Japan, January 15, 2013, Tokyo.
82. Author's email interview with Professor Masanori Kondo, April 23, 2013.
83. "Indian PM seeks greater investment, cooperation with Japan," *Mainichi Daily*, October 25, 2010.
84. "India, Japan lift economic ties" (Editorial), *The Japan Times*, October 28, 2010.
85. "Bolstering Japan-India ties," *The Japan Times* (Editorial), January 21, 2012.
86. "Japan, India must deepen security, economic ties," *The Yomiuri Shimbun*, (editorial), October 26, 2010.
87. Yuzuru Takano, "Japan needs strategic view of EPA with India," Opinion, *The Asahi Shimbun*, October 20, 2010.
88. CII Report, "India-Japan Business Summit: Celebrating 60 years of India-Japan diplomatic relations," p. 7.
89. Amitabh K. Kanth, "Delhi-Mumbai Industrial Corridor: Challenges and Prospects, lecture delivered at the Observer Research Foundation," New Delhi on October 11, 2012.
90. DMIC website available on line at http://www.dmic.co.in/dmic-introduction.php (Accessed on September 23, 2016).
91. Amitabh K. Kanth, "Delhi-Mumbai Industrial Corridor: Challenges and Prospects, lecture delivered at Observer Research Foundation," New Delhi on October 11, 2012.
92. "Govt moves cabinet note on 26% stake of Japanese govt in DMIDC," *The Indian Express*, May 1, 2012.
93. Rajaram Panda and Shamshad A.Khan, "The Implications of Noda's visit to India," *IDSA Issue Brief*, January 13, 2012, p.3 available online at http://idsa.in/system/files/IB_TheImplicationsofNodasVisittoIndia.pdf (Accessed on September 23, 2016).
94. K.V. Kesavan, "Indo-Japanese partnership at a new stage: PM Yukio Hatoyama's visit" *ORF analysis*, January 09, 2011 available online at http://www.orfonline.com/cms/sites/orfonline/modules/analysis/AnalysisDetail.html?cmaid=18114&mmacmaid=18115 (Accessed on September 23, 2016).
95. National Alliance for peoples 'Movement, "Ploy to Plunder Resources and People's Sovereignty," (Press Release accessed by author) March 26, 2016.
96. "Lalu has a date with Japan's Bullet Train," *The Hindustan Times*, January 13, 2009.
97. "Joint Statement on Prime Minister's visit to Japan: Strengthening the Strategic and Global Partnership between India and Japan beyond the 60th Anniversary of Diplomatic Relations," Ministry of External Affairs, Government of India, May 29, 2013. Full text available at http://mea.gov.in/bilateral-documents.htm?dtl/21755 (Accessed on September 23, 2016).
98. Ibid.
99. "India near deal to use Shinkansen," *The Yomiuri Shimbun*, March 11, 2013.
100. India agrees to adopt Shinkansen technology on major routes, *The Yomiuri Shimbun*, December 8, 2015.
101. Ibid.

102. IMM Jeong-Seong, "Why do Japanese companies go for joint ventures in India?," *POSRI Chindia Quarterly*, Spring 2011, Vol.2, p.74.
103. Suggestion for Government of India by JCCI, 2011, a copy of JCCII suggestion was obtained by this researcher during a Roundtable discussion at ICRIER, New Delhi on July 25th 2011.
104. "Reform and we will invest, India told," *Kyodo News/The Japan Times*, April 3, 2013.
105. Saurabh Naruka, "Households and amenities survey," *Competition 360*, Pathfinder publication, New Delhi, May 2012, p. 49.

6

INDIA-JAPAN COOPERATION AND THEIR QUEST FOR A RULE-BASED ORDER

In 2006, when India and Japan signed their strategic partnership, they agreed to have dialogue not only between themselves but also with "other like-minded countries in the Asia-Pacific region on themes of mutual interest."[1] By using terms such as "like-minded countries" and having dialogue on the themes of "mutual interest," they maintained ambivalence about the objective of this dialogue. But with their statements and speeches delivered by the leadership of the two countries at different fora, it became apparent that with the "like-minded" countries they meant regional democracies and the objective of the dialogue on mutual interest was to forge a rule based order in the region and beyond.[2] The calls from the regional powers to create a rule based order, is based on their assumption that when a new power rises, it changes the status quo of the existing order. Moreover, it tries to dominate the region by undermining the existing internationally accepted norms and laws. The new power that is being debated in the strategic and political circles across the globe is none other than China.[3] Concerns are being expressed about Beijing's expansive behaviour and its assertions in the South China Sea and the East China Sea. At the international forums various leaders and statesmen have expressed unease over these developments.

In Asia, Japan and India have been at the forefront in urging the democracies to come forward to create a rule based regional order. To assess strategic thinking of India and Japan and their objectives to create a new order, this chapter identifies three key variables, a) the leadership, b) the strategic thinkers, and c) the media. The researcher considers that these three variables play an important role in formulating and influencing the strategic debate in the democracies. The chapter attempts to evaluate the statements and speeches of Japanese and Indian leaderships to assess how they envisage the rule based order for the Asia-Pacific and beyond. The chapter also analyses Indian and Japanese strategic thinking using the opinion pieces written by strategic experts and editorials that appeared in the leading newspapers. Since the popular debate generated by the media and strategic thinkers help influence the decision making process of the states, the analyses of their debates would help understand various converging and diverging points of the different constituencies in both the countries towards creating a new rule based order. This in turn will help assess whether this goal can be achieved.

This chapter has been divided into various sub-themes to understand the issues involved towards creating a new order in the Asia-Pacific (also referred as Indo-Pacific). The first sub-theme attempts to define the concept and it analyses the statements and speeches of leaders in India and Japan regarding the concept of a rule-based order. Then it goes on to analyse and compare different shades of Indian and Japanese strategic thinking expressed through opinion articles and editorials in order to understand the convergences and divergences of their approaches vis-à-visa rule-based order or anew security architecture.

Quest for a Rule-Based Order in the Asia-Pacific: Defining the concept

While several interpretations of the term 'rule-based order' or 'the new world order' have been in use in strategic circles, it remains an ideological notion associated with the concept of global governance through collective efforts.[4] At the core of the debate are the new developing relationships among various democracies, including India and Japan. Notably, India and Japan, the two Asian democracies, have developed a global and strategic partnership and have made commitments to work together on various regional and international issues.

Japan and India view themselves as complementary to each other in both economic and security matters. In their strategic and global partnership agreement signed in 2006, they identified a strong and prosperous India is in the interest of Japan and vice versa. Both countries are networked internationally. Japan has used its different foreign policy tools, including its overseas financial aid and Overseas Development Assistance (ODA), to remain engaged with the international community. India, since the end of the Cold War, has signed a number of strategic partnerships with countries across the globe, which is reflective of the fact that India is much more engaged with the world than ever before. Because of their growing interdependence with the international community both politically and economically, it is quite natural that both India and Japan are cooperating for a rule-based order to safeguard the global commons. Of late, both India and Japan have argued for creating a global economic and security environment that could benefit all nations in the international community. Their demand that freedom of navigation and over-flights be safeguarded as global commons stems from their common understanding.

Japanese and Indian Leaders' Quest for a Rule-based Order

Various statesmen have called for creating a rule-based order and have presented their views on how to achieve this goal. Japan's search to create a new architecture based on the "rule of law" can be traced to a 2006 speech by Taro Aso when he was the Foreign Minister of Japan. In 2006, Aso enunciated the idea of an "arc of freedom and prosperity." He argued that, in its diplomacy, Japan should lay emphasis on "universal values" such as "democracy, freedom, human rights, the rule of law, and the market economy."[5] This statement was one of the rare "pro-active" foreign policy pronouncements by Japan, which is widely considered a "reactive state." Japan at that time wanted to "design" an "arc of freedom and prosperity" by forging stronger ties with "budding democracies." Presenting his views towards creating this arc, Aso included budding democracies that "line the outer rim of the Eurasian continent." Apart from the budding democracies, his value-oriented diplomacy also included the friendly nations sharing common views and interests. He argued:

> I firmly believe that Japan must make its ties even firmer with friendly nations that share common views and interests, namely of course, the United States as well as Australia, India, and the member states of the EU and NATO, and at the same time work with these friends towards the expansion of this "arc of freedom and prosperity."[6]

It was clear from Aso's pronouncement that Japan wanted to create an exclusive global architecture in which countries not espousing democracy and the rule of law had no place. Taking the idea forward, Prime Minister Shinzo Abe, during his first stint in office, mooted the idea of a "broader Asia" at the confluence of the Indian and Pacific oceans and urged that the democratic nations located at the opposite edges of these seas deepen the friendship among their citizens at every possible level. He highlighted that "this 'broader Asia' will evolve into an immense network spanning the entirety of the Pacific Ocean, incorporating the United States of America and Australia."[7]

These pronouncements and ideas from Japanese leaders were generally appreciated by other democracies as well, but they did not take concrete steps to shape a value based order. By then, China had already started voicing concerns, terming these ideas an attempt to encircle China. With the change of government in Japan in 2009, these terminologies were dropped from Japanese Foreign policy pronouncements as the new government was eager to forge a closer relations with China and South Korea and it was cautious in making statements which could give them misperception that their policies are aimed at containing China.

But after the LDP regained power, the Japanese leadership gave yet another push to revive the idea of creating a regional security architecture consisting of democracies. Just before resuming office for his second term as Prime Minister of Japan at the end of 2012, Abe mooted the idea of a "Democratic Security Diamond." In his oft-quoted article published by the Project Syndicate, he argued:

> I envisage a strategy whereby Australia, India, Japan, and the US state of Hawaii form a diamond to safeguard the maritime commons stretching from the Indian Ocean region to the western Pacific. I am prepared to invest, to the greatest possible extent, Japan's capabilities in this security diamond.[8]

It was not surprising when Japan adopted its first National Security Strategy, a new doctrine combining its military and diplomatic strategy to secure its national interest, it talked about forging a rule based order. It stated:

> The key of national security is to create a stable and predictable international environment, and prevent the emergence of threats. It is thus necessary for Japan to realize an international order and security environment that are desirable for Japan, by playing an even more proactive role in achieving peace, stability and prosperity of the international community as a "Proactive Contributor to Peace" based on the principle of international cooperation.[9]

Moreover, in his speech at the 13th Shangri-La Dialogue in 2014, Abe urged the international community to resolve disputes in light of "international law." Clearly, Abe's exhortations to the international community to uphold the "rule of law" were reiterations of statements made by previous Japanese administrations. At the Shangri-La Dialogue, he presented three principles of the "rule of law" at sea for "states" to resolve their disputes:

(a) states shall make and clarify their claims based on international law;
(b) states shall not use force or coercion in trying to drive their claims; and
(c) states shall seek to settle disputes by peaceful means.[10]

These three principles of the "rule of law" at sea for the resolution of disputes were also reiterated by Abe during his maiden speech before the US Congress. Abe's enunciation of these three principles for the resolution of disputes was in consonance with the Japanese government's policy of creating a rule-based order. By renewing this pledge before the US Congress, Abe made it clear that he considers the US an important partner in achieving a rule-based order in the Asia-Pacific. Later, in an opinion article contributed to *Project Syndicate* which was later published in various newspapers, Abe presented this idea more emphatically:

> We must make the vast seas stretching from the Pacific to the Indian Ocean a zone of peace and freedom, where all adhere to the rule of

> law. For this reason, too, it is our responsibility to fortify the US-Japan alliance.[11]

As regards statements from Indian leadership towards the rule based order are concerned, Indian leaders have not been as emphatic as their Japanese counterparts. However, they have presented a vision somewhat similar to that of Japan toward creating a new world order in their speeches and statements. The then Indian Prime Minister Manmohan Singh, while addressing a gathering of serving Indian diplomats, underscored the need for creating "a global economic and security environment"[12] in the changing world order. He said that India is "prepared to work with the international community" to create this kind of global environment "beneficial to all nations."[13] Notably, the seminar was entitled "India's Place in the Changing World Order: Where Do We See Ourselves? What Do We Wish to Achieve?" The seminar attended by Singh was aimed at identifying the way forward for promoting India's key foreign policy interests across the regions.

In the context of India-Japan relations, Indian leaders have also voiced their support for creating a stable regional order in Asia. Manmohan Singh argued:

> India's relations with Japan are important not only for our economic development, but also because we see Japan as a natural and indispensable partner in our quest for stability and peace in the vast region in Asia....[14]

He further emphasised that "there are strong synergies between our economies, which need an open, rule-based international trading system to prosper."[15]

Similarly, Prime Minister Narendra Modi voiced concerns about the "expansionist" tendencies of some Asian states. His reference to expansionist tendencies was taken as an apparent reference to China. While addressing business leaders in Tokyo, Modi stated that the world is divided into "two camps." He stated:

> One camp believes in expansionist policies, while the other believes in development. We have to decide whether the world should get caught in the grip of expansionist policies or we should lead it on the path of development and create opportunities that take it to greater heights.[16]

The "rule-based" Global Maritime Order: Understanding Convergences and Divergences

With the rise of China, successive turbulence is being witnessed at sea and in the air. Beijing's expansive behaviour and its claims in the South China Sea and the East China Sea have drawn concerns from various countries. India, Japan, the US and other democracies around the world argue that seas (especially the high seas) are part of the global commons and that all nations have the right to freely transit through the seas. The leaders of India and Japan have also time and again reiterated their demand that China abide by the internationally-accepted laws and norms on the freedom of navigation. As mentioned in the previous section, Japanese leaders mooted the idea of an "Arc of Freedom and Prosperity," the "Confluence of Two Seas" and most recently a "Democratic Security Diamond" primarily aimed at establishing a rule-based maritime order. Nevertheless, India was a little circumspect about embracing this idea. But gradually the issue crept in their joint statements. Finally, the South China Sea issue also surfaced in India-Japan joint statement signed. The joint statement signed during Shinzo Abe's Delhi visit in December 2015 stated that "the two Prime Ministers noting the developments in the South China Sea called upon all States to avoid unilateral actions that could lead to tensions in the region."[17] The statement was reiterated in the India-Japan joint statement signed in 2016.

It may be noted that when the concerns were raised by various states about China's maritime assertions, it has started acknowledging the concept of freedom of navigation. China's stance on the freedom of navigation, however, differs with that of the US, Japan and India. The Chinese stance can be best understood by a statement by its Ministry of Foreign Affairs that argues "The Chinese side advocates the freedom of navigation in the South China Sea, yet the freedom definitely does not mean that foreign military vessels and aircrafts can enter one country's territorial waters and airspace at will."[18]

Apparently, China is pushing for a new norm by asking that military vessels seek permission from the coastal state before innocent passage. Citing UNCLOS, which extends the sovereignty of coastal states on waters up to

12 nautical miles, China is building new man-made islands by reclaiming sea in the South China Sea. However, the international community at large has expressed concern over China's reclamation activities and has argued that the 12 nautical mile stipulation of UNCLOS should not be applied to artificial islands to interfere with the innocent passage.

Considering China's expansion in South China Sea, Philippines, one of the aggrieved parties took the case to Permanent Attribution Council (PAC) at The Hague. The PAC has given verdict in favour of Philippine. Japan has accepted the verdict and asked the parties to abide by the verdict.[19] Unlike Japan, India did not comment on the legality of the verdict but following the verdict in a statement it urged all the parties to respect the UNCLOS. The statement noted: "Sea lanes of communication passing through the South China Sea are critical for peace, stability, prosperity and development. As a State Party to the UNCLOS, India urges all parties to show utmost respect for the UNCLOS, which establishes the international legal order of the seas and oceans."[20]

Assessing Indian and Japanese Strategic Thinking on the New Order/Architecture[21]

Reactions among the strategic thinkers about the regional order, both from India and Japan, have been mixed. While the leaders of the two leading democracies of Asia in their speeches have presented broader outlines of cooperation, the strategic thinkers have been quick to suggest how the two democracies, India and Japan, should interact with each other as well as what their level of cooperation with another nations in the region should be to realise this goal. To maintain diplomatic niceties, the leaders of the two countries have omitted references to China when they envision a new order in Asia but the strategic thinkers have been quite explicit in naming the pillars upon which the new order or security architecture should be built.

Some Indian strategic thinkers welcome closer partnership among the US, Japan, India and other nations to hedge China. This kind of argument has been put forward by leading Indian strategic thinkers such as Brahama Chellaney and C. Raja Mohan. Chellaney, who has written a number of articles on this issue in the last few years, sees the relationship between India and Japan as a significant milestone in building "Asian power equilibrium." He opines that "concerned over China's lengthening shadow, Japan and India are bracing for a strategic challenge in the Asian heartland." However, he believes that the partnership between the two countries is not aimed at gaining preeminence but to "thwart preeminence."[22]

K. Shankar Bajpai, a strategic thinker and a former Indian diplomat, in the context of burgeoning India-Japan relations states that "power-politics and balance-of-power calculations...are facts of life." He further states that "in our totally changed world, we ourselves have evolved to cooperate strategically with the US. Doing so with Japan is no less important." Bajpai, clearly sees the relationship between Japan and India as a byproduct of an assertive China and opines that "we can both (India and Japan) honestly say we are not building relations in hostility against China; but it is right and proper for us to examine what to do if China acts in hostility against us."[23]

Similarly, C. Raja Mohan sees India and Japan as important players in the evolving security architecture in the region. Raja Mohan has been critical of India's slow approach towards embracing Japan in the event of a rising China. In an opinion piece, he states that "don't provoke China" has been the "mantra behind New Delhi's recent 'go slow' strategy with Japan." He asserts that "holding it back until now was the political fecklessness in Tokyo and Delhi." Raja Mohan further opines that "at the very moment when many Asian countries are frightened by the prospect of China's non-peaceful rise and are looking to Indian leadership in constructing a stable Asian balance of power, Delhi seems trapped in strategic hesitation." He is of the view that "a genuine strategic partnership between India and Japan will be a game changer for Asian geopolitics."[24] On similar lines, Harsh V. Pant believes that "the rise of China in the Asia-Pacific and beyond has altered the strategic calculus of India and Japan, forcing them to rethink their attitudes toward each other." As regards the emerging regional order, Pant opines that "India seems most willing to acknowledge Japan's centrality in shaping the evolving Asia-Pacific security architecture."[25]

A number of Indian columnists have also seen India-Japan relations through the prism of ongoing power politics in the Asia-Pacific. An Indian observer commenting on the geopolitics of Asia stated that "Japanese seek greater cooperation in trade with India while India is attempting to forge a larger relationship so that Japan could act as a counterfoil to China once it rises to the pinnacle of its power."[26] Similarly, another observer opined that China's "peaceful rise" is unlikely to remain "peaceful" for much longer. He suggests that "in its own interest, and in the larger equation of maintaining the balance of power in Asia, Japan must take the lead in such a way that the Chinese behemoth does not swallow the world with its influence."[27]

A group of Indian academicians, including Rajesh Rajagopalan, also views ongoing India-Japan relations purely from a realist paradigm. In the context of China's rise, Rajagopalan writes:

> To paraphrase the Athenian historian, philosopher and General Thucydides, China's rise and the fear this causes in Asia and elsewhere is at the root of India's importance. China's aggressiveness has frightened even the more powerful Asian powers such as Japan.[28]

He is among those scholars who debunk the theory that economic interdependence between China and India will help moderate China's aggressive behavior vis-à-vis India and the region. He opines that "a strong and welcome new theme in India's foreign policy is a focus on the economic side of diplomacy. But it would be a mistake to assume that closer economic relations will minimise strategic challenges."[29]

Like Indian strategic thinking, a group of Japanese strategic thinkers argue that foreign and security policy of both Japan and India should be based on their values such as freedom, democracy, human rights and the rule of law, which they espouse. Yoshiko Sakurai, a close aide of Abe and President of Tokyo based think tank Japan Institute of National Fundamentals, opines that "[T]he countries best suited to articulating these values (of freedom, democracy, human rights and the rule of law) are Japan and India. In Asia, it is in fact Japan and India that have sufficient latent strength to deploy their foreign policy on the basis of their values. I believe that in their partnership with the US, both countries will become cognizant of their own values and strength and forge the way forward for Asia."[30]

Yuriko Koike, a former defence minister of Japan and present Governor of Tokyo, has been one of the leading voices in Japan who argue the need to construct security architecture without China. She argues that "America alone cannot construct a viable security structure for the region. From India to Japan, every Asian country must play its part." Koike is aware that various countries in the region face a dilemma over how to deal with China. She suggests that "...fear of provoking China should not stop Asia's leaders from seeking a regional security consensus, such as the proposed code of conduct for disputes in the South China Sea."[31]

Similarly, Takashi Shiraishi and others argue for a strong partnership among democracies in the Asia-Pacific region to check China's dominating tendencies. In an article in *Japan Echo*, Shiraishi considers India as one of the important elements in forging a regional balance. He argues that "Japan's relations with India should remain grounded in the Japan-US alliance. Engaging with India within the framework of the Japan-US alliance is a balancing act in some aspects...."[32] Pointing to the quadrilateral partnership among Australia, India, Japan and the US, he states that "whatever the actual intentions were, the scheme was quite naturally regarded as a strategy for containing or encircling China." As regards India's role as a balancer to China, Shiraishi opined that "while using India to counterbalance China may appear sound in theory, it will not work in practice because India is unlikely to allow itself to be used in that manner."[33] Tomohiko Taniguchi, Prime Minister Abe's political adviser, believes that containing China is not feasible as China is economically interlinked with the region. However, India and Japan must engage with each other wherever their interests converge.[34]

On the other hand, there is another strand of strategic thinking both in India and Japan that believe in creating inclusive regional security architecture for the Asian subcontinent. This group of strategic thinkers argues that India, Japan and China are key players in the Asia-Pacific region and that, without China, forming a regional architecture would not be possible. They consider that, since the US is an outside power, it does not fit into the inclusive security architecture of the Asia-Pacific. More importantly, they believe that both Japan and China are equally important for India.

Siddharth Varadarajan, a well-known journalist and strategic thinker, argues that "India, Japan, South Korea and China, which have emerged as principal powers in Asia, should have multilateral and bilateral interactions with each other."[35] Varadarajan adds that "without these four countries and Russia establishing a relationship of comfort among and between themselves, it will not be possible to develop the security architecture of Asia."[36]

How should India interact with Japan in forging the new security architecture? Varadarajan is of the view that "in its interaction with Japan, the Indian side needs to encourage a constructive approach to Asian security based on addressing current concerns as well as the lingering burdens of history."[37]

While others argue that the US should be an inalienable partner of the emerging Asian security architecture, Varadarajan is apprehensive of a "trilateral element" (read the US) creeping into the bilateral arrangement between India and Japan. He has reasons for this apprehension:

> The trilateral idea has two dimensions. At the military level, the United States would like to enhance the inter-operability of Asian forces loosely aligned with Washington. And at the political and strategic level, it would like to demonstrate that India, Japan, and the US will provide the nucleus around which any emerging security architecture in Asia must be built.[38]

Varadarajan suggests that the government maintain a balance in its policy towards Japan and China:

> Modi might represent a party that has traditionally favoured a more muscular Indian approach towards China and that is not averse to the neo-containment talk currently fashionable in Tokyo, but the last thing India wants is to be forced to choose between Japan and China.[39]

Similarly, "Non-Alignment 2.0," a policy paper compiled by a group of Indian strategic thinkers including a former Indian diplomat, also suggests India to maintain a balanced approach in its foreign policy in the changing world order. This semi-official policy paper offers various alternative proposals to the government of India for crafting its foreign policy. It argues:

> Alongside the US and China, there will be several other centers and hubs of power that will be relevant, particularly in regional contexts.

> This means that Non-Alignment will no longer be limited to avoiding becoming a frontline state in a conflict between two powers.[40]

As mentioned previously, various Indian strategic thinkers have seen the blossoming India-Japan ties as a response to a rising and aggressive China. In opposition to this, Srinath Raghavan, who is among the co-authors of "Non-Alignment 2.0," opines that "from a strategic standpoint, it would be unwise to convey an impression to China that our relationship with Japan is primarily directed against it."[41] Raghavan has suggested that India should not bandwagon with any country to balance another. He opines that "it is certainly not in India's interest to convey an impression that its security partnerships are subordinate parts of the US 'pivot' to Asia."[42] Notably, he suggests India to "avoid making sharp choices or premature commitments" in its dealings with Japan and China.[43]

Yet another Indian strategic thinker suggests India to adopt a cooperative foreign policy approach to the regional order. Ramesh Thakur opines that "China, India, and Japan should join forces to construct an architecture of regional order that fosters peace and promotes prosperity across Asia and the world without cutting across existing bilateral relations of any of the three."[44]

Thakur warns that rivalry among them will have an adverse impact on the world. "The destiny of Asia in this century will be shaped by the triangular relationship between China, India, and Japan. The 'strategic footprint' of that triangle will cover the world. Cooperation between them will help to anchor peace and prosperity in Asia. Rivalry and conflict will roil the world."[45]

Atul Aneja, a Beijing-based correspondent for *The Hindu*, an influential Indian newspaper, while writing his opinion piece on Prime Minister Modi's visit to China opined that "in redefining India's geopolitical relationship, Mr. Modi would have to take a call on balance of power in the Asia-Pacific."[46] Within the context of an emerging balance of power in the region, Aneja observed that "While it is tempting to enmesh in security arrangements that have Japan, Australia and the United States as the major players, a more prudent and bolder course that the Prime Minister can pursue is to propose and push for an integrated dialogue that involves all the major players in the region on a single dialogue platform."[47]

Within Japan too, there are observers, who caution the government not to use relationship with India to counter China. Yoichi Funabashi is one of the strong advocates who argue that the bilateral relationship between India and Japan should not be aimed at counterbalancing China. He opines that "in both Tokyo and New Delhi, there are people seeking to elevate Indo-Japanese relations to the status of a de facto alliance and to pursue a strategy of encircling China."[48] Funabashi adds that "it is not necessary, however, to look for the China factor in every new initiative in Indo-Japanese relations."[49] He suggests that both Asian democracies "should exercise restraint and take a stance of "quiet deterrence" to avoid provoking China."[50]

In another opinion piece, Yoichi Funabashi argues, "Japan's long-term strategic aim must be the formation of a world and regional order based upon the model of a "liberal international order" and "rooted in the rule of law." More importantly, he suggests Japan to "hone" its geo-political skills and avoid becoming a strategic pawn "in someone else's game."[51] Norio Kondo, Takenori Horimoto and some young scholars such as Ryohei Kasai and Kazutoshi Tamari have views similar to that of Yoichi Funabashi. Japanese Indologists believe that India and Japan should not pursue a strategy of encircling China. Their arguments are in favour of accommodating China in the regional architecture wherever possible. Norio Kondo on the issue of growing trilateral engagement among the US, India and Japan believes that "such a trilateral arrangement will probably work against alleviating tension between China and neighbouring countries."[52]

The analysis above clearly suggests that there is no uniformity on views among Indian and Japanese strategic thinkers whether to forge a new order with or without China. However, both the strands of strategic thinkers consider Japan and India among the common player around whom the new order can be formed.

Towards a Rule-based Order in Asia: Mapping the Views of the Indian and Japanese Press

In the Indian press, including the vernacular Hindi press, various articles and editorials have come to the fore highlighting the level of interactions between India and the world. Like the country's strategic thinkers, the media in India are also divided over the issue of forging a new security architecture. Some are favouring a hedging of China with the help of Japan and the US as well as other like-minded countries while others are arguing against stoking insecurity in China by forging a partnership with other countries.

The Hindu in its editorials has been urging caution on not letting India-Japan ties affect India's relationship with China. In one of its editorials, *The Hindu* argues that "New Delhi needs to guard against allowing ties with Japan to get underpinned by the shared wariness of Beijing. There is nothing to be gained for India, Japan and China in a polarised Asia."[53] Following Prime Minister Abe's India visit in 2015, the Hindu reminded that "India should be wary of the great game going on in Asia."[54] It argues that rather than joining any geopolitical alliance "India should build strong ties with each power, instead of aligning with any particular bloc."[55]

Business Standard, on the other hand, opines that "fear of China's reaction cannot be allowed to stand in the way of natural cooperation with Japan." The daily suggests that India forging closer ties with other regional powers to check an assertive China is the "only option." It adds that "India so far has had a distressing habit of refusing to commit itself all the way, although realpolitik in this case clearly suggests that closer alliances with other regional powers concerned about an assertive China is the only option."[56] The *Indian Express*, yet another leading Indian daily, states that the "India-Japan partnership cannot, however, be explored without reference to the China factor" adding that "...it is undeniable that China's rise is reordering the Asian balance of power. Japan and India are both adapting to that fact and trying to improve their individual prospects through a deeper strategic collaboration."[57]

In the context of an emerging regional order in the Asia-Pacific, *The Asian Age* in its editorial opines that "the build-up (between India and Japan) has been gradual but focussed. But it is exaggerated to see in this a threat to China, with which India as well as Japan actually desires the bettering of ties."[58] On the similar lines, The *Hindustan Times* opines that "symbolically closer ties would help put China on warning that its increasingly imperialist actions will inevitably lead to bandwagonning against it in the Asia-Pacific area." It further argues that "at a time when the US cannot seem to make up its mind whether it is prepared to stand up to China and the Southeast Asian countries are selling out to Beijing's money power, the India-Japan relationship should be seen as being ultimately about ensuring the stability of Asia as a whole."[59]

The vernacular press also has shown keen interest in India-Japan ties and their possible impact on relations with China. The *Navbharat Times*, in this context, states that "a stronger relationship with Japan should not be forged at the cost of China as momentary benefits may later result into loss."[60] The daily *Hindustan* in an editorial views India-Japan relations in the context of Chinese claims in the Asia-Pacific. It opines that one of the reasons for the growing ties between India and Japan is to "counter China's growing preeminence in the Asia-Pacific region." The *Hindustan* further states that "in this region India is the only country which can confront China and for this, Japan needs India's cooperation."[61]

Similarly, the Japanese media is also divided into two opposing camps. Analyses of editorials in the *Yomiuri Shimbun* and the *Asahi Shimbun* show that, while both favour a closer partnership between India and Japan, the former recommends a strong partnership with India to counterbalance China while the latter has maintained ambivalence over this issue.

The Japanese press has mostly highlighted the economic benefits of stronger Japan-India relations in its editorials and analysis. At times, though, they have seen this relationship in the context of China. For example the *Japan Times* in one of its editorials opines that "by deepening ties with India, Japan can counter China, which is trying to increase its maritime influence, and can reduce the risk of excessive economic reliance on China." However, the leading Japanese daily asks the government not to antagonise China. It adds that "Japan must act carefully to avoid antagonising China."[62] *The Asahi Shimbun* is of the view that "India has been expanding military exchanges with the United States, Australia and Southeast Asian countries. They all have a common objective to keep China in check." Against this context, *The Asahi Shimbun* opined that "intensifying bilateral relations to counter China is risky."[63] On the other hand, the *Yomiuri Shimbun* asserts that "India is an important partner for Japan in the regional cooperative framework centered on the East Asia Summit." Given this context, it asks Japan to "call on India to play constructive roles that fit its new status as a major power."[64] *The Yomiuri Shimbun* states that "Japan faces a direct threat from China's maritime expansion in the East China Sea, while India is exposed to a similar threat in the Indian Ocean." The editorial asks Japan and India "to actively utilise vice-ministerial talks between their foreign and defence ministries, to discuss common strategy regarding China, such as measures to ensure the safety of sea lanes." *The Yomiuri Shimbun* calls on India and Japan to widen their cooperation to achieve this goal:

> The two countries also need to seek partnerships with the United States, and then with the Southeast Asian countries that stand at the forefront of friction with China. To realise this goal, Japan and India, regional powers in Asia, must further deepen bilateral relations.[65]

Conclusion

The analyses in this chapter suggest that although the leaders of the Asian democracies espouse the idealism of the so-called value-based order, a significant gap remains among them over how to forge this order. From the analyses above it is apparent that both Indian and Japanese leaders have sounded positive on forming a rule-based order to check China's assertive behaviour; however, they have not hesitated to embrace China wherever their national interests converged with those of Beijing. For example, Tokyo denounces China's aggressive behaviour but, when it comes to restraining Pyongyang, it has been amenable to the idea that Beijing should play an influential role in the Six-party Talks.[66] Japan has also opened up negotiations with North Korea and eased sanctions on the country, despite the US and South Korea urging Japan not to do so. These tendencies have weakened Japan's campaign for a "rule based" and "value based" order in the region.[67]

Secondly, the talks on forming a new architecture/order remain heavily focussed on security, especially maritime security. A number of other factors, including the economic order, the global nuclear order, and climate change have not been taken into account.[68] These are the factors that act as intervening variables and hinder India and Japan's goals in forging a rule based order. These are issues on which states, especially India and Japan, are not necessarily in accord with each other. While Japan finds itself comfortable with the European—and US-led economic order, India is uncomfortable with this order. India argues that Western-led financial institutions based on the Breton Woods system do not represent the changing realities of the present economic system. India wants more say in these financial institutions commensurate with its present economic status. China, more or less, has similar grievances with the international financial systems and wants more say in the decision-making process. China has been taking various steps to challenge the existing financial order by mooting the idea of establishing a BRICS bank and the Asian Infrastructure Investment Bank (AIIB). Apparently, this is the reason that, rather than allying with Japan on the issue of the AIIB, New Delhi has gone with Beijing to forge a new alternative economic order. India has joined the China-led AIIB as a founding member but Japan has gone with the US and opted not to join the Bank. Japan argues that the AIIB's loan disbursement mechanism is opaque while that of the ADB is very transparent, and that the AIIB may be "nothing more than a policy instrument of the Communist regime." Moreover, a number of Japanese strategic thinkers consider the AIIB to be an institution that will help establish "China's regional hegemony."[69]

Furthermore, Japan is of the view that the AIIB is competing with existing lending banks, including the Asian Development Bank (ADB) led by Japan. On the other hand, India thinks that the AIIB is not necessarily a rival to the Japan-led ADB and that in fact it can complement the ADB. It seems that India has accepted China's invitation to join the AIIB as a founding member to gain more say in forging a new financial order in the region as well as an acknowledgement of its growing economic stature.

While India and Japan talk about democratic ideals to achieve a rule-based order in Asia, their differing national interests sometimes compel them to take different steps and they thus have to compromise their own ideals giving preference to their own national interests. Although India and Japan take an identical position on United Nations Security Council reform and the issue of freedom of navigation and over-flight bind them together, their national interests differ on various key issues, including the nuclear order, climate change and the emerging economic architecture. Therefore, the two Asian democracies should bridge their perceptions over various global and regional issues in order to forge a strongly-knit rule-based order.

It may be noted that at present Japan and India are at different levels in their economic development. While Japan is a developed country, India is still a developing economy. The gap between them over different global issues will persist until they reach the same level of economic development. Japan should help India, by way of sharing key technologies and providing economic and infrastructure aid, to achieve parity with the developed world. Undoubtedly, India is aligning with major powers, and its global outlook has substantially changed in the post-Cold War period. It is willing to embrace and respond to the changing global order but, at the same time, it is seeking greater participation and say in shaping the emerging global order. It is seeking membership in various forums, including the Asia-Pacific Economic Community, the Nuclear Supplier Group, the Wassenar Group, etc. It is also asking for a greater voice in various global financial institutions commensurate with its economic power. Japan has made commitments to bring India on the table in these bodies in its joint statements issued after summit level meeting at Prime Ministerial levels and it must be welcomed. However, it should move beyond commitment and should take a leading and supporting role to facilitate India's entry into these bodies and organisations. India's participation in these institutions will help it gain greater participation and say in shaping the emerging global order, paving the way for a greater partnership between Japan and India on various global and regional issues.

END NOTES

1. "Joint Statement Towards India-Japan Strategic and Global Partnership," December 15, 2006, available at http://meaindia.nic.in/mystart.php?id=100512192 (Accessed on November 1, 2015)
2. The previous version of this chapter was published at the JIIA website in November 2015. The author thanks Professor Marie Izuyama for her useful insights and her comments on the previous draft. This Chapter has been modified and the developments after November 2015 have also been incorporated.
3. John J. Mearsheimer, a professor of political science at the University of Chicago argues that message—that China is a benign power—will be drowned out by China's

behaviour, which will be much more oriented towards altering the status quo, and by military force, if necessary. Full interview of Mearsheimer to *Nikkei Asia Review* is available at http://asia.nikkei.com/Politics-Economy/International-Relations/US-China-heading-toward-face-off-says-Mearsheimer (Accessed on November 1, 2015)

4. This definition was adopted in the concept note of a seminar held in November 2014 organised by the School Of International Studies, Jawaharlal Nehru University, New Delhi on the theme of "India in the Emerging Global Order: Political, Strategic and Economic Dynamics."
5. "Arc of Freedom and Prosperity: Japan's Expanding Diplomatic Horizon," Speech by Taro Aso, Foreign Minister of Japan, delivered at the Japan Institute of International Affairs, on November 30, 2006; speech available at http://www.mofa.go.jp/announce/fm/aso/speech0611.html (Accessed on November 3, 2015).
6. Ibid.
7. "Confluence of Two Seas," Speech by Shinzo Abe, Prime Minister of Japan at the Parliament of the Republic of India, Ministry of Foreign Affairs, Government of Japan, August 22, 2007.
8. Shinzo Abe, "Asia's Democratic Security Diamond," *Project Syndicate*, December 27, 2012.
9. National Security Strategy, *Ministry of Foreign Affairs*, Government of Japan, 2013, p.5.
10. For details please refer to Shinzo Abe's keynote address at the IISS Shangrila Dialogue, 2014, available online athttps://www.iiss.org/en/events/shangri%20la%20dialogue/archive/2014-c20c/opening-remarks-and-keynote-address-b0b2/keynote-address-shinzo-abe-a787 (Accessed on November 3, 2015).
11. Shinzo Abe, "Towards an Alliance of Hope," *Project Syndicate/The Japan Times*, May 12, 2015.
12. Highlight of Prime Minister's address at the Annual Conclave of Indian Ambassadors/High Commissioners abroad in New Delhi; full speech of Prime Minister Manmohan Singh is available at http://www.mea.gov.in/Speeches-Statements.htm?dtl/22428/Highlights+of+Prime+Ministers+address+at+the+Annual+Conclave+of+Indian+AmbassadorsHigh+ Commissioners+ abroad+in+New+Delhi (Accessed on November 4, 2015).
13. Ibid.
14. Prime Minister's address to Japan-India Association, Japan-India Parliamentary Friendship League and International Friendship Exchange Council; full text of Manmohan Singh's speech is available at http://www.mea.gov.in/Speeches-Statements.htm?dtl/21754/Prime+Ministers+address+to+JapanIndia+ Association + JapanIndia + Parliamentary+ Friendship+ League+ and+International+Friendship+Exchange+Council (Accessed on November 4, 2015).
15. Ibid.
16. Quoted in Bruce Einhorn, "Visiting Japan, India's Modi pokes at China," Bloomberg, September 2, 2014, available online at http://www.bloomberg.com/bw/articles/2014-09-02/visiting-japan-indias-modi-pokes-at-china (Accessed on November 5, 2015).

17. "Japan India vision 2025 Special Strategic and Global Partnership Working Together for Peace and Prosperity of the Indo-Pacific region and the World" (joint statement), Ministry of Foreign Affairs, Government of Japan, December 12, 2015, available at http://www.mofa.go.jp/s_sa/sw/in/page3e_000432.html (Accessed on December 13, 2015).
18. Hua Chunying of the Chinese Ministry of Foreign Affairs quoted in Graham Webster, "South China Sea: What 12 nautical miles really means," *The Japan Times*, October 18, 2015.
19. "Japan, US, South Korea recognizes the South China ruling legality," *Yomiuri Shimbun*, July 15, 2016.
20. "Statement on Award of Arbitral Tribunal on South China Sea Under Annexure VII of UNCLOS," Ministry of External Affairs, Government of India, July 12, 2016, full text available at http://www.mea.gov.in/press-releases.htm?dtl/27019/Statement_on_Award_of_Arbitral_Tribunal_on_South_China_Sea_Under_Annexure_VII_of_UNCLOS (Accessed on November 5, 2015).
21. The term architecture and order has been used by Indian strategic thinkers interchangeably.
22. Brahama Chellaney, "Japan, India: Natural allies," *The Japan Times*, August 16, 2007.
23. K Shankar Bajpai, "Japan, India and the balance of power," *The Hindu*, January 27, 2014.
24. C. Raja Mohan, "Talking Tokyo," *The Indian Express*, May 27, 2013.
25. Harsh V. Pant, "Turning towards Tokyo," *Business Standards*, January 1, 2012.
26. Rahul K. Bhonsle, "Indo-Japan Relations: Strategic Realignment in Asia," *News Blaze*, January 1, 2007.
27. Rajeev Sharma, "How Japan should tackle China's 'peaceful' rise," *The Asahi Shimbun*, June 21, 2010.
28. Rajesh Rajagopalan, "India needs to deftly deal with multiple strategic partners, including China," *The Economic Times*, September 18, 2014.
29. Ibid.
30. Yoshiko Sakurai, quoted in Takenori Horimoto, "Japan-India rapprochement and its future issues," Japan Institute of International Affairs, Tokyo, 2016.
31. Yoriko Koike, "To kowtow or cooperate in Asia," *The Japan Times*, November 29, 2012.
32. Shirashi Takashi, "Crafting Japan's Asia Policy in a Multipolar World," *Japan Echo*, August 2008, p.29.
33. Ibid. Shirashi offered similar views on these issues during an interview with the author on January 7, 2015.
34. Author's interview with Tomohiko Taniguchi, January 16, 2015.
35. Siddharth Varadarajan, "Perils of Three-way Security Cooperation," *The Hindu*, February 14, 2006.
36. Ibid.
37. Ibid.

38. Ibid.
39. Siddharth Varadarajan, "Calibrating India's term of engagement with Japan," *Business Standards*, August 30, 2014.
40. Sunil Khilnani, et al., "Non-Alignment 2.0:A Foreign and Strategic Policy for India in the 21st Century," Center for Policy Research, New Delhi, 2012, available online at http://www.cprindia.org/sites/default/files/working_papers/NonAlignment%202.0_1.pdf. (Accessed on November 5, 2015).
41. Srinath Raghavan, "China is most important for India, Japan," *The Economic Times*, October 29, 2010.
42. Srinath Raghavan, "Why China and Japan are wooing India," *The Business Line*, May 31, 2013.
43. Ibid.
44. Ramesh Thakur, "Asia's strategic triangle: China, Japan and India," *The Hindu*, September 14, 2007.
45. Ibid.
46. Atul Aneja, "In China, going beyond optics," *The Hindu*, May 14, 2015.
47. Ibid.
48. Yoichi Funabashi, "Build strong Japan, India ties without taking aim on China," *The Japan Times*, August 14, 2014.
49. Ibid
50. Author's interview with Yoichi Funabashi, January 23, 2015, Tokyo, Japan.
51. Yoichi Funabashi, "Japan needs geopolitical skills," *The Japan Times*, April 15, 2015.
52. Author's interview with Norio Kondo, December 30, 2014.
53. "Love in Tokyo," *The Hindu*, May 31, 2013.
54. Cautious cooperation with Japan, *The Hindu*, December 14, 2015.
55. Ibid.
56. "Natural partners: Closer relations with Japan are a strategic must," *Business Standards*, May 29, 2013.
57. "Stronger together," *The Indian Express*, December 15, 2015.
58. "Indo-Japan ties no threat to China," *The Asian Age*, January 28, 2014.
59. "India-Japan relations: Ties that ensures stability in Asia," *The Hindustan Times*, December 15, 2015.
60. "Ugte Suraj Kesath (with the rising sun)," *Navbharat Times*, Hindi Daily, May 29, 2013.
61. "Japan se Dosti (Friendship with Japan)," *Hindustan*, May 30, 2013.
62. "Bolstering Japan-India ties," *The Japan Times*, January 21, 2012.
63. "Japan-India relations aimed at countering China" (analysis), *The Asahi Shimbun*, December 29, 2011.
64. "Japan should cement ties with new big power India," *The Yomiuri Shimbun*, December 29, 2009.
65. "Japan-India must deepen security, economic ties," *The Yomiuri Shimbun*, October 26, 2010.

66. Author's interview with Yasushi Watanabe, Professor, Keio University, Japan on January 13, 2015 at International House, Tokyo.
67. Ibid.
68. Because of paucity of space in this chapter, India and Japan's stance on these issues have not been analysed here.
69. Masahiro Matsumura, "The AIIB has little to offer to Japan and the US," *The Japan Times*, May 20, 2015.

7

India-Japan Nuclear Cooperation: Between Economic Gains and Ideal Principles

Introduction

Nuclear issue has been one of the thorny issues in India-Japan relations. Although they have signed a civil nuclear cooperation agreement in 2016, they took longer time than expected to ink the deal. The conclusion of the deal was delayed mainly because of their differing perceptions on the global nuclear order and the nuclear technology regime. Although Japan stands for a nuclear free world, by joining the US led nuclear umbrella it has accepted the legitimacy of the possession of nuclear weapons by P-5 countries.[1] India on the other hand, considers this global nuclear order discriminatory as it allows the possession of nuclear weapons to a selected number of countries while denying the same privilege to others.[2] India argues for a total abolition of the nuclear weapon and therefore has not signed the Nuclear non-Proliferation Treaty (NPT). Similarly, on the issue of generating nuclear energy, Japan and a section of its anti-nuclear lobbies had been arguing that the nuclear technology to generate energy should be given to only those countries who are signatory to the NPT. After rounds of hectic parleys between India and Japan, Tokyo finally gave its nod to allow access to its nuclear technology and has finalized the deal in November 2016.

Various factors can be attributed to Japan's slow approach that delayed the process of granting access to India of its nuclear technology. To understand these factors, it is important to understand how Japan and its domestic constituencies have reacted to India's nuclear programmes and what are their concerns regarding India-Japan nuclear cooperation? This Chapter against this context, attempts to examine the issue and analyses various pull and push factors which helped determine the fate of nuclear cooperation agreement between the two countries.

India's Nuclear Program: Reactions and Response from Different Japanese Constituencies

As has been discussed in Chapter 3, both Japan and India came together and pledged to eliminate weapons of mass destructions including nuclear weapons. The joint statements signed between Nehru and his Japanese counterpart and later between Indira Gandhi and her Japanese counterpart indicate that the nuclear weapons elimination was one of the key agenda of India-Japan cooperation. But when India conducted its nuclear test in 1974, without taking Japan into confidence, it came as a shock and surprise for Japan. Following the nuclear test, Japan criticized India for the test and almost all the political parties also joined the government in condemning New Delhi for the act. The people from Hiroshima and Nagasaki, the two cities on which nuclear bomb was dropped during the World War II, also reacted harshly. While the former's municipality sent a telegram to Prime Minister Indira Gandhi expressing its shock and anger; the later lodged a protest to Indian embassy in Tokyo.[3] In a similarly response, Japan protested India's 1998 nuclear test. Its response can be analysed at three different levels, i) Japanese government condemned the test and withdrew its ambassador, ii) it lobbied internationally to stop nuclear proliferation and tried to put pressure on India to sign the NPT, and iii) Japanese NGOs and civil society protested India and Pakistan's move to conduct the nuclear test.

In a harsher response to India's nuclear test in 1998, Tokyo froze new grants and suspended yen loans to India. It also withdrew its offer to host the annual donors' conference; India Development Forum (IDF).[4]

However, it did not suspend humanitarian aid and grant assistance for grass root projects. Japan's reactions to these tests was termed "unusually harsh" within New Delhi's strategic circles.[5] Satu P. Limaye, an Asian expert, argues that the measures adopted by the Japanese government on India were harsher than those imposed on China following its five nuclear tests in 1996. In China's case, Japan suspended only grant aid after serious intra-governmental debate, and yen loans to Beijing were unaffected.[6] But why Japan's reaction to Indian nuclear test was so harsh? This answer can be found in J.N. Dixit's observations. Dixit, India's top envoy, who visited Tokyo to brief Japanese officials about the circumstances under which New Delhi took decision to conduct the Pokhran test, opines that "the impression I got was of a profound dichotomy affecting Japan's attitude towards India. On the one hand, there's a deeply-felt emotional and moral objection to India's nuclear weaponisation rooted in their experience and memories of the Hiroshima-Nagasaki bombings."[7]

Dixit further added that "on the other hand, there are genuine strategic and security apprehensions that the horizontal proliferation of nuclear weapons is likely to become an incremental phenomenon, especially in the Asian region, and can pose a general threat to security and stability in Asia. North Korea getting out of control, an assertive China, ...the possibilities of Indo-Pak nuclear confrontation on Kashmir, and the likelihood of countries like Iraq and Iran acquiring nuclear weapons, all worry Japan."[8] An Indian diplomat then based in Japan, however, in an article on Japan's reaction following Pokhran II opined that "the stark reality of 1998 was that India was less relevant to Japan's economy, its security, culture, even leisure and entertainment, than say the European Union."[9] He also notes that bilateral relations were at the minimal level both economically and culturally that these were "not a significant restraining factor as Japan's leaders contemplated a response to Pokhran II. In the event, Japanese reaction to the Indian nuclear tests was surprisingly swift and exceptionally harsh."[10] Dixit, on the other hand, noted a perceptible change in Japanese mind as they realized that Japanese reactions were "excessive" and added that:

> There is, however, a realisation that Japan's punitive political and economic responses to the Indian nuclear tests were perhaps excessive. This realisation is underpinned by the fact that while the other

> important powers have resumed dialogue with India in one form or another, Japan for some time has remained stuck in its political posture towards India.[11]

It may be noted that when India conducted 1998 Pokhran nuclear test, Japan was a non-permanent member of the United Nations Security Council (UNSC). Using this international body, Japan called for an emergency meeting following India and Pakistan's nuclear tests. It introduced a resolution in the UNSC which was co-sponsored by Sweden and Costa Rica. The resolution condemned the test and demanded that India and Pakistan join the NPT regime. The UNSC unanimously adopted this resolution. At the same time, Japan urged P-5 nuclear capable countries as well as G-8 countries to take strong interest in resolving root causes for the tension between India and Pakistan.[12] Japanese Prime Minister Ryotaro Hashmito called for the need of international community to "take strong interest in the root causes for the tensions between India and Pakistan, including Kashmir, and consider how to maintain the security of the South Asia region."[13] However, the P-5 and G-8 countries did not evince much interest in Japan's initiatives and did not impose sanctions on India and Pakistan. Japan was deeply dissatisfied by the response of the international community. A publication by then Japan Defense Agency (presently Ministry of Defense) argued, "In the case of the recent nuclear tests by India and Pakistan, the United Kingdom, France, and Russia opposed, or have taken a negative attitude toward, sanctions from the outset, and the Security Council was thus prevented from even taking up the issue on the agenda. Such an attitude of the Security Council, a body that bears the primary responsibility to ensure peace and security of the international community, is a matter of debate."[14] The Japanese civil society also protested the test by India and Pakistan launching protests demonstrations especially in Nagasaki and Hiroshima. They pressurised the Ministry of Foreign Affairs to mobilise opinions to stop nuclear proliferation.

Japanese think tanks also lobbied with the international think tanks to create a wider consensus to stop proliferation of nuclear weapons. The Institute of International Policy Studies (IIPS), a Tokyo based think tank, in collaboration of Adenauer Foundation presented following points to stop nuclear proliferation after nuclear tests by India and Pakistan:

- No first use of nuclear weapons by any and all nuclear weapon states (NWS).
- Governments of nuclear weapon states should pledge not to use nuclear weapons against non-nuclear weapon states.
- All nuclear weapon states should sign and ratify the Nuclear Non-Proliferation Treaty (NPT) and the Comprehensive Test Ban Treaty (CTBT).
- All states should agree on reduction in the number of nuclear weapons, implementation of nuclear disarmament measures, the eventual elimination of all nuclear weapons, and the immediate implementation of START.[15]

Later, the IIPS adopted another proposal known as Nakasone Initiative and suggested ways to check the proliferation of the nuclear weapons. Commenting on the test conducted by two South Asian countries, the Nakasone Proposal argued that "The nuclear tests conducted by India and Pakistan in May 1998 took the somewhat complacent post-CTBT (Comprehensive Test Ban Treaty) world with surprise, and reminded the international community of the importance of nuclear non-proliferation in South Asia as well as in the rest of the Third World."[16] It argued that "It is important to place international safeguards on peaceful nuclear fuel cycles in order to avoid diversion for military purposes, but it is equally important to place similar safeguards on military fuel cycles, to avoid any leakage."[17]

With special reference to India and Pakistan, Nakasone proposal argued that "It may be worthwhile to try to bring India and Pakistan into the CTBT with a firm pledge not to carry out any more nuclear tests and to cooperate in furthering the international non-proliferation regime. They should also pledge to abide strictly by the London Guidelines, the Missile Technology Control Regime (MTCR), and the Wassenar Arrangements, as may be appropriate."[18]

The Japanese government, taking cognizance of demands made by its think tank and influential strategic thinkers, took concerted efforts to raise the issue of nuclear non-proliferation and asked for sanctions against those who break these norms. But Japan failed to garner enough support in the international forum. Nakasone, who had held series of such seminars and deliberations, in and outside Tokyo was obviously disappointed. In an article published in *Japan Echo,* he opined that "Japan responded [to the tests] by trying to have a United Nations resolution passed. But behind the scenes Russia was supporting India, and similarly China was supporting Pakistan. The United States, meanwhile, seemed to take a low-key approach to the UN resolution; the Americans felt that the balance of power among China, India, and Pakistan was working to prevent any of the countries from pursuing expansionist ambitions. The resolution that was finally adopted was vague and had no teeth."[19]

The Pokhran Test and its Impact on India-Japan Relations

Obviously, following Pokhran test, relations between India and Japan touched the lowest ebb. Indian Diplomat Muchkund Dubey argues that "the initiative taken by Japan both unilaterally and jointly with other major powers caused great deal of disquiet and consternation in India and severely strained Indo-Japan relations."[20] But soon, Japan realised that India cannot be "ignored for a long as it is a big country in Asia."[21] Meanwhile, India was also making efforts to put the bilateral ties back on track. The then Foreign Minister Jaswant Singh visited Japan in December 1999 which was followed by a visit by Defence Minister George Fernandes in January 2000. These efforts resulted in melting of ice between India and Japan.

Japan's Commitment to Forge a Nuclear Cooperation with India

Perceptible change in Japan's foreign policy initiative was noticed during Prime Minister Yoshiro Mori's visit to New Delhi in 2000. Mori's visit paved way for a global and strategic partnership signed between the two countries in 2006. Interestingly, in the same year India and Japan agreed in their joint statement that "nuclear energy can play an important role as a safe, sustainable and non-polluting source of energy." The Joint statement signed by Japanese Prime Minister Shinzo Abe and his Indian counterpart Manmohan Singh made a commitment to enhance civil nuclear energy cooperation "through constructive approaches under appropriate IAEA safeguards."[22] However, they kept it vague whether they will go for a civil nuclear cooperation agreement. There remained a basic disagreement on the approaches of the two counties. Japan, looked the nuclear cooperation purely from strategic angle, while India viewed it from an economic perspective and considered Japan's approval of a nuclear deal important for going ahead with the installation of nuclear power plants within the country. This is primarily because Japanese companies enjoy a monopoly over certain key components including "reactor vessels" required for nuclear reactors.[23]

Meanwhile, India had signed agreements with General Electrics, Areva SA and Westinghouse to set up nuclear power plants following the Indo-US nuclear deal and the waiver granted by the Nuclear Suppliers Group to pursue its civil nuclear programme in 2008. In all these companies, Japanese companies have major stakes. Japan's reluctance to sign the nuclear cooperation until November 2016 with India, has delayed these companies nuclear reactor installation plans. India at that time wanted to explore various means and resources including the nuclear energy to meet its energy requirements. Statistics suggest that India needs 3128 Trillion Watt hours of electricity annually to sustain its economic growth.[24] India considers nuclear energy as one of the important components of its energy mix. At present, share of nuclear energy in India's "energy mix" is roughly 2 percent. Coal and oil remains major contributor in India's energy mix. 42 percent of India's total energy comes from coal and 24 percent from oil. As a result, carbon emission also remains high. To cut the carbon emission and to achieve self-sufficiency in energy, India wants to set up another 20 nuclear reactors in near future with a target of producing 20,000 Megawatt nuclear energy by 2020. Therefore, India looked at Japan for nuclear energy cooperation to meet its energy demands.

Although India and Japan took different approaches on the nuclear order and nuclear technology regime and failed to bridge their differences over these issues, they made some headway as a result of sustained dialogue at the level of political leadership. The then Foreign Minister of Japan, Katsuya Okada, during his New Delhi visit in 2010 agreed to launch a negotiation on nuclear agreement. Okada stated that "the decision to launch the negotiation for the nuclear cooperation agreement was probably one of the toughest decisions that I had to make as Foreign Minister."[25] Japan took almost four years to move from commitment to negotiation stage. As pointed previously, Japan showed its willingness to cooperate in nuclear energy field in 2006. But it took almost a decade to sign the deal. To understand why Japan took longer time than expected and what were the factors that acted as a drag in signing the deal, it is important to analyse various push and pull factors. The following section identifies and discusses those factors in details.

India-Japan Nuclear Cooperation: The Push Factors

There has been sustained pressure on Tokyo from certain policy circles to go for the nuclear deal with India. The Japan Forum for International Relations, a leading Japanese think tank, was the first to underscore the need for nuclear cooperation with India. In a 2007 policy recommendation, the think tank suggested to the Japanese government to forge an agreement with India. It argued:

> ...because of the need to reduce global warming, India will presumably want to depend much more heavily on nuclear power in the future. Japan's technology and expertise in generating and ensuring the safety of nuclear power is among the best in the world, so it is in an excellent position to cooperate with India in these areas.[26]

To allay Tokyo's nuclear proliferation concerns, the think tank argued:

> ...even though India developed nuclear weaponry..., it has always called for global nuclear disarmament, it has strongly maintained policies promoting nuclear non-proliferation and it has not abandoned those policies even after it had acquired a nuclear force. For these reasons we call upon the Japanese government to cooperate with India on this issue...[27]

Influential academicians in Japan also argued for forging cooperation with India in nuclear technology trade and argued that Japan should approach nuclear cooperation with India looking at a long term strategic perspective. For example, Takashi Shiraishi, the President of Institute for Developing Economies as well as Graduate Institute of Policy Studies, in an article published in 2008, opined that "Japan has yet to make a move in this direction [signing a civil nuclear cooperation with India] owing to concerns about India's status vis-à-vis the Nuclear Proliferation Treaty." He opines that India has the potential to develop into an "economic Power" and suggests Japan to engage India from "a long term strategic perspective." He believes a key means of the long term perspective would be forging "nuclear energy cooperation" with India.[28] He is also of the view that Nuclear Cooperation would be great enabler in enhancing strategic partnership with India.[29]

The push to forge a nuclear cooperation also came from Ministry of Economy, Trade and Industry (METI) and its policy to export nuclear technology for Japan's economic revival. It may be noted that the Japanese government under the supervision of METI has set up International Nuclear Energy Development of Japan Co. (JINED) with an aim to form a centralized platform to increase Japan's competitiveness in winning contracts for nuclear power projects overseas. This enterprise is eyeing the nuclear energy potentials of UAE, Jordan, Saudi Arabia and India. Indian nuclear energy market alone offers US Dollar 150 billion. Therefore, they were continuously pushing their case arguing to swiftly conclude the deal with India.

The support to the deal also came from the *Yomiuri Daily* which had been advocating for not abandoning the Japanese nuclear industry. The daily wrote in its editorial, after Noda's visit to India, that "we think it appropriate that the two leaders also agreed to make more efforts toward an agreement on peaceful nuclear energy cooperation between the two countries."[30]

People in the Japanese establishments were also amenable to the idea of nuclear technology trade with India but had been treading very cautiously owing to the concerns expressed by its nuclear allergic public, majority of whom remained unaware of India's "unilateral moratorium on nuclear testing." To assuage their concerns, Japan had been asking India to include a clause in the pact: "Tokyo would halt nuclear energy cooperation if New Delhi conducts a nuclear test." They continued with this demand in their negotiations till 2015 delaying the prospect of the deal. But a section of the Japanese trade lobby was worried that prolongation of negotiation may lead to a supply chain not dependent on Japan. A Japanese media report stated that "Japan Steel Works Limited produces nearly 80 percent of global supplies of forged nuclear reactor parts."[31] Since General Electrics and Areva SA also depend on Japanese components, they cannot start new nuclear power generation projects they have bagged contract for setting up nuclear reactors in India. So Japan had "considerable leverage" on Indian civil nuclear program. However, a group of Japanese, especially from the nuclear industry, expressed unease that more suppliers would surface in the future and there will be "global supply chain without Japanese makers"[32] which would put Japanese nuclear power industry in a disadvantageous position. Therefore, they were pressurizing Japanese government not to prolong the negotiation with India further and seize the opportunity as soon as possible.

India-Japan Nuclear Cooperation: The Pull Factors

The obstacle to sign the deal with India was never posed by the Japanese government, as it was viewed in New Delhi prior to signing the deal and the stalemate that continued over the contents of the agreement. In fact the Japanese government, like any other government, supported by its trade lobbies wanted to sign the nuclear deal to earn economic dividend offered by huge Indian nuclear market estimated to be over 150 billion US Dollar. But it was proceeding cautiously owing to the concerns expressed by its anti-nuclear lobby supported by a large number of people including the *Hibakushas* (victim of Hiroshima and Nagasaki atomic bomb radiation). A section of the Japanese domestic constituency remains opposed to government policy of nuclear technology trade. This constituency can be divided into two broader trends of thinking; the one which opposes Japan's nuclear technology trade with countries which has not signed the NPT. However, this constituency is not India centric. But whenever the issue of nuclear technology trade with India came to the fore, this constituency considered India among the first state to test nuclear weapons after the institutionalization of the NPT in 1970s and thus argued that Japan should not sign the nuclear accord with India till it joins the NPT.[33] The second strand of thinking which emerged following Fukushima nuclear disaster likens nuclear reactor trade as "selling of opium"[34] to other countries. People associating themselves with this trend of thinking had been arguing that the export of this technology will likely bring similar disaster in the host countries.[35] Domestically, they remained opposed to reactivation of existing nuclear reactors and have held a number of protests calling the government to phase out nuclear technology. Put together, both these trends of thinking constituted a large electorate and a political party could not ignore their concerns while deciding its foreign and economic policy priorities. This was an apparent reason for Japanese establishment for treading cautiously on a nuclear cooperation deal with India.

To assuage the concerns of the anti-nuclear domestic constituencies, the previous Democratic Party of Japan (DPJ) which started negotiation with the then UPA government in 2010 over a prospective nuclear accord had been asking a specific nullification clause in the final agreement.[36] It had asked India to include a clause in the deal saying that Japan will cancel the nuclear cooperation agreement with India if the latter conducts nuclear tests in future. India reminded Japan that it already has adopted a moratorium on nuclear testing in 2008.

The media also joined the anti-nuclear lobbies in opposing the nuclear technology trade with India and openly expressed concerns about the deal. Japanese leading dailies which help construct opinion on certain issues had been consistently asking the Japanese government to proceed cautiously over the issue of nuclear cooperation with India. *The Japan Times*, *The Asahi Shimbun* and the *Mainichi Daily* have not approved the idea of a nuclear deal with India. When the Japanese administration started negotiation with India, the *Japan Times* in one of its editorial opined that "Japan, which has advocated for a nuclear weapons-free world ... has started talks with India on a pact to allow India to import civilian nuclear technology and equipment from Japan."[37] The daily suggested that "before agreeing to civilian nuclear cooperation...Japan should impose strict conditions on India so that Japan's nuclear technology does not proliferate to other countries and thus the NPT regime is not undermined."[38] Similarly, the *Asahi Shimbun* argued:

> We must not forget that lax export controls are responsible for nuclear proliferation to India, Pakistan and North Korea. Exporting nuclear power plants is big business, and it can also help curb global warming. But is it right to develop this business at the price of damaging the NPT?[39]

The *Mainichi* editorialised that "Japan should stop working with India on atomic energy if it conducts nuke test."[40] All these media organizations have expressed similar opinion in their latter editorials also. And when Japan signed a Memorandum of Understanding (MOU) with India in December 2015 to look at the technicalities of a prospective nuclear deal, Japanese media and the anti-nuclear bodies renewed their demand following the MOU by asking the government not to give concessions to India. The Hiroshima and Nagasaki Mayors in their joint statement demanded Abe government to "suspend" negotiations to conclude nuclear agreement with India noting that "this agreement raises serious concerns about nuclear materials and nuclear-related technology and equipment being diverted toward nuclear weapons development."[41] The statement emphasized that the nuclear agreement with a non-NPT country would tantamount to "hollowing out of the NPT regime." Similarly, the leading dailies of Japan in their editorials on a prospective India-Japan nuclear deal have expressed their reservations.

The *Asahi Shimbun*, which had written a series of editorials raising concerns on India-Japan nuclear agreement in the past few years, in an editorial following the MOU called this development as an "act of folly" and noted that signing the deal would further "emasculate the nonproliferation regime."[42] It also opined that following this agreement it would become difficult to explain to "North Korea and Iran,... why we are dealing differently with India. We could lose our convincing power for dissuading other nations from following in their footsteps."[43] The *Mainichi Daily* stated that that Japanese government "must not give tacit approval to India's possession of nuclear arms or facilitate nuclear proliferation."[44] The *Japan Times* in its editorial termed this deal "risky" noting that "a major problem with the planned pact is that Japan would allow India to reprocess nuclear fuel burned in a plant built with Japanese components and materials."[45] It urged government of Japan to take "utmost efforts" to stop India from "reinforcing its nuclear arsenal by taking advantage of this pact."[46] The *Yomiuri Daily* was the lone voice among the Japanese English media which has been supportive of conclusion of a nuclear agreement with India to strengthen the strategic partnership. However, in the editorial post Abe's India visit, the Daily noted that the "accord should limit the cooperation to solely peaceful purposes, while a clear-cut brake should be put in place to prevent the fruits of the cooperation from being applied militarily."[47] Like its other counterpart, this media group also urged Japan to persuade India to join the NPT. It opined; It is important for Japan to persistently urge India to join an international framework of nuclear nonproliferation and to promote nuclear disarmament.[48]

India-Japan Memorandum on Nuclear Cooperation 2015

As a result of repeated demand on Japan to sign a nuclear deal with India by the Indian leadership and its trade lobbies, Japan signed a Memorandum on Nuclear Cooperation with India during Prime Minister Shinzo Abe's New Delhi visit in December 2015.[49] Apart from the domestic trade lobbies, external factors also acted as a pressure on the government of Japan. It may be noted that after the Indo-US nuclear deal signed in 2006, and thereby waiver granted to India by the Nuclear Supplier Group (NSG) to undertake nuclear technology trade outside the Nuclear non-Proliferation Treaty regime, a number of countries considering their business interests in Indian nuclear market had signed the similar deals with New Delhi one after the other in line with the Indo-US nuclear deal. Australia and Japan remained cautious to sign the deal with India despite the waiver granted by the NSG and were of the view that doing so would undermine the NPT regime.

In a significant departure from its long held policy, Australia announced in 2014 that it will sign a nuclear agreement with India with which it has established a relationship of "trust." This prompted the people in Delhi's strategic circles to conclude that despite the elevation of India-Japan strategic partnership to a "special strategic partnership" the 'trust' in the bilateral partnership is still missing. Echoing similar concerns, Yasukuni Enoki, a former Japanese ambassador, who served in Japanese embassy in Delhi also termed the ongoing stalemate over nuclear issue between India and Japan as a "bone stuck in the throat"[50] implying that it will hamper overall strategic partnership between the two Asian countries. The understanding reached between Japanese and Indian leadership in December 2015 to sign the civil nuclear cooperation agreement after finalizing the "technical details"[51] was apparently aimed at allaying the deepening concerns of an existing "trust deficit" over the nuclear issue between the two countries' political leadership.

India-Japan Nuclear Agreement 2016: Deconstructing the Texts

As has been mentioned above, India-Japan in their joint statement in 2006 signed between Japanese Prime Minister Abe and his Indian counterpart Manmohan Singh noted the importance of nuclear energy "as a safe, sustainable and non-polluting source of energy." It seems, they deliberately kept the meaning vague and did not specify that they are trying to harness each others' potential to forge a nuclear cooperation. The same sentence has appeared in the opening paragraph of India-Japan nuclear agreement signed by Indian Foreign Secretary S. Jaishankar and his Japanese counterpart Kenji Hiramatsu in November 2016 during Prime Minister Modi's visit to Tokyo. In nutshell, it can be said that the commitment to forge nuclear cooperation in 2006 between Abe and Singh reach to a logical conclusion during summit level talk between Abe and Modi. The nuclear agreement, however, attaches a number of conditions on the contracting parties. In other words, Japan has kept options open to "terminate" the agreement. To understand the texts of the agreement one needs to deconstruct two separate documents signed between Amandeep Gill and Osuga Takeshi and S. Jaishankar and Kenji Hiramatsu.

A separate "Note on Views and Understanding" signed between India and Japan suggest that Japan has considered the statement made by Pranab Mukherjee, the then External Affairs Minister in Indian Parliament on September 5, 2008 as a basis to sign the nuclear deal. The September 5, 2008 statement make commitment on "unilateral moratorium on nuclear testing" and states that India will remain firm on its "no-first-use of nuclear weapons."[52] The Note states that the September 5 statement "constitutes and essential basis for cooperation between the states under the Agreement."[53] The document also notes that "India reiterates the September 5 statement."[54] And if India violates September 5 agreement, Japan will view it a "serious departure from the prevailing situation. In that situation, reprocessing of nuclear material subject to the Agreement will be suspended..."[55]

In addition to this, the document notes that Japan will implement the provision of Article 14 of the Agreement and may "exercise its rights and initiate the procedures stipulated in the aforementioned article where there is any change in this basis." Article 14 of the India-Japan cooperation for the peaceful use nuclear cooperation, divided into 9 paragraphs, remains an important clause to understand the provisions of the deal. It stipulates that both the parties have the right to terminate this Agreement by giving "one year's written notice to the other Party and citing the reasons for seeking such "termination."[56] Paragraph 2 of the Article 14, however, keeps the option open to salvage the agreement by "promptly hold[ing] consultations" and they will "consider carefully the circumstances that may lead to termination..." Paragraph 3 of the Article stipulates that the parties shall consider whether the action was caused "inadvertently" and whether the violation could be considered "material." This indicates that though Japan reserves the right to terminate and suspend the nuclear cooperation agreement with India, it cannot exercise this right until the violation is proven material.

Paragraph 4 of Article 14 notes that in the event of "cessation" of the nuclear cooperation agreement, the contracting parties would have the right to require the return of "nuclear material, non-nuclear material and equipment transferred pursuant to this Agreement and any special fissionable material recovered or produced as a by-product." The next paragraph, however, adds a proviso, "[B]oth Parties shall take into account the potential negative consequences of termination of this Agreement on the on-going contacts and projects initiated under this Agreement of significance for the respective nuclear programmes of either Party." Since the deal is largely driven by Japan's entrepreneurial objectives, it would be difficult for Tokyo to exercise the nullification rights and it will not only impact on Japan's interest but also impact on India-Japan relations as a whole.

In addition to the measures that have been put in place in the nuclear cooperation Agreement to guarantee that Japan's nuclear technology is used for peaceful purposes, Japan has impressed upon India to abide by its protocols signed with International Atomic Energy Agency (IAEA). The

Agreement notes that their nuclear cooperation will require "the application of safeguards by the Agency as applicable to Japan and the Republic of India in accordance with their respective relevant agreements with the Agency." Japan reminds India that "nuclear material recovered or produced as a by-product may be reprocessed within the jurisdiction of the Republic of India" using its technology under "the Application of Safeguards to Civilian Nuclear Facilities, done on February 2, 2009 as supplemented by the Protocol Additional to the said Agreement, done on May 15, 2009, where applicable, is in force for the Republic of India."[57]

These two agreements that have been signed between India and the IAEA have been mentioned many times in the text of the India-Japan civil nuclear cooperation Agreement. In addition to this, Japan expects from India to put "two national processing facilities, as well as additional new reprocessing facilities"[58] under safeguards of the IAEA. India, if desired by the IAEA, will provide it "access to safeguard relevant operator data, such as authenticated process control data."[59]

In addition to this, the Agreement put restriction on India for carrying out enrichment through the use of Japanese equipment. It expects India to limit enrichment "up to less than twenty percent" A written consent of the "supplying Party" (Japan) would be required for "enrichment of twenty percent and above in the isotope 235 of uranium transferred pursuant to this Agreement, as well as uranium used in or produced through the use of equipment transferred pursuant to this Agreement...."[60]

A careful reading of the two texts of the nuclear cooperation Agreement signed between India and Japan, analysed above, suggest that Japan has tried to include conditions apparently to assuage the concerns of its anti-nuclear constituencies. The deal, however, has failed to assuage their concerns. The leading Japanese dailies in their editorial expressed doubts whether the restrictions would prevent India in diverting the nuclear materials for other purposes. *The Japan Times* opined, "doubts persist that these provisions will guarantee that India will not resume nuclear weapons testing or divert plutonium extracted by reprocessing spent fuel to use in nuclear arms."[61] *The Mainichi* daily in its editorial stated, "the latest agreement has tarnished the moral principles that Japan has maintained as the world's only atomic-bombed country."[62] Echoing similar concerns, the *Asahi Shimbun* stated that "signing a nuclear trade deal with a country that has shunned the treaty designed to stop the spread of nuclear weapons is itself a big mistake." It further added that "as a country that has first-hand experiences of nuclear devastation, Japan must never take an action that can ruin the global nonproliferation safeguards."[63] The mayors of Hiroshima and Nagasaki also expressed their opposition to the deal which reflected their traditional stance on nuclear proliferation. The *Hibakusha* (victims of nuclear radiation) also registered their protest taking out a rally on the streets of Tokyo. One of the Hibakushas observed: "the proliferation of nuclear weapons goes against the spirit of the NPT and could lead to the creation of more hibakusha."[64]

Conclusion

As has been argued previously, both the countries have differing perceptions on global nuclear order and global technology regime and these differing stances acted as an impediment in concluding the civil nuclear cooperation agreement. To break the stalemate to conclude the agreement, both reached a middle ground to seal the deal. They agreed that September 8, 2008 statement made by the then External Affairs Minister Pranab Mukherjee "constitutes and essential basis for cooperation between the states under the Agreement." Notably, the statement by Mukherjee had made commitment on "unilateral moratorium on nuclear testing" and stated that India will remain firm on its "no-first-use of nuclear weapons." Inclusion of the September 8 statement has partially fulfilled Japan's demand which had been asking India to agree that Tokyo will terminate the nuclear cooperation if New Delhi conducts further nuclear tests. The domestic constituencies, especially the anti-nuclear groups, however, still doubt that Japanese nuclear material may be diverted and would be used in making nuclear arms.

Various opinion articles within India and outside India, especially after Fukushima crisis, have come to the fore urging Indian leadership to take cue from the nuclear crisis and not to install nuclear reactors. The nuclear deal with Japan has reignited the debate within India. Since India does not fall under the similar seismic zone with that of Japan, India still can consider using nuclear energy for its overall energy mix given that it is struggling to control carbon emission because of its heavy reliance on coal to meet its growing energy requirements. However, while selecting the nuclear reactors installation sites it should pay attention that the reactors should not sit atop the seismic fault. Also it should employ the safety standards that Japan had adopted following Fukushima nuclear crisis.[65] But again these safety standards that Japan has adopted are based on the shortcomings and causes of the nuclear accident identified by the nuclear operators and it is being contested by a section of Japanese scientists.[66] Ambassador Shyam Saran points that "the ratio of nuclear energy in India's total energy mix remains modest and a future cooperation with Japan in this sector is not likely to change this ratio dramatically."[67] He asserts that "immediate opportunities for growth are thus on other fuels."[68] Therefore, considering the vulnerability of nuclear reactors as well as external political and domestic hurdles in installing nuclear reactors, India should be cautious not to put all eggs in one basket that is nuclear energy and should also explore other sources of renewable energy to meet its energy demand.

END NOTES

1. Muchkund Dubey, "India's Foreign Policy: Coping with the Changing World," Pearson, New Delhi, 2013, p.267.
2. Text of statement of the External affairs Minister (Atal Behari Vajpayee) laid before the Parliament of India on the visit of the Foreign Minister of Japan to India, July 28, 1977. For the text of the statement please refer to, P.A. Narsimha Murthy, "India and Japan: Dimensions of their Relations (Documents)," pp.338-339.
3. Frank C. Langdon, "Japanese reactions to India's nuclear explosion," *Pacific Affairs*, Vol. 48, No.2, p. 174.
4. Satu P. Limaye, "Tokyo's Dynamic Diplomacy: Japan and the Subcontinent's Nuclear test," *Contemporary Southeast Asia*, Vol. 22, No.2, August 2000, p. 324.
5. Muchkund Dubey, "India's Foreign Policy: Coping with the Changing World," Pearson, New Delhi, 2013, pp.267.
6. Satu P. Limaye, "Tokyo's Dynamic Diplomacy: Japan and the Subcontinent's Nuclear test," *Contemporary Southeast Asia*, Vol. 22, No.2, August 2000, p. 324.
7. J.N.Dixit, "Pride and Pragmatism,"*Outlook*, December 28, 1998 available on http://www.outlookindia.com/article.aspx?206766 (accessed on October 5, 2016).
8. Ibid.
9. S Jaishankar, "India-Japan relations after Pokhran II," *Seminar*, No. 487, March 2000.
10. Ibid.
11. JN Dixit, "Pride and Pragmatism," *Outlook*, New Delhi, December 28, 1998 available

online at http://www.outlookindia.com/article.aspx?206766 (Accessed on October 5, 2016).

12. Muchkund Dubey, "India's Foreign Policy: Coping with the Changing World."
13. Hashimoto quoted by Satu P. Limaye in "Tokyo's Dynamic Diplomacy: Japan and the Subcontinent's Nuclear test," *Contemporary Southeast Asia*, Vol. 22, No.2, August 2000, p. 326.
14. East Asian Strategic Review, 1998-1999, National Institute of Defense Studies, Japan's Defense Agency, Government of Japan, Tokyo, pp 56-57.
15. Ryukichi Imai, "IIPS initiative regarding the nuclear tests by India and Pakistan," *Asia Pacific Review*, Vol 5, No.3, 1998, pp 167-168.
16. Ibid, p.171.
17. Ibid, p.176
18. Ibid, p.177.
19. Yasuhiro Nakasone, "Japan's firm non-nuclear resolve," *Japan Echo*, October 1998, p. 28.
20. Muchkund Dubey, 2013, p. 265.
21. Remarks by former Prime Minister Yoshiro Mori during inaugural ceremony of India-Japan relations on January 19, 2011, Embassy of India, Tokyo. Author's personal note. The author visited Tokyo as a panelist to participate in the panel discussion that followed Mori's remarks.
22. For details, see "Towards Japan-India Strategic and Global Partnership (Joint Statement)," December 2006, available at http://www.kantei.go.jp/foreign/abespeech/2006/12/15joint.pdf. (Accessed on October 5, 2016).
23. For details see, Takenori Horimoto, "The India-Japan nuclear agreement: Enhancing Bilateral Relations?, *Asia Pacific Bulletin*, No. 107, April 15, 2011.
24. Eshita Mukherjee, "Signing not so bright: Solar Energy in India," *IDSA commentary*, February 10, 2012, available online at http://www.idsa.in/idsacomments/SolarEnergyinIndia_emukherjee_100213. (Accessed on October 5, 2016)
25. Joint Press Interaction of EAM and FM of Japan, available at http://www.mea.gov.in/. (Accessed on October 5, 2016).
26. "India's leap forward and Japan," (September 2007), 29th Policy recommendation, *The Japan Forum for International Relations*, Tokyo.
27. Ibid.
28. Shiraishi Takashi, "Crafting Japan's Asia Policy in a Multipolar World," *Japan Echo*, August 2008, p.29.
29. Author's interview on Shiraishi Takashi, January 7, 2015.
30. "Japan and India's strategic ties vital for economy, security" (Editorial), *The Yomiuri Shimbun*, January 3, 2012.
31. "Uncertainty over test stymies India nuclear pact," *Kyodo News/Japan Times*, October 26, 2010.
32. Ibid.
33. "Japanese Groups Protest NSG Exemption for India," September 17, 2008. Also available online at http://www.cnic.jp/english/?s=Statement+Concerning+an+

Amendment + to+NSG+Guidelines+Granting+an+Exemption+for+India (Accessed on October 3, 2016)

34. An aggrieved Japanese equated Japanese reactor's sale abroad with opium trade. See Hiroshi Matsuoka, "Do Not Export What you will not use" (Readers in Council), *The Japan Times*, August 28, 2011.
35. "The people of Fukushima are still suffering and spent nuclear fuel cannot be disposed of properly. It is wrong to sell nuclear plant technology overseas by emphasizing only its safety and convenience," told a Hiroshima nuclear radiation victim to *Asahi Shimbun* in her reaction to India-Japan nuclear deal. For details see "Japan's nuclear power deal in principle with India a first with an NPT non-signer," *The Asahi Shimbun*, December 13, 2015.
36. For details see Shamshad A. Khan, "Towards India-Japan nuclear agreement: Prospects and Challenges," IDSA Comment, August 24, 2010, available online at http://www.idsa.in/idsacomments/TowardsIndoJapannuclearagreement Prospects andChallenges_sakhan_240810 (Accessed on October 2, 2016).
37. "Exporting Nuclear Technology" (Editorial), *The Japan Times*, July 2, 2010.
38. Ibid.
39. "NPT Framework in Peril" (Editorial), *The Asahi Shimbun*, July 15, 2010.
40. "Japan should stop working with India on atomic energy if it conducts nuke test" (Editorial), *Mainichi Japan*, August 24, 2010.
41. Translated text of Hiroshima and Nagasaki Mayor's joint appeal to Japanese government on nuclear deal with India can be accessed online at
42. "Japan India nuclear cooperation a slap in the face of NPT" (Editorial), *The Asahi Shimbun*, December 14, 2015.
43. Ibid.
44. "Japan-India atomic cooperation agreement lacks guarantee for peaceful use," (Editorial) *The Mainichi Daily*, December 16, 2015.
45. "The risky nuclear deal with India," (Editorial), *The Japan Times*, December 16, 2015.
46. Ibid.
47. "Cooperation on building N-plants a pillar of Japan-India strategic ties," *The Yomiuri Shimbun*, December 15, 2015.
48. Ibid.
49. Also see, Shamshad A. Khan, "India-Japan Memorandum on Civil Nuclear Cooperation: Concerns and Challenges," *Economic and Political Weekly*, Vol.51, No.14, April 02, 2016.
50. Author's personal interview with Yasukuni Enoki on January 13, 2015.
51. The Memorandum on civil nuclear cooperation notes that "The two governments confirm that the Agreement will be signed after the technical details are finalized, including those related to internal procedure." The full text can be accessed online at http://www.mofa.go.jp/files/000117783.pdf (Accessed on January 5, 2016).
52. The author in a policy brief has suggested that if Japan insists on the specific abrogation clause in the proposed nuclear deal, both the parties, as a last resort, should consider

a special clause in the pact, conveying the essence of the statement made by Pranab Mukherjee made on September 8, 2008 in the Indian Parliament. See for the details, Shamhad A. Khan, "The Elusive India-Japan nuclear Deal: It is time to bridge the difference to clinch the deal," Policy Brief, Indian Council of World Affairs, New Delhi, December 5, 2014, available online at http://www.icwa.in/pdfs/PB/2014/PBshamdec2014.pdf (Accessed on January 5, 2016).

53. "Note on Views and Understanding," Ministry of Foreign Affairs, Government of Japan, Tokyo, 2016, available online at http://www.mofa.go.jp/mofaj/files/000202921.pdf (Accessed on November 25, 2016)
54. Ibid, paragraph 5.
55. Ibid, paragraph 3.
56. "Agreement Between the Government of Japan and the Government of India for Cooperation in the Peaceful Uses of Nuclear Energy," Article 14, Paragraph 1, Ministry of Foreign Affairs, Government of Japan, Tokyo, 2016, available online at http://www.mofa.go.jp/mofaj/files/000202920.pdf
57. Ibid.
58. Ibid, Annex B, Para 3.
59. Annex B, Article 6 b(iv).
60. "Agreement Between the Government of Japan and the Government of India for Cooperation in the Peaceful Uses of Nuclear Energy," Article 11.
61. "A Questionable Nuclear Deal" (Editorial), *The Japan Times,* November 15, 2016.
62. "Japan-India nuclear accord shows Japan's lacking will as A-bombed nation," (Editorial), *The Mainichi Daily*, November 12, 2016.
63. "Japan's nuclear deal with India undermines its key principles," (Editorial), *The Asahi Shimbun*, November 12, 2016.
64. Hibakusha's observations quoted in, "Nuclear accord with India draws fire from A-bomb survivors, others," *The Asahi Shimbun*, November 12, 2016.
65. Japan's Nuclear Regulatory authority has adopted a new nuclear safety regime following the Fukushima crisis. For details see, Shamshad A. Khan, "Fukushima Impact: A New Nuclear Safety Regulations in Japan," IDSA Comment, July 22, 2013, available online at http://www.idsa.in/idsacomments/FukushimaImpactinJapan sakhan_220713 (Accessed on October 5, 2016).
66. The operator of the Fukushima nuclear power plant has cited that it was the unprecedented tsunami which caused the nuclear crisis. While a section of nuclear experts has asserted that the nuclear plant was damaged by the quake even before the tsunami hit the plant. For details see, Shamshad A. Khan, "Japan's Nuclear Energy Debate: A Year after Fukushima Nuclear Crisis," IDSA Issue Brief, March 22, 2012 available online at http://www.idsa.in/issuebrief/JapansNuclearEnergyDebate_Shamshad (Accessed on October 5, 2016).
67. Shyam Saran and Radhika Khosla, "Energizing India-Japan Cooperation on Clean Energy and Climate Change," in Rohan Mukherjee and Anthony Yazaki (Eds), *"Poised for Partnership: Deepening India-Japan Relations in the Asian Century,"* Oxford University Press, New Delhi, p.145.
68. Ibid.

8

Conclusion and Policy Suggestions

An analysis of evolution of India-Japan relations, discussed in the previous chapters, suggest that the bilateral relationship between the two Asian countries have been driven by different factors in different periods ranging from religious/cultural factors, economic factor and presently a mix of economic and strategic factors. Moreover, the bilateral relationship witnessed various phases of estrangements, during which there were negligible contacts between the two countries as well as phases of engagements during which they had an excellent interaction. With the institutionalisation of a Prime Ministerial level annual dialogue in 2006, the phases of "estrangement" that was witnessed in the bilateral relationship was over. Thus, institutionalisation of summit level dialogues can be considered an important landmark in the history of India-Japan relations.

Since the institutionalisation of annual dialogue, the summit level meetings between the two prime ministers have held almost every year and from 2006 onwards bilateral relations have been moving in an upward trajectory. As part of the strategic partnership, both the countries have identified a number of areas of bilateral interests where they are cooperating mutually. These include; trade, economics, infrastructure, security and defence and energy security. During Indian Prime Minister, Narendra Modi's Japan visit in September 2014, the existing strategic partnership has been elevated to a "special" strategic and global partnership. The up-gradation of the partnership is not simply a change in the nomenclature of bilateral relationship, rather it is an indication that India attaches utmost importance to its ties with Japan and, in the coming decades, Tokyo will remain on the top of New Delhi's foreign policy priorities. Japan also accords similar priorities in its relationship with India. However, to make the "special and strategic partnership" more relevant, both the countries should take practical steps to make it more substantive. This concluding chapter offers various suggestions and recommendations to further bolster this relationship.

How the Bilateral Partnership is Being Viewed?

Various comparative studies on India's strategic partnerships have given low ranking to the India-Japan strategic partnership. In a study conducted by New Delhi based Foundation of National Security Research, Japan has been given a low ranking. The comparative study conducted by some of the former Indian diplomats and strategic thinkers assessed India's strategic partnership with the US, the UK, France, Russia, Japan and Germany. In the study, Japan was rated fifth and slightly above Germany which stood last. The US and Russia gained first and second positions respectively. The report notes that "on 10-point scale, ..., Japan's support to India can be graded at four in respect of how substantial it was, four on how sustained it was, and six on how much potential it has for future."[1] Yet another study conducted by the Institute of Defense Studies and Analyses also gave lesser ranking to India-Japan strategic partnership as compared to other strategic partnership that India has signed. The study looked at India's relationship with the United States, Russia, Japan, UK and China, on the basis of "five parameters, namely economics, politics, defence, technology and people-to-people and ranked them in order of importance."[2]

According to this study, Japan was placed on fourth place just above UK and surprisingly a place lower than China. Japan fared better amongst the five strategic partners of India in the economic partnership, while in the fields of defense cooperation, politics, technology and people-to-people cooperation, Japan was ranked lower than other partners.[3] This is indicative of the fact that both India and Japan need lots of ground work to lift the status of the partnership at par with the US or Russia. Despite the low ranking given by the Indian strategic thinkers' to Japan, India has elevated its strategic partnership with a chosen few to a "special strategic partnership." These include Russia, Japan and South Korea.

Despite the shortcomings identified by Indian strategic thinkers in the strategic partnership, the Japanese thinkers believe that it has much more scope to broaden and strengthen it further. Professor Tomohiko Taniguchi, who is speech writer of Prime Minister Abe and an adviser to his cabinet, believes that the "sky is the limit" of India-Japan relationship. He believes that elites in Delhi puts caution on Anglo-American led institutions and they are still in the mindset of "Non-Alignment." He is of the view that this mindset serves as a kind of stumbling blocks that needs to be gradually removed, though they are getting smaller.[4]

Yoichi Funabashi, former Editor in Chief of the *Asahi Shimbun* and present President of Rebuild Japan Foundation, suggest that the existing prime ministerial level engagement needs to be broadened to a "Cabinet Level" engagements consisting of all the ministers. Ministries of both the countries should hold an annual consultation. This will help strengthen dialogue and implement decisions.[5] Professor Takashi Shiraishi, President of Institute of Developing Economies as well as Graduate Institute of Policy Studies, however, believes that Japanese entrepreneurs and industrialists will play key role in uplifting India-Japan relations to a new height, a role they played in strengthening Japan-China relations. To achieve that objective, India needs to consistently engage Japanese entrepreneurs for a decade or so. He is of the view that while others take one year to reach to a final decision, the Japanese take a decade to reach the same decision. But once they take a decision, they do not look back.[6] Emi Mifune, suggests that India and Japan should partner each other in several multi-national frameworks including APEC, of which India is not a member yet. She opines that "it is necessary for Japan to encourage India to join APEC and to play a greater role in a diplomatic strategy to confine Chinese hard-line policies in multilayered frameworks."[7] Some of the suggestions offered by these experts, who observe India-Japan relations mostly from an international relations perspective, must also be reflected by the policy planners while formulating futuristic agenda of India-Japan relationship. Against this context, following areas need particular attention from policy planners.

1. Strengthen the Partnership

As has been discussed in the previous chapters, India and Japan are cooperating in almost all the fields and sectors. There is no field left where they are not cooperating. From Space to Deep Ocean and from cyber security to future technologies; they have made commitment to tap each others' potentials. So where will the bilateral relationship reach beyond this point?

A bird's eye view on evolution of India-Japan relations and the areas in which they are cooperating, may lead to a conclusion that they have reached the optimum potentials. But there are some areas where they need to deepen the existing relationship and move beyond their statements and commitments they have made before they expand it further by identifying new areas.

One area could be upgrading the existing India-Japan 2 plus 2 strategic dialogues at par with the US-Japan and Japan-Australia.[8] The strategic dialogue between Japan and Australia and Japan and the US has been steered by their Defence and Foreign Ministers, commonly known as 2 plus 2 dialogues. However, in India-Japan strategic partnership, this dialogue till 2016 has taken place at the level of defence and foreign securities and their Japanese counterparts. Japan is eager to upgrade the existing India-Japan 2 plus 2 dialogue, apparently to expedite the decision making process. India, in principle, is amenable to "intensify" strategic dialogue between the two governments. However, it is treading cautiously, apparently due to China's concerns regarding growing India-Japan strategic ties, which views these measures between India and Japan as "encirclement" of China.

China has similar concerns about the US-Japan, and Japan-Australia 2 plus 2 mechanisms. All the three countries have deep economic interests with China; however, it has not stopped them from institutionalising their bilateral strategic dialogues and discussing global security threats and issues related to their security interests. India and Japan should also do some groundwork to institutionalise a 2 plus 2 dialogues at the ministerial level, keeping the two countries' bureaucracy involved. The elevation of the 2 plus 2 dialogue at the ministerial level will not only expedite the decision making process, but will also bring India-Japan 2 plus 2 strategic dialogue at par with Japan-Australia and Japan-US strategic dialogues.

The strategic partnership signed between other democracies, such as Japan and Australia and Japan and the US, has been driven by their defence and security interests. However, in India-Japan strategic partnership, economic cooperation has been the dominant factor so far and security and defence issues have found lesser priorities. It is partly because Japan, due to its pacifist policies, was averse to selling its defence equipments overseas; hence, stringent domestic laws were put in place on Japanese companies to export arms and arms related technologies. Also, both India and Japan wanted to keep their defence and security partnership low profile in an attempt not to affront China. However, domestic changes in both Japan and India have provided new opportunity for them to cooperate in defence and security areas. In 2014, Japan has eased the restrictions on the export of arms and arms related technologies and the Japanese companies have started entering into joint ventures with Australian and French companies. Indian defence companies had been eager to undertake joint defence production with Japanese companies, as they have cutting edge defence technologies. The internal changes in Japan may pave way for joint defence production between Indian and Japanese companies to help cut defence expenditures. However, India should be cautious not to send the message that this mechanism with Japan is aimed at dominating the region militarily as it will likely lead to an arms race in the region. It may also likely shift focus from the development projects undertaken by Japan and India.

The Indian defence companies are especially interested in Japan's US-2 amphibious aircraft, the only one of its kind available in the world for advanced air–sea search and rescue operations, as well as the Soryu submarine, which is one of the world's largest conventional submarines that is not nuclear-powered, and is one of the best in terms of the depth of undersea cruising and range. A section of Japanese defence manufacturers are also interested in Indian market given its vast potential. However, some others are very cautious in sharing these technologies. Their concern is that if these technologies are leaked to a third country, Japanese companies' competitive edge in the global market would be compromised. To assuage these concerns, India should assure Japan that these technologies would be protected and the government will take all necessary measures to prevent the leakage of these technologies to a third country.

There are various areas where India and Japan have to move beyond stated commitments and seek ways to implement those commitments. India and Japan, following their Defence Ministers' meeting in 2009, had expressed commitments to jointly work in the UN Peacekeeping missions, peace building and disaster relief works. Both Japan and India reiterated similar commitments following their Defence Ministers' meeting in 2011. Both the countries have also expressed their desire to transform the strategic partnership into a global partnership and cooperate with each other in UN Peacekeeping operations and disaster response overseas. In cases, such as Indian troops' participation in disaster response and cooperation with Japanese troops in these areas, both would require sharing of resources and logistics jointly.

There is a general practice of signing of Acquisition and Cross-Service Agreement (ACSA) among the two governments desiring to mutually cooperate in large scale disasters. Despite commitments that the contingents of the two countries' security forces will mutually cooperate in Peace Keeping Operations (PKOs) and Humanitarian and Disaster Response (HADR), India and Japan are yet to start negotiation on a bilateral logistic sharing agreement or the ACSA. Given their commitments to participate in United Nations PKOs and disaster relief operation overseas, India and Japan should consider signing an agreement for reciprocal supplies during such activities. The signing of ACSA between India and Japan will certainly promote closer cooperation between the two strategic partners, who are keen to play an active role in the promotion of peace and security of the international community.

Both India and Japan depend on Sea Lanes of Communication for their exports and imports. The Indian Navy and Coastguards have been safeguarding the Indian and Japanese vessels from pirates' attacks and have used force to repel the incidences of piracy, while the Japanese Maritime Self Defence Forces have not been undertaking these activities, as Japan has been keeping restraints on exercising the use of force. Thus, the entire India-Japan maritime cooperation, so far, has been uni-dimensional. However, the Japanese Parliament has lifted the ban and has allowed its defence forces to exercise the right of collective defence. Moreover, Japan has stated that Japanese naval forces would be able to undertake anti-piracy and minesweeping activities from the Straits of Hormuz to Malacca Straits. India should take note of these internal changes in Japan and review the bilateral maritime security mechanism to make India-Japan maritime cooperation inter-operable.

2. Make the Trade and Economic Partnership Mutually Beneficial

Apart from the Security and Defense fields, India and Japan are cooperating in the field of economics and trade. Economic and Trade ties between the two countries have deepened but it is yet to achieve "complementarities."[9] An independent India always wanted to forge a complimentary relationship with Japan in the fields of economy and trade. To achieve this objective, India offered key minerals and raw resources to war ravaged Japan in the 1950s, hoping that latter's economic recovery will lead to its own economic development.

However, India-Japan relationship could not transform into a complimentary relationship till the end of the Cold War. After the end of the Cold War, which coincided with India's economic liberalisation, New Delhi once again decided that the economy should be the "bedrock" of a stronger and complementary relationship with Tokyo. It decided to uplift the abysmally low bilateral trade volume between the two Asian economies by signing a Comprehensive Economic Partnership Agreement (CEPA) in 2011, which covers trade in goods and services between the two countries. Moreover, India termed this agreement as an "alliance between Japanese technology and capital and a young Indian labour force." Both the countries had decided to take the low trade volume of US Dollar 10 billion to 20 billion by 2010. But they have missed the target and instead of going up, bilateral trade is on a downward spiral. Also, because of certain non-tariff barriers imposed by Japan, the inflow of Indian goods in Japan remain limited. Though, the investment flows from Japan as well as increasing number of Japanese companies setting up their industry in India are encouraging signs. However, a comprehensive and complementary economic relationship, which was envisioned by the leaderships of the two countries, is yet to be achieved. The following section of this chapter, in this regard, offers some suggestions to give a new fillip to economic and trade relationship between India and Japan.

One of the many objectives of the India-Japan CEPA was to exponentially enhance the bilateral trade volume between the two countries and deepen the economic ties. CEPA did bring impressive results and within a year of this agreement coming into effect in 2011, the bilateral trade touched US dollar 18.32 billion in the fiscal year 2011-12 as compared to US dollar 13.72 billion in 2010-11. However, after two consecutive years of touching new heights, the bilateral trade has decelerated and has come down to US dollar 14.51 billion in fiscal 2015-16.[10] If the trend continues, it may reach the level of 2010, in another few years, defeating the purpose of the CEPA.

Keeping this in mind, both Indian and Japanese governments should find ways to make the CEPA relevant and should consider a few options in this context. One of the options could be to "re-open" and review the CEPA. Recently, India and South Korea have agreed to review their CEPA as they realized that their bilateral trade has stagnated. Since the bilateral trade between India and Japan is also showing signs of stagnation, both the countries should also think to review their CEPA and make it more inclusive to once again push the trade volume on an upward trajectory.

The second option could be to conclude some of the "inconclusive" parts of the CEPA signed in 2010.[11] It may be reminded that Japan has signed similar CEPA (known as EPA in Japan) with Indonesia and Philippines, where it has allowed nurses and careworkers to work in Japan as part of the EPA. India was also asking similar treatment for its nurses and caregivers in the India-Japan CEPA. Japan, in principle, had agreed to give the same treatment to Indian workers, but sought more time, as it found that majority of the nurses and careworkers from Indonesia and Philippines are finding it difficult to attain language proficiency after their two years of internship in Japan. Passing the language test was a pre-requisite to start a full-fledged work in the service sectors catering to the medical requirements of Japan's ageing society. However, Japan has revisited this policy and has simplified the language tests for expats,[12] which has resulted in a large number of those expats clearing the Japanese language test. Since Japan is no more facing the difficulties it cited to India, it should conclude this "inconclusive" aspect of India-Japan CEPA. This will allow more Indians to work in the Japanese service sectors, as CEPA promises trade not only in goods, but also in services.

Thirdly, India should look at the new avenues and openings in Japan and should try to tap these opportunities. Recently, Japan has announced a New Industrial Policy under which it plans to allow some 60,000 high technology skilled workers by 2020 to revitalize Japan's industry.[13] Since the CEPA promises trade in services and assures flow of human resources between the two countries, it would be pertinent for India to request Japan to give preferential treatment to countries with which it has signed CEPA. Moreover, India should ask Japan to fix a quota for Indian high skilled workers under this New Industrial Policy.

It may be recalled that India-Japan strategic partnership was aimed at creating a "win-win" situation for both the countries. It has certainly resulted in a much more concerted response by the two countries on the issues and challenges faced by the world, including the freedom of navigation and security of sea lanes of communication. However, in the field of economy and trade, it has brought more advantage to Japan than to India. For example, in the India-Japan bilateral trade, which stands at US dollar 14.51 billion at present, India's share is only 5.38 billion US dollar. The efforts should be made to achieve a balance in trade so that it does not lead to "trade frictions" in future.

Japan has allowed the entry of some of the Indian vegetables, fruits, poultry and fisheries. However, some of the Indian agricultural produce as well as fisheries and shrimps do not come up to the Sanitary and Phyto Sanitary (SPS) measures applied by Japan. There are reports that suggest that some of the Indian shipments to Japan had to be taken back as they could not come up to the Japanese SPS standards. Similarly, India's generic medicines' share in Japanese markets is less than one percent of the total consumption of generic drugs. It is said that the "whiteness" of Indian medicines does not match with that of the Japanese ones; because of this, the local consumers shy away from buying these medicines. Therefore, till India overcomes these Non-Tariff Barriers (NTBs) on its food products as well as generic medicines, it would be difficult to gain access to the Japanese market and, in that case, it would be difficult to achieve a trade balance with Japan. To overcome these NTBs imposed by Japan, India should ask Japan to share and facilitate the technologies, application of which would lead to improvement in Indian products' SPS measure standards as well as

Indian medicines could match the colours including the whiteness of the Japanese generic medicines.

One of the objectives of India-Japan strategic partnership was to harness Japan's technological prowess. India's focus so far had been on gaining high-end technologies including civil nuclear technology, technology related to US-2 amphibious aircrafts and Soryu class submarines. Japan attaches too much political sensitivities to these technologies. India would need sustained efforts to break the stalemate to gain access to these technologies.

However, it is appreciable that Japan has shared some of its technology with India, especially those related to renewable energy (nuclear, solar, hydro power and wind, etc.) as well as technology to cut carbon emissions from coal based power plants. Apart from these high-end expensive technologies, India should try to harness Green House technology for farming and food reprocessing. Japan has developed cost effective Green House method for producing vegetables and fruits on small tracts of land. India should collaborate with Japan to gain the knowhow related to this technology. Using this technology for vegetable and food production may not be economically viable at this point of time for India, but given the large scale urbanization that is being planned in India, early adoption of this technology would be very helpful in future.

Food processing could be another area in which India needs Japanese technology and knowhow. Estimates suggest that some 40 percent of vegetables and fruits go waste in India, while Japan has been able to minimize the wastage by using food processing technology and an effective supply chain. Collaboration with Japan in this field would help India improve its food security.

India should also make sincere effort to pass on the benefit of India-Japan technological cooperation to masses, though with the introduction of the mass transportation system such as metro in different Indian cities, common people are witnessing the impact of bilateral technological cooperation. But much more can be done to uplift the facilities in Indian cities and semi urban areas by deepening the technological cooperation with Japan. Japan has used technology to provide clean water, uninterrupted piped gas and power supply to every house hold as well as built excellent garbage disposal system and sewage treatment system. India and Indian agencies should collaborate with Japan and its agencies to implement similar technology to upgrade these facilities within India so that general masses also benefit from India-Japan cooperation.

Needless to say, Japan has acknowledged that "a strong, prosperous and dynamic India is in the interest of Japan and vice versa." Both the governments have undertaken various measures to upgrade their economic relations. However, there are vast potential and opportunities, some of them cited above, which remain untapped. Collaboration in these fields between the two countries will certainly impart momentum to their economic growth and prosperity.

3. Invest in People-to-People Relationship

As has been mentioned previously, those who study India-Japan relationship from area studies perspective consider much more needs to be done to deepen the current level of ties between India and Japan. Apart from the political and strategic issue discussed in previous section, people-to-people ties remain a weak link between India and Japan. The promotion of human exchange is vital for improvement of mutual understanding and thereby consolidating further expansion of India-Japan relations, argues Makoto Kojima.[14] Statistics suggest that only 23,000 Indians were living in Japan on a long term visa, far less than other smaller South Asian countries such as Nepal, Bangladesh and Pakistan. Kojima suggests that Japanese Universities should increase English based courses in its campuses to attract the Indian students to uplift the people-to-people ties. Similarly, P.A. George suggests implementing "the eight fold initiative" signed between India and Japan in 2005 to strengthen people-to-people ties. One of the components of the initiative was to "strengthening of people-to-people contacts to raise the visibility and profile of one country in the other" through cultural and academic initiatives.[15] George's study suggests, however, that the Japanese language studies have grown in India through non-governmental initiatives.

The interest among Indian youths in Japan remains high as is reflective from the growing number of Japanese language institutes as well as number of students appearing for Japanese Language Proficiency test. The same cannot be said about Japanese youths' interest in India. There are few universities offering courses on India and the Indian literatures. Private schools teaching Indian languages are also negligible in Japan. Among the Japanese youth the interest to learn Indian languages—Hindi, Urdu and Bengali, remains low while the same cannot be said about the European and East Asian languages. This can be assessed by visiting the major Japanese book stores particularly their corners where language learning books are available. Self help books to learn English, Italian, French, German, Portuguese, Spanish as well as Chinese and Koreans can be found in good numbers from different publishers. However, the self help books on Indian languages can rarely be found.[16] Both the governments should take effort to deepen youths' interests in each other's language, culture and society.

Japan has made an effort to expose Indian youths to different aspects of Japan by offering visits under its JENESYS programme. However, India is yet to reciprocate the same by inviting Japanese youth for excursion and study tours. The Indian and Japanese universities should start joint courses to bridge this deficit. Pakistan, despite not having an excellent strategic partnership with Japan, has taken lead in this regard. Japan's Waseda University has joined with Pakistan's Lahore University of Management Science. They invite each others' students for a semester and transfer the credits to each others' students participating in such programme. The same should be emulated between Indian and Japanese universities.

4. Make Efforts to End "visibility deficit"

India and Japan, despite forging an excellent relationship, face "visibility deficit" in each other's countries. While other countries who have signed similar partnership have invested in establishing institutions, cultural centers and targeted TV channels for each other's audiences which in turn lead to enhancing better understanding between the two countries. Such institutions and mechanisms supported by government are missing in India and Japan and thus they face "visibility deficit" in each other countries. This should be filled by taking new initiatives.

Japan has, Japan Foundation in New Delhi which is doing excellent work in introducing different aspects of Japan to Indian audiences. But its reach remains limited to Delhi and the capital region. It should open up new centers in different metropolitan cities to fill the existing gap. Japan is planning to open up new Japan Centre as parts of its soft power diplomacy and intends to establish this centre in countries such as Washington, Sao Polo and Manila. But it would be wise to open one such centre in India where it faces visibility deficit. Similarly, India should also expand its cultural diplomacy in Japan by opening new cultural centres in Japanese cities. It has started opening India Chair in different Japanese universities but its number remains very limited. This initiative must be expanded.

Satellite TVs are playing an important role in bridging visibility deficit. Various international channels such as BBC, CNN, Russian TV, Duetsche Welle TV of Germany, F-5 of France, Airang TV of South Korea and CCTV of China can easily be watched in India. Despite having free to air channel, Japan's national TV channel the NHK, is not widely available in India. Only one cable service provider, the Dish TV, provides the NHK in its basket of TV channels. Japan and its agencies should take effort so that other cable providers should include the NHK in its basket of channels. While China has made efforts to reach out to the masses informing them about the availability of its TV channel by giving a full page advertisement about CCTV in Indian newspapers, no such effort has been made by Japan or the NHK to reach out Indian audience using advertisement strategy. India, however, is lagging much behind other countries in using such technology. India's national TV channel, Door Darshan had announced that it will go global. But it is yet to take off. Once it takes off, it should air targeted programme aimed at Japan, devoting few hours in Japanese language. Though All India Radio and its overseas services is still continuing some of its overseas foreign language programs including in Arabic, French, Chinese, Bhasha Indonesia but Japanese stands out. They should reach out to Japanese audience not through the outdated terrestrial broadcasts but using the internet broadcasts/podcasts which its other counterparts, including the NHK Radio, have already been using.

Conclusion

The relationship between the people of India and Japan that was built through a cultural-religious connect, and later nurtured by the ideas of Okakura Tenshin and Rabindranath Tagore, has transformed into a "special strategic and global partnership." The two countries are cooperating with each others in various fields. Though in the past, the relationship between the two countries have drifted from the path and have witnessed various road blocks impacting the overall relationship, it is not likely to witness the similar trend in the future as the relationship is "institutionalised" through the annual summit level meeting between the leaderships of the two countries. In the coming few decades, India-Japan relations would be driven by three factors; cultural-religious, political and economic. Both the countries should try to deepen their relationship in these fields and try to find the "complementarities" to take the relationship to a new depth and a new height.

END NOTES

1. Satish Kumar et al, "India's Strategic Partners: A Comparative Assessment," Foundation for National Security Research, New Delhi, 2011, p. 8.
2. Arvind Gupta and Sarita Azada, "Evaluating India's Strategic Partnerships using Analytic Hierarchy Process," Institute of Defense Studies and Analyses, New Delhi, September 17, 2011.
3. Ibid.
4. Author's interview with Professor Tomohiko Taniguchi on February 5, 2016 at Raiosha building, Keio University, Hiyoshi Campus, Kanagawa, Japan.
5. Author's interview with Yoichi Funabashi at Rebuild Japan Foundation office, Roppongi Hills, Tokyo on January 23, 2015.
6. Author's interview with Professor Takashi Shiraishi at Graduate Institute of Policy Studies, Tokyo on Januray 7, 2015.
7. Emi Mifune, "Japan-India-US Relations and Rising China," in (eds) Takenori Horimoto and Lalima Varma, India-Japan Relations in Emerging Asia, Manohar, 2013, p.109.
8. Also see, Shamshad A. Khan, "India-Japan Relations: Suggestions to further deepen bilateral strategic partnership," *ICWA Policy Brief*, Indian Council of World Affairs, New Delhi, December 5, 2014.
9. Also see, Shamshad A. Khan, "India-Japan Economic and trade partnership: Suggestions to make it balanced and mutually beneficial," *ICWA Policy Brief*, Indian Council of World Affairs, New Delhi, July 9, 2015.
10. Export Import Data, India-Japan Bilateral trade, Ministry of Commerce, Government of India, Data available online at http://www.commerce.nic.in/eidb/iecnt.asp. (accessed August 6, 2016).
11. The official document of India-Japan CEPA in this regard notes that "Japan shall enter into negotiation with India...regarding the acceptance of Indian qualified nurses and certified care-workers by Japan, with a view to reaching a conclusion of the negotiations within one year if possible, but not later than two years, after the entry into force of this Agreement." Please refer to "Comprehensive Economic Partnership

Agreement Between Republic of India and Japan," Ministry of Commerce, Government of India, 2010, p.972.

12. "Nursing exam held with English terms to help foreign hopefuls," *The Japan Times*, February 21, 2011.
13. "Japan eyes more foreign workers, challenging taboo on immigration," *The Asahi Shimbun*, April 26, 2016.
14. Makoto Kojima, "Expanding Japan-India Economic Relations," in (eds) Takenori Horimoto and Lalima Varma, India-Japan Relations in Emerging Asia, Manohar, 2013, p.215.
15. P.A. George, "Present Status of Japanese Studies in India," in (eds) Takenori Horimoto and Lalima Varma, India-Japan Relations in Emerging Asia, Manohar, 2013, p.251.
16. Author's personal observation based on visits of various Book stores in Tokyo area in June 2016.

INDEX